AMERICAN
CLASSIC CARS

AMERICAN
CLASSIC CARS

RICHARD NICHOLLS

Grange
BOOKS

First published in 2002 for Grange Books
An imprint of Grange Books plc
The Grange
Kingsnorth Industrial Estate
Hoo, Nr Rochester
Kent ME3 9ND
www.grangebooks.co.uk

Reprinted in 2003

ISBN: 1-84013-502-6

Editorial and design by
Amber Books Ltd
Bradley's Close
74–77 White Lion Street
London N1 9PF

Project Editor: Chris Stone
Design: Stylus Design

Printed in Singapore

PICTURE CREDITS
Aerospace Publishing: 15, 16, 18, 19, 20, 21, 22, 23, 25, 26, 28, 29, 30, 31, 32, 33, 34, 35, 39,
40, 41, 42, 43, 45, 46, 49, 50, 53, 54, 55, 57, 59, 61, 62, 63, 66, 67, 69, 70, 71, 72, 73, 74, 75, 77,
79, 81, 84, 85, 86, 87, 90, 91, 92, 98, 99, 102, 103, 104, 105, 106, 111, 112, 113, 114, 117, 120,
121, 122, 123, 128, 130, 131, 133, 134, 135, 137, 138, 139, 141, 144, 145, 146, 147, 148, 152,
155, 157, 158, 160, 161, 163, 166, 167, 168, 172, 173, 174, 175, 176, 179, 180, 181, 183, 187,
190, 192, 193, 194, 196, 197, 200, 204, 205, 206, 207, 209, 211, 214, 215, 217, 218. 219, 222,
223, 226, 227, 229, 230, 232, 233, 234, 235, 236, 237, 238, 239, 240, 241, 242, 243, 245, 247,
248, 250, 251, 253, 254, 255, 257, 261, 262, 264, 266, 268, 273, 274, 276, 277, 278, 281, 284,
289, 294, 297, 298, 299, 301, 303, 305, 306, 307, 308, 309, 312.

International Masters Publishing BV: 14, 17, 24, 27, 36, 37, 38, 44, 47, 48, 51, 52, 56, 58, 60,
64, 65, 68, 76, 78, 80, 82, 83, 88, 89, 93, 94, 95, 96, 97, 100, 101, 107, 108, 109, 110, 115, 116,
118, 119, 124, 125, 126, 127, 129, 132, 136, 140, 142, 143, 149, 150, 151, 153, 154, 156, 159,
162, 164, 165, 169, 170, 171, 177, 178, 182, 184, 185, 186, 188, 189, 191, 195, 198, 199, 201,
202, 203, 208, 210, 212, 213, 216, 220, 221, 224, 225, 228, 231, 244, 246, 249, 252, 256, 258,
259, 262, 263, 265, 267, 269, 270, 271, 272, 275, 279, 280, 282, 283, 285, 286, 287, 288, 292,
293, 295, 296, 300, 302, 303, 310, 311.

TRH Pictures: 6, 10, 12, 13.

TRH/John Cadman: 8.

CONTENTS

Introduction

In 1923, 30 years after the start of mass car production, some 15 million vehicles were registered in the world, and over 80 percent of those were in the USA. This may come as no surprise to either those who live in America or to those who have visited it, because the country is vast.

As the land became increasingly populated during the 19th and 20th century, it demanded more forms of transport, and between 1805 and 1942 there were simply thousands of different car manufacturers in and out of business. Some produced just the one model before succumbing to failure; others, like Henry Ford, went from strength to strength. Ford invented the production line and literally flooded the market with cheap Model Ts, which became the backbone of the American car industry between 1913 and 1927.

Oldsmobile is America's oldest car brand; when their 1930 sedan arrived the company had already been in business for over 30 years. The sedans were popular, selling over 32,000 in their first year.

In fact, of the 12 million vehicles registered in the USA in the early 1920s, over half were Fords, which shows just how popular and significant the Model T was.

But there were standout vehicles prior to the Ford's Tin Lizzy Model T. The Stutz Bearcat, which this book starts with, was remarkable, even though today it looks like a vintage car with barely enough power to beat a jogging pace. In fact, the Bearcat could travel at 80 mph (129 km/h) and cruise at 60 mph (97 km/h), making it one of the supercars of its day. And it was built to such a degree that when, in 1915, one customer returned his car, complaining that the new 16v overheadcam engine was no good, Harry C. Stutz gave the car to dare-devil motorcyclist Erwin 'Cannonball' Baker, who consequently drove across America on little more than dirt tracks, doing 3,700 miles (5,953 km) at an average of 13.7 mph (22 km/h), taking just over 11 days to complete the trip and breaking every record in the process, with a broken shock-absorber clip the only casualty! This feat swamped the manufacturer with orders, and it was only the attempt at floating the company on the US stockmarket which eventually destroyed the brand.

FINANCIAL ASSETS

It was the Wall Street Crash of 1929 which also saw the end of the revolutionary Cord L29, so called as it was launched in 1929. Head of the company, Erret Lobban Cord, worked his engineers and designers hard to come up with the car in just eight months, even though, as a great salesmen, he embellished the truth and said the prototype had taken years of development. That car used a frontwheel-drive configuration, the first for any production vehicle, though racers had used it previously and had been beating rearwheel-drive machines. What Cord did was make the FWD set-up workable with a tight turning circle and strong chassis, while creating a car which was beautiful in proportion and very low because it didn't require a transmission tunnel.

It was E.L. Cord who also headed the Duesenberg company, having acquired it in 1926. He ordered the engineers to make a car which would rival the best in the world. They duly did with the Model J, and not just the car but the model gained a reputation for being the finest the US had ever produced. But here was another victim of Wall Street, while the larger manufacturers soldiered on.

Chevrolet was one of those giants, and the company had, since 1912, tried to produce more innovative cars than Ford and, hence, top their sales

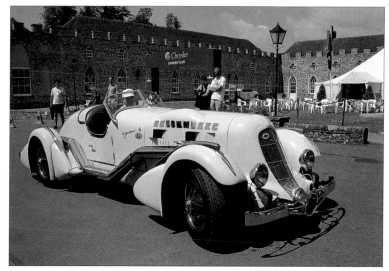

'He drives a Duesenberg' was the advertising slogan the company used, which said it all. The cars were expensive, lavish and driven by glamorous film stars such as Gary Cooper.

figures. Ford had been at the top of the sales in the US car market since 1906, and they were to stay there until 1926. The following year Chevrolet won over buyers through its Capitol series, and partly because of the ageing design of the Model T. The following years saw Chevrolet offer four-wheel brakes and a six-cylinder engine over Ford's four, which again put the brand at the top of the sales pile. But Ford were able to hit back with full Model A production (after initial delays) in 1929 and 1930, though the see-saw continued in 1931 with a new series from Chevrolet called Independence. So it went on, though Chevy had the better grab of the market until World War II.

POST-WAR DEVELOPMENT

Both the crash of 1929 and World War II sorted the wheat from the chaff in the car market, and saw many names either disappear altogether or be swallowed up by bigger companies. However they went, far fewer made it through to the late 1940s, but it remained a significant time in car production. Technology was fast developing and the engineering practices became more refined as, more than ever, costcutting was essential in an increasingly competitive market. Developments in casting techniques led to stronger and lighter components which cost less to make, plus advances in fuel refinement meant that engines could produce more power reliably.

But the post-war period was certainly not about gearing down; it was about gearing up for an increasing number of drivers, and that brought about more diverse machines as an offshoot. Unusual cars like the Studebaker Champion came along, as did unlikely collaborations such as that between the American George Mason, president of Nash, and Briton Donald Healey, who simply met on the Queen Elizabeth liner and decide to make the Nash Healey car between them for the US market.

Cars like the 1949 Mercury defined a new way for styling, because, like the Fords of the same year, they used slab sides. This marked them out as quite radical to the separately fendered cars which dated back to the 1940s, and even 1930s in some cases. Another significant move for the era was provided by Hudson, who introduced their Step Down chassis which allowed their cars to sit much lower and, therefore, have a lower centre of gravity, which improved handling immensely.

The early 1950s saw the rise and rise of chrome on cars, as an increasingly opulent society flourished in the States. The more chrome you had, it seemed, the more successful you were in life. But chrome wasn't the only addition, as many of the cars of the time were designed by stylists who took their influence from the transport industry in general, and therefore used ideas from both planes and trains of the era. Cars were given bold noses and fintailed rears, and arguably the most celebrated of these brash vehicles was the Cadillac Series 62 of 1959. With fins over 1 ft (0.3 m) high and twin bullet lenses protruding rearwards, the 1959 Caddy was every bit a design icon and easily rates among the top five of all-time American classics.

The 1950s also saw the birth of two American sportscars: Ford's Thunderbird and Chevrolet's Corvette. Again the two companies were fighting for the same market, but fortunately it was a huge one and sales of both vehicles flourished; at least the Corvettes did after a couple of years in production, and once Chevrolet had slotted in their new compact small-block V8 of nearly 275 ci (4.5 litres). The Americans then had some serious sports machine on their hands, enough to give plenty of sleepless nights to the European bosses of Ferrari and Jaguar.

Outrageous styling reached its peak in 1959, as this Pontiac Bonneville shows. Fins and excessive chrome attracted an opulent post-war American society.

THE V8 AND MUSCLE BOOM

Performance became a big part of car-marketing in the 1950s and 1960s. While the sporty two-seaters from two major manufacturers were indeed fast (the Corvette held the fastest production-car record for some years), the sedans weren't exactly far behind. Engine displacement had been getting larger ever since the war, and Chrysler had been adding cubic inches as well as developing their engines internally. The advent of their 'Hemispherical' design combustion chamber left other manufacturers reeling at the outputs possible, though fortunately for them, the engines were designed for full-sized sedans, and hence all the performance was needed to stay level with other, lighter vehicles.

Other manufacturers began to add the cubic inches, but it was the unlikely and fairly staid Pontiac who really came up with the goods in 1964. That year, John DeLorean was the general manager, and he knew that America's youth weren't satisfied with the cars that had pleased their parents in the previous decade. Hence, when a young advertising executive in the business, Jim Wangers, approached him about a concept which involved fitting the company's 389 ci (6.3-litre) engine in the mid-sized LeMans/Tempest bodyshell, DeLorean gave it the go-ahead immediately and, in doing so, created the muscle car. Called the GTO after the Ferraris of the same name, it was an instant success, and this sent shockwaves through the industry as manufacturers scrabbled to jump on the bandwagon and grab a share of the booming market.

Ford were ahead of most because they were already in the process of producing a new model, and it was to be in the same vein as the GTO, but much more readily available to America's youth. The Mustang stole the show as soon as it was released: it was truly a sensation, and very few cars since have created such an impression. While based on the rather ordinary Falcon, the new sheet metalwork was striking, and the name Mustang was a marketing dream as it conjured images of the hard-working steeds of the American cowboys: fast, tough and entirely dependable. The fact that the car came in coupe, fastback and convertible styles merely added to the all-round appeal.

Chevrolet and, later, both Dodge and Plymouth, produced cars to rival the Ford's new machine and all became known, after the Mustang, as pony cars. But later in the 1960s the barebones nature of many muscle cars developed with the market as young people grew older. They wanted more creature comforts and hence later muscle cars became more refined. The power remained, of course, and both Dodge and Plymouth made a big impression on the market, not just with the Hemi 426 ci (6.9-litre) motor, but with 440 ci (7.2-litre) Wedge engines and torquey small-blocks powering compact fastbacks such as the Challenger. But this was all about to change.

FUEL AND ENVIRONMENT

The muscle era peaked in 1970, but while these boulevard bruisers were busy burning fossil fuels, environmentalists were growing increasingly unhappy with pollution and, with Americans being by far the biggest users of internal combustion-engined vehicles, they were targeted. This led to the introduction of lead-free fuel and, due to the lack of refinement in this new fuel, cars' compression ratios needed to be decreased. Hence power outputs dropped and sales slumped. The fuel crisis of 1973 further depressed the market and most manufacturers simply withdrew their muscle cars.

The following years of the 1970s marked several changes, the most

Chevrolet's first Impala in 1958 came after a trio of successful models from 1955–1957. The new car was even more popular and the Impala name remained until the 1990s.

prominent being the development of smaller and therefore more lightweight models, which had improved fuel economy. By the middle of that decade the country also saw import cars on a severe rise, with Golf's new hatchback of 1975 making big impressions on the youth of America and also those who were more practically minded. The US didn't sit on its laurels for too long, introducing its own compact cars which won over buyers, even though they had no performance bias. Somewhat tamer muscle cars were still built during the 1970s, it's just that they were in far fewer numbers (though they are mentioned in this book) and weren't hyped as much by the manufacturers.

As the 1980s dawned, computer technology found its way into cars and made them far more efficient. The bonus was with computer engine-management that power could be found while keeping the cars environmentally friendly, hence the whole performance saga went off with a bang again early that decade. Ford released a new Mustang in 1979 and it steadily gained more power through the 1980s, while Chevrolet were close on their heels with the Camaro in its third-generation guise.

Turbo technology also had its part to play at this time, as factory cars found the sort of power usually associated with muscle cars, but with engines far smaller and many times more efficient. What it all led to is one of the greatest car-producing decades with the 1990s. More than ever, cars became easier to produce with computer aid. And while the days of chrome and huge engine-displacement might be long gone, America remains at the forefront of car production with the biggest car companies in the world, which looks promising for many future classics.

Finally, throughout the decades covered in this book, many one-off specials built by individuals or small companies have been produced. Hot rodders who have developed their cars for speed and style, drag racers who have simply built for the fastest acceleration possible, and cruisers who have put style way ahead of content, are all praised here. It is they who, along with the manufacturers, have kept the American classics alive and will continue to do so in the years ahead.

The luxury of a car plus the practicality of a small pick-up, Chevrolet's El Camino was bought by many small businesses. Many of the trucks had V8 engines, so were performance bargains.

Stutz Bearcat (1914)

Fundamentally a road-going race car, the Bearcat was developed from Stutz's Indy racer which came 11th in 1911 at the very first Indy 500. The race car inspired Harry Clayton Stutz to start production, and he was clever in the design of his Bearcat, make it lightweight and with good weight distribution to make the car handle, albeit it had standard wooden 'cart' wheels, though wire-spoked rims were optional. The Bearcat had a basic but strong twin rail design, and used the engine solid-mounted to make it a stressed member, a trick that's still used in racing cars today. The gearbox was mounted at the rear as part of the transaxle, helping offset the huge cast-iron engine's weight up front. The car could easily cruise at 60mph (96km/h), making it the supercar of its day. In 1915 Erwin 'Cannonball' Baker crossed America in one, doing 3,700 miles (5,953km) at 13.7mph (22km/h), without proper roads.

Top speed:	80 mph (128 km/h)
0–60 mph (0–96 km/h):	N/A
Engine type:	In-line four
Displacement:	390 ci (6,3902 cc)
Transmission	3–speed manual
Max power:	60 bhp (44 kW) @ 1,500 rpm
Max torque:	N/A
Weight:	2,500 lb (1,136 kg)
Economy:	13.8 mpg (4.88 km/l)

Ford Model T (1918)

The Model T is arguably one of the most famous of all American cars, and therefore has a place in everyone's heart. Hot rodders have taken to it since the 1920s, stripping the car from its already basic specification to make it lighter and therefore turning it into more of a racer. Though at first the cars received tuned versions of the standard four cylinder 183ci (3-litre) motors, by 1932 the Flathead V8 was in production, and it wasn't long before that found its way into the stripped Model Ts, which were then raced on the dry lakes of southern California. The T Bucket, as shown here, came about in the 1960s as a development of the stripped-out cars, though by then more often than not they had Chevy's small-block, and strong rear axles with huge tyres to get maximum straight-line performance. The skinny front wheels were purely to keep it lightweight.

Top speed:	115 mph (184 km/h)
0–60 mph (0–96 km/h):	5.2 sec
Engine type:	V8
Displacement:	350 ci (5,735 cc)
Transmission	4–speed auto
Max power:	250 bhp (186 kW) @ 5,000 rpm
Max torque:	328 lb ft (444 Nm) @ 3,200 rpm
Weight:	2,198 lb (999 kg)
Economy:	18.1 mpg (6.4 km/l)

Willys 65-Knight (1925)

Willys prided themselves on building quality cars, and it was this, plus a number of special design points, which made the company's 65-Knight a great seller in the 1920s. Whereas engines had been rough and noisy up until this point in the majority of machines, Willys added internal balancing which comprised two extra cylinders rotating in the opposite direction to the main engine. Also, it used sleeve valves which improved the seal of the combustion as carbon built up inside the engine, thus giving the car more power as it used it, which independent testing endorsed. It also produced plenty of torque which meant the drive could get away with the minimum gear changes for an almost effortless drive. The sedan was one of few hardtops built at the time, and it maximized internal space, plus had 'suicide' style opening rear doors to ease passenger entry.

Top speed:	60 mph (96 km/h)
0–60 mph (0–96 km/h):	31.0 sec
Engine type:	In-line four
Displacement:	186 ci (3,047 cc)
Transmission	3–speed manual
Max power:	40 bhp (30 kW) @ 2,600 rpm
Max torque:	N/A
Weight:	3,060 lb (1,390 kg)
Economy:	16 mpg (5.6 km/l)

Duesenberg Model J (1928)

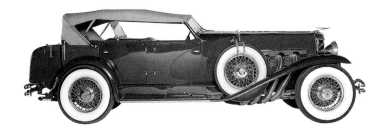

While Rolls Royce garnered much praise for luxury motoring in Britain, it was Duesenberg who were top of the pile in the USA, though their machines were recognized and respected throughout Europe. The Model J was more than just a luxury car, as Duesenberg intended it to be a sporting drive for keen drivers. The engine was mighty, being a straight-eight cylinder with twin overhead camshafts and four valves per cylinder, plus a mercury-filled crank damper which kept it smooth running while being incredibly powerful. The suspension was developed too and the company invented the phrase about its Duesenberg taking curves 'as though on rails'. For those people with the money to buy one but who got bored with the performance, there was always a supercharger kit which could boost power up to 320bhp (238kW), which filmstar Gary Cooper did to his SSJ roadster.

Top speed:	116 mph (186 km/h)
0–60 mph (0–96 km/h):	11.0 sec
Engine type:	In-line eight
Displacement:	420 ci (6,882 cc)
Transmission	3–speed manual
Max power:	265 bhp (198 kW) @ 4,250 rpm
Max torque:	N/A
Weight:	4,895 lb (2,225 kg)
Economy:	9.4 mpg (3.3 km/l)

Ford Model A (1928)

After sales of over 15 million cars, the Model T made way for the Model A in 1928. While the previous car had done well, it was dated in technology by the late 1920s, but the A more than made up for it with new-found refinement and an all-new engine. In fact it had double the power of the Model T and the extra torque was because of a longer stroke crankshaft. Another development was the use of battery-fed ignition. Further changes occurred in the chassis, which had four-wheel brakes against the two rears which had featured on T, plus higher effort steering and 19-inch (482mm) wheels in place of the 21-inchers (533mm) to give a lower ride height and more suspension travel. By 1929, two million Model As had been produced, but in 1931 sales dropped due to competition from Chevy and the Great Depression. There were also rumours of a new V8 Ford for 1932.

Top speed:	65 mph (104 km/h)
0–60 mph (0–96 km/h):	32.0 sec
Engine type:	In-line four
Displacement:	201 ci (3,293 cc)
Transmission	3–speed manual
Max power:	40 bhp (30 kW) @ 2,200 rpm
Max torque:	128 lb ft (173 Nm) @ 1,000 rpm
Weight:	2,212 lb (1,005 kg)
Economy:	18 mpg (6.4 km/l)

Ford Model A Pick-up (1929)

Like most early Fords, the Model A was subject to much modification but still remained in the shadow of the 1932 Ford, which could naturally take a V8 engine as it had a Flathead eight-cylinder as standard. The A could just about take one at a squeeze, though many hot rodders used the 1932's chassis with the lighter A body on it to make their hot rods. This particular car uses a virtually stock Model A pick-up body mounted on a separate chassis based on the dimensions of the original frame. At the front, this car uses a beam axle which is similar to the original set-up, but which has kick-ups either side of the beam in order to allow the body to sit lower. The engine is a mildly tuned version of Ford's much later Windsor small-block V8 engine, and the power is handled by a 9-inch (227mm) live axle, which is of similar vintage to the motor.

Top speed:	129 mph (206 km/h)
0–60 mph (0–96 km/h):	5.3 sec
Engine type:	V8
Displacement:	351 ci (5,751 cc)
Transmission	4–speed auto
Max power:	304 bhp (227 kW) @ 4,900 rpm
Max torque:	380 lb ft (515 Nm) @ 3,200 rpm
Weight:	2,470 lb (1,122 kg)
Economy:	13.8 mpg (4.88 km/l)

Cord L-29 (1930)

Spoilt by arriving just a day before the USA's famous stock market crash in 1930, the Cord L-29 was nonetheless extremely stylish. It was put together by the Auburn Automobile Company and named after the firm's president, E.L Cord. It was revolutionary in that it used front-wheel drive with a de Dion axle mounted under the grille, and the massive straight-eight engine had an alloy head and was set back in the chassis for good weight-distribution. Because of the drive configuration, chief design engineer John Oswald was able to style the L-29 very long and low, which made it look sleek against its contemporaries. Because of the market crash, the car sold poorly, so its price was slashed to help boost sales. Even so, the car was finished by 1931but it had done well in the Europe Concours d' Elegance shows, and paved the way for the most coveted of all Cords, the 812.

Top speed:	78 mph (125 km/h)
0–60 mph (0–96 km/h):	24.0 sec
Engine type:	in-line eight
Displacement:	299 ci (4,899 cc)
Transmission	3–speed manual
Max power:	115 bhp (86 kW) @ 3,350 rpm
Max torque:	N/A
Weight:	4,710 lb (2,140 kg)
Economy:	12 mpg (4.2 km/l)

Chevrolet Independence (1931)

While Ford sold more than twice as many cars as Chevy, the exclusivity is what has drawn many hot rodders to their early cars. However, this hot rod couldn't be more far removed from the original Independence, which came with a 50bhp (37kW) motor which made just over 50mph (80km/h) possible. This car has a chopped five-window body channelled over the lightweight tube-frame chassis to get the car as close to the ground as possible. The front end has a drop beam connected via four locating bars and a transverse leaf spring, while the rear consists of a 9-inch (229mm) Ford live axle, again located by four adjustable bars. The 'Rat' motor is from a late 1960s Chevelle, being the big-block Chevy reworked to accept a Weiand supercharger with intercooler for more power. Made for acceleration, this car does the quarter-mile in 9.9 seconds at nearly 140mph (224km/h).

Top speed:	170 mph (272 km/h)
0–60 mph (0–96 km/h):	4.5 sec
Engine type:	V8
Displacement:	460 ci (7,538 cc)
Transmission	2–speed auto
Max power:	900 bhp (67 kW) @ 6,400 rpm
Max torque:	710 lb ft (963 Nm) @ 3,800 rpm
Weight:	2,850 lb (1,295 kg)
Economy:	4 mpg (1.4 km/l)

Duesenberg SJ (1932)

Like most luxury and expensive machines of the time, the Duesenberg SJ came only as a rolling chassis to which the customer would add their choice of coachbuilt body. Fred Deusenberg pushed for quality and durability and the frame consisted of strong 8-inch (203mm) deep rails with vacuum-assisted four-wheel brakes with aluminium brake shoes and a variable effort dash lever for dry to icy roads. Aluminium was, in fact, used where possible because at 20ft (6m) long the car needed as many weight-saving measures as it could get. The engine was the most powerful in production in the world at the time and made the supercharged version of the SJ one of the fastest road cars available. In 1935 A.B. Jenkins averaged 135mph (216km/h) on a 24-hour Bonneville run and clocked a 160mph (258km/h) top speed. Sadly Duesenberg never knew, as he died driving one of his SJs in 1932.

Top speed:	130 mph (208 km/h)
0–60 mph (0–96 km/h):	8.5 sec
Engine type:	In-line eight
Displacement:	420 ci (6,882 cc)
Transmission	3–speed manual
Max power:	320 bhp (239 kW) @ 4,200 rpm
Max torque:	425 lb ft (576 Nm) @ 2,400 rpm
Weight:	5,000 lb (2,272 kg)
Economy:	10 mpg (3.54 km/l)

Ford Hi-Boy Roadster (1932)

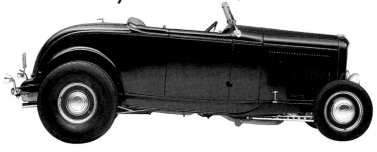

The term 'hot rod' to most people conjures up images of one particular model – the 1932 Ford roadster. It was the most sophisticated of the 'flat sided Fords' and so quickly became a backbone of the rodding scene. The trend for building them began in the late 1930s. Back then, young guys were picking them up very cheap, stripping everything but the essentials off of them, fitting the Flathead V8s from the '34 model then racing their cars on the street or on the dry lake beds of Southern California, which were both flat and vast. The hot rod scene has grown to incorporate all manner of cars, but the 1932 roadster remains a favourite. This example is typical of the cars built in the 1960s, with split wishbone front arms, a beam front axle, live rear axle and a small-block V8 for power, though in this case it's Ford and not Chevy. Modifications include wide steels and fenderless body, which save weight.

Top speed:	120 mph (192 km/h)
0–60 mph (0–96 km/h):	6.0 sec
Engine type:	V8
Displacement:	302 ci (4,948 cc)
Transmission	3–speed manual
Max power:	250 bhp (186 kW) @ 4,500 rpm
Max torque:	275 lb ft (373 Nm) @ 3,000 rpm
Weight:	2,250 lb (1,022 kg)
Economy:	15 mpg (5.3 km/l)

Ford Model 18 Coupe (1932)

The line 'You gonna go after him John', is from the immortal film *American Graffiti*, where John Milner (played by Paul LeMat) is asked whether he's going to chase the tuned 1955 Chevy of Bob Falfa (a young Harrison Ford). The two square up in the final scene, with Milner in this five-window coupe hot rod. Set in 1962, the film centres around one night in a southern Californian town. Milner paroles the main cruise in his 'Deuce coupe' powered by a 1966 327ci (5.3-litre) Corvette engine with 'Fuelie' (fuel injection) heads and a Man-a-Fre quad carb manifold. The car used a Chevy sedan rear axle with a transverse leaf spring and ladder bars for optimum traction, while the front used the original beam axle but kicked-up either end to lower the nose of the car. The wheels were reversed versions of what was available on larger Chevy sedans, but chromed here for show.

Top speed:	125 mph (200 km/h)
0–60 mph (0–96 km/h):	6.2 sec
Engine type:	V8
Displacement:	327 ci (5,358 cc)
Transmission	4–speed manual
Max power:	370 bhp (283 kW) @ 6,000 rpm
Max torque:	380 lb ft (515 Nm) @ 3,800 rpm
Weight:	2,680 lb (1,218 kg)
Economy:	15 mpg (5.3 km/l)

Ford Roadster (1932)

Hot rodding became huge throughout the 1950s and '60s, and never really stopped even into the 1990s. What it did as time went on is used new technology and it seemedd like as soon as a new engine was debuted, within months one had found its way into a hot rod. However, in a turn against the high-tech cars, some owners built their cars using the parts they grew up with, which began a trend to a new style called 'nostalgia' cars. This example shows the style well, using a Nailhead Buick engine (because of the small vertical intake valves) to provide much torque. A drop beam axle with four bar location and transverse leaf spring support the front, while out back a 9-inch (229mm) Ford live axle rear is situated on coilovers and a four-bar racing set-up. In a further nod towards the rods and aeroplanes of the 1950s, this owner has painted flames on the side of his car.

Top speed:	120 mph (192 km/h)
0–60 mph (0–96 km/h):	5.8 sec
Engine type:	V8
Displacement:	401 ci (6,571 cc)
Transmission	4–speed auto
Max power:	410 bhp (305 kW) @ 4,400 rpm
Max torque:	445 lb ft (603 Nm) @ 2,800 rpm
Weight:	2,338 lb (1,062 kg)
Economy:	7 mpg (2.5 km/l)

Chrysler Airflow (1934)

The Airflow was the first production car to use wind-tunnel design testing, but it also had a number of other advances. The body was built in a similar way to an aircraft, with a steel beam and truss framework for the panels to mount on. It was very aerodynamic and helped a 1934 Imperial coupe model complete a flying mile of 95.6mph (154km/h) at Bonneville salt flats. The Airflow also had a unique gearbox, fitted with helical gears to make it exceptionally quiet. Later examples were fitted with hypoid rear axles and above 45mph (72km/h) when your foot was lifted off the accelerator, an overdrive gear would automatically engage. Another first was the puncture-proof tyres, which comprised Lifeguard tyres with heavy-duty tubes and a second floating tube inside that. The car was considered too radical for its time, and had poor sales, even when the front end was restyled in 1935.

Top speed:	88 mph (141 km/h)
0–60 mph (0–96 km/h):	19.5 sec
Engine type:	In-line eight
Displacement:	298 ci (4,883 cc)
Transmission	3–speed manual
Max power:	122 bhp (91 kW) @ 3,400 rpm
Max torque:	N/A
Weight:	4,166 lb (1,893 kg)
Economy:	16 mpg (5.66 km/l)

Ford Coupe (1934)

The first mass production car to use a V8, the 1934 Ford also went away from the slab–sided look which had dated previous models to horse-drawn carriages. The swept-back grille and swooping fenders gained many fans, and because all 1934 models came with a V8 they were also popular to tune up or at least use for their upgraded parts. As such, hot rodders loved them. The 1934 used an era-typical separate steel chassis, and these remain on many of the hot rodded cars even now. This car even uses the stock beam front axle, but with modern telescopic dampers. At the rear it's more high-tech with the use of a late-model Corvette independent suspension. This hot rod has a period appearance with many accessories of the era. It goes like a modern supercar though, thanks to a tuned small-block Chevy which has been bored out to 358ci (5.8 litres).

Top speed:	127 mph (203 km/h)
0–60 mph (0–96 km/h):	8.7 sec
Engine type:	V8
Displacement:	358 ci (5,866 cc)
Transmission	4-speed manual
Max power:	330 bhp (246 kW) @ 5,500 rpm
Max torque:	339 lb ft (460 Nm) @ 3,400 rpm
Weight:	2,403 lb (1,092 kg)
Economy:	13.8 mpg (4.88 km/l)

Ford Model 830 Pick-up (1935)

Pick-ups have always been a part of the American way of life, and this extends to hot rods. Their lightweight bodies and utilitarian looks go against the grain but that's part of their attraction. They also came with strong chassis and uprated suspension so could take a lot of modifying without major component renewal. Saying that, for the ultimate in style and performance, you have to build any car from the ground up, and that means completely new underpinnings. This pick-up uses a custom steel separate chassis with a Mustang II independent wishbone front end and live axle rear with semi-elliptical springs and traction bars. The engine is the hot rodder's favourite, a small-block Chevy giving mid-14 second potential on the quarter-mile. In typical street rod fashion, this pick-up features a custom interior with leather and air-conditioning for the ultimate in cruising.

Top speed:	110 mph (176 km/h)
0–60 mph (0–96 km/h):	6.4 sec
Engine type:	V8
Displacement:	350 ci (5,735 cc)
Transmission	3-speed auto
Max power:	320 bhp (238 kW) @ 5,400 rpm
Max torque:	360 lb ft (488 Nm) @ 3,800 rpm
Weight:	3,280 lb (1,491 kg)
Economy:	15 mpg (5.31 km/l)

Ford Roadster (1936)

By 1936 cars from Ford had started to swell in size and each new year brought a
model with great advances in both technology and design. But every example
was well liked by the public, who flocked to Ford like no other manufacturer as they
offered cheap yet good-quality transport. As the street rodding industry saw a
revival in the 1980s, many firms went into the reproduction of early Ford bodies as
they were becoming so difficult to find in good-condition steel. Offering them in
glass-fibre which wouldn't rot and was lightweight seemed perfect for the majority
of builders who wanted to construct their own cars from kit form at home. This car
uses one such body on a vintage shaped chassis but with extra strength. The front
and rear suspension are beam and live axle respectively, while power comes from a
basic tune small-block Chevy which can still pull the car to quick speeds.

Top speed:	120 mph (192 km/h)
0–60 mph (0–96 km/h):	6.9 sec
Engine type:	V8
Displacement:	350 ci (5,735 cc)
Transmission	4-speed auto
Max power:	250 bhp (186 kW) @ 4,800 rpm
Max torque:	320 lb ft (434 Nm) @ 3,200 rpm
Weight:	2,350 lb (1,068 kg)
Economy:	13 mpg (4.60 km/l)

Hudson Terraplane (1936)

While competing with the likes of the more mainstream Fords and Chevrolets, the Hudson Terraplane offered a number of interesting design features that put it ahead of its rivals and marked the models as rugged and reliable transport. The chassis was incredibly strong, but whereas most cars had their bodies bolted to the frame, the Terraplane had its welded at around 30 points to make the whole structure very rigid and thus the ride quality better. Also, the company favoured wider tyres than most, then ran them at a lower pressure to further enhance the ride. At the front the beam axle was located by radius arms which improved feel and gave a measure of anti-dive under hard braking. Finishing the car off were the brakes which were hydraulic; in case these failed and the pedal went to the floor, a mechanical set of brakes was activated on the rear only.

Top speed:	80 mph (128 km/h)
0–60 mph (0–96 km/h):	23.2 sec
Engine type:	In-line six
Displacement:	212 ci (3,474 cc)
Transmission	3-speed manual
Max power:	88 bhp (65 kW) @ 3,800 rpm
Max torque:	N/A
Weight:	2,740 lb (1,245 kg)
Economy:	16 mpg (5.66 km/l)

Chevrolet Coupe (1938)

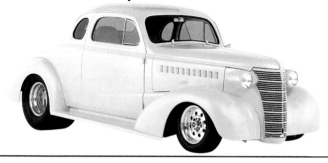

Towards the end of the 1930s Chevrolet excelled in making simple yet rugged cars for the masses, often outnumbering Ford in sales. Their cars became very popular with the hot-rodding fraternity who used them and started off the trend in 'fat fendered' rods which continued with cars built in the late 1940s. Such cars could take major suspension changes and wider tyres without a great deal of bodywork modification and, with their wide engine bays, handled motor transplants with ease too. This car has been fitted with a Generation V big-block Chevy under the hood and to put all the torque down the rear's been equipped with a pair of 18.5-inch (470mm) wide tyres. A Mustang II front suspension clip has been installed along with airbag springs to alter the ride height whilst giving supreme comfort, and at the back a live axle is located with four links and coilover dampers.

Top speed:	143 mph (229 km/h)
0–60 mph (0–96 km/h):	5.1 sec
Engine type:	V8
Displacement:	454 ci (7,439 cc)
Transmission:	3-speed auto
Max power:	410 bhp (306 kW) @ 6,000 rpm
Max torque:	520 lb ft (705 Nm) @ 3,400 rpm
Weight:	2,980 lb (1,354 kg)
Economy:	8 mpg (2.83 km/l)

Ford Model 81A (1938)

Ford were the first company to introduce a V8 in a mass production car in the early 1930s, and they continued thanks to massive public demand. By 1938 the engines were standard across the board, but other manufacturers were using them too and in particular Chevy, who regularly overtook Ford in sales. To compensate, Ford split its models into two distinctly different version, the Deluxe and Standard. This car is the Deluxe, shown by the grille splitting into two distinct arcs at the top, whereas the Standard had a vertical top. Little remains of the standard car underneath, except for a strengthened version of the stock chassis. A Mustang II wishbone suspension clip is fitted at the front, while the rear uses leaf spring on a live axle. Its Chevy V8 has received the mildest of tune-ups but still has plenty of power to make this a boulevard bruiser.

Top speed:	122 mph (195 km/h)
0–60 mph (0–96 km/h):	6.1 sec
Engine type:	V8
Displacement:	350 ci (5,735 cc)
Transmission	4-speed auto
Max power:	345 bhp (257 kW) @ 5,600 rpm
Max torque:	360 lb ft (488 Nm) @ 4,000 rpm
Weight:	2,350 lb (1,068 kg)
Economy:	14 mpg (4.95 km/l)

Ford Deluxe V8 (1939)

Often regarded as Ford's finest pre-war cars, the 1939–1940 V8s had up-to-the-minute styling and plenty of power, thanks to the latest developments of the V8 Flathead engine. In this car's case, the optional 85bhp (63kW) motor was up 20bhp (15kW) thanks to a new intake manifold and carburettor. Underneath, the car used a similar chassis to that which had been developed for the 1934 model year, with an X-braced twin rail design. The suspension it used went even further back in time, being almost identical to the Model T's set-up of a beam front and live rear axle supported on transverse leaf springs, but then Henry Ford always did believe in keeping his cars simple and therefore cheap. New for 1939 were four-wheel hydraulic brakes, which made the Fords much safer and more reassuring to drive. By the later 1930s the popular airflow look was evident on Ford's designs.

Top speed:	87 mph (139 km/h)
0–60 mph (0–96 km/h):	17.4 sec
Engine type:	V8
Displacement:	221 ci (3,621 cc)
Transmission:	3-speed manual
Max power:	85 bhp (63 kW) @ 3,800 rpm
Max torque:	155lb ft (210 Nm) @ 2,200 rpm
Weight:	2,898 lb (1,317 kg)
Economy:	18 mpg (6.37 km/l)

Lincoln Zephyr (1939)

While the 1939 and 1940 Lincoln Zephyr looked much like the Ford designs of the same era, underneath they were significantly different. The Zepyr was the base model Lincoln and was to use a Flathead V8 like the Fords, but under the order of Henry Ford instead they had a V12 engine developed from the V8 but with a 75-degree angle. Early models suffered from overheating, warped bores and oil sludge build-up due to inadequate crankcase ventilation, but this was solved and later engines also had hydraulic lifters for quieter, more reliable, running. The Zephyr was revolutionary in that it used unitary construction as opposed to a separate chassis, but aside from that, it was basic and dated with solid axles and transverse leaf springs. What was different was the Columbia two-speed rear axle which effectively doubled the gears to six forward speeds.

Top speed:	87 mph (139 km/h)
0–60 mph (0–96 km/h):	16.0 sec
Engine type:	V8
Displacement:	267 ci (4,375 cc)
Transmission	3-speed manual
Max power:	110 bhp (82 kW) @ 3,900 rpm
Max torque:	180 lb ft (244 Nm) @ 3,500 rpm
Weight:	3,790 lb (1,722 kg)
Economy:	16 mpg (5.66 km/l)

Packard 6/110 (1940)

While most luxury cars were using a V8 or, in some cases, a V12, Packard shunned these for its junior car, the 6/110, the name of which denoted six cylinders and 110bhp (82kW). Packard customers expected smooth, silent and ultra-refined engines, and the 110 still met those requirements whilst being less punchy than the V8 cars. The cars were designed to be luxurious rather than lightweight or sporting, hence most of the time a few extra pounds here or there didn't matter. However, in the case of the X-braces chassis, the crossmember was drilled to save weight. At the front the car was hi-tech for the time, as it had an independent double wishbone set-up with coil springs which gave an excellent ride quality. The rear consisted of a live axle on two longitudinal leaf springs. Other useful extras were air-conditioning, an overdrive gearbox and electrical windshield wipers.

Top speed:	75 mph (120 km/h)
0–60 mph (0–96 km/h):	20.1 sec
Engine type:	V8
Displacement:	245 ci (4,014 cc)
Transmission	3-speed manual
Max power:	100 bhp (74 kW) @ 3,600 rpm
Max torque:	195 lb ft (264 Nm) @ 4,500 rpm
Weight:	3,200 lb (1,454 kg)
Economy:	16 mpg (5.66 km/l)

Chevrolet Coupe (1940)

Chevrolet hailed the new for '40 model as significant because it was their first car to use both plastics and stainless steel in its construction. While it used a basic chassis and suspension, it was rugged and reliable and racing driver Juan Manual Fangio won the 6,000-mile (9,654km) Gran Primo Internacional Del Norte race in Argentina, South America in a Business Coupe like the one shown. Chevrolets are often chosen over Ford by hot rodders who want a more individual car. This version has had a separate chassis based on the original rails, with independent A-arm front and Jaguar sedan independent rear suspension. The brakes are discs all around with an upgrade to four-pot callipers. The engine is a Corvette small-block Chevy with three two-barrel carburettors, known as Tri-Power, and uses the centre carb on light throttle then all three on full throttle. Inside it uses all-electric Corvette seats.

Top speed:	125 mph (200 km/h)
0–60 mph (0–96 km/h):	6.8 sec
Engine type:	V8
Displacement:	327 ci (5,358 cc)
Transmission	4-speed auto
Max power:	300 bhp (224 kW) @ 5,000 rpm
Max torque:	321 lb ft (435 Nm) @ 3,200 rpm
Weight:	2,900 lb (1,318 kg)
Economy:	14.7 mpg (5.20 km/l)

Ford Coupe (1940)

Ford evolved their separate fender design ever since the '34 model appeared, but by the 1940 Ford coupe they'd become rounded and this pretty much steered car design into the next decade. While once proving affordable and simple transportation for many Americans, the 1940 coupe went on to be a hot rodders' favourite, as its Flathead V8 was tuner friendly. The V8 engine developed as time went on, and when Chevrolet's small-block appeared in '55 it was an instant hit with hot rodders. This car uses one sitting in the 40 Coupe's basic rails, strengthened to take Mustang II front suspension and a 9-inch (229mm) Ford live rear axle on semi–elliptical leaf springs. The small-block has been treated to a high-lift camshaft, modified heads, a dual plane intake manifold, Holley four-barrel carb and can now do the quarter in 14 seconds while providing cruising family comfort.

Top speed:	123 mph (197 km/h)
0–60 mph (0–96 km/h):	6.4 sec
Engine type:	V8
Displacement:	350 ci (5,735 cc)
Transmission	3-speed auto
Max power:	345 bhp (257 kW) @ 5,600 rpm
Max torque:	360 lb ft (488 Nm) @ 4,000 rpm
Weight:	2,769 lb (1,258 kg)
Economy:	15 mpg (5.31 km/l)

Willys Coupe (1940)

Drag-racing started getting very popular in 1960's USA, because pre-war cars were cheap and plentiful and so were used on the strip. They used large V8s run on pump gas and ran high in order to fit both large wheels under the stock rear bodywork and to allow a big engine up front without major body alterations. The 1940–1941 Willys was a favourite to modify, but as time went on an aerodyanamics played a bigger part, the cars sat lower. Hot rodders have long used the Willys coupe but they've been most popular in the 1980s and 1990s. This car is typical of the finest built, and uses a separate box steel chassis with a custom double A-arm suspension at the front and a four-bar located live axle at the rear. A blown Chrysler Hemi engine provides power enough for 10-second quarter miles through the 18.5-inch (470mm) wide Mickey Thompson street/strip tyres.

Top speed:	150 mph (240 km/h)
0–60 mph (0–96 km/h):	3.4 sec
Engine type:	V8
Displacement:	392 ci (6,423 cc)
Transmission	3-speed manual
Max power:	700 bhp (522 kW) @ 6,800 rpm
Max torque:	509 lb ft (690 Nm) @ 3,200 rpm
Weight:	2,872 lb (1,305 kg)
Economy:	5 mpg (1.77 km/l)

Graham Hollywood (1941)

When Auburn-Cord-Duesenberg went out of the business in the late 1930s two companies battled to save the incredible Cord, and one of those was Graham-Paige. They took the front-wheel drive 810/812 and turned it into a rear-wheel drive before fitting their own restyled body called the Hollywood. They needed a new front axle to replace the driveshaft-equipped front-wheel drive set-up, so chose a simple but rather ancient (by then) beam axle on leaf springs, matched at the rear with leaf springs either end of a live axle. The ride offered was best cruising at speed, where the car was in a class of its own. The engine wasn't particularly large but with a supercharger, it did offer plenty of torque and the three-speed gearbox smoothed out its operation well. While the car seemed to offer an afterlife for the Cord, it was too costly to produce, and by late 1941 it was finished.

Top speed:	89 mph (142.4 km/h)
0–60 mph (0–96 km/h):	14.6 sec
Engine type:	In-line six
Displacement:	218 ci (3,572 cc)
Transmission	3-speed manual
Max power:	124 bhp (92 kW) @ 4,000 rpm
Max torque:	182 lb ft (247 Nm) @ 2,400 rpm
Weight:	3,240 lb (1,472 kg)
Economy:	17 mpg (6.01 km/l)

Pontiac Torpedo Eight (1941)

Prior to World War II, Pontiac had long battled with Buick in the intermediate-priced market, but in 1941 it came up with a winner that put it ahead, so much so that the company continued the car's production up until 1948, when many companies were trying to leave their pre-war designs behind. The wide low grille was a sign of things to come in car design, as were the blended-in sealed beam headlamps and tail lights. While still using a separate chassis, the Torpedo did have independent wishbones suspension and telescopic shocks on the rear axle which Pontiac promoted as reducing sway on corners. The engine offered extremely relaxed performance thanks to its low-down torque and almost silent revving. It went well with the car's smooth cruising ability and flat cornering prowess with neutral handling. The interior was a work of art, thanks to hand-made dash details.

Top speed:	88 mph (141 km/h)
0–60 mph (0–96 km/h):	18.9 sec
Engine type:	In-line eight
Displacement:	294 ci (4,817 cc)
Transmission	3-speed manual
Max power:	103 bhp (77 kW) @ 3,500 rpm
Max torque:	190 lb ft (258 Nm) @ 2,200 rpm
Weight:	3,325 lb (1,511 kg)
Economy:	16 mpg (5.66 km/l)

Willys Jeep (1941)

When the US Army needed an all-purpose in World War II, Bantam came up with the right 4WD design but production was also given to both Ford and Willys. Each company produced virtually the same vehicle, though Willys produced the most with 361,349, Ford being second with 277,896, and Bantam last with just 2,675. The frame was simple but very rugged and everything had to be bolt-on for ease of maintenance. Fully floating Spicer axles were used at either end with multi-leaf springs for durability and strength to carry heavy loads as these cars were adapted to many uses. As the idea was to keep the components simple and reliable, the engine was a four-cylinder unit with high torque and low output. The Jeep could pull up steep inclines, thanks to a two-speed transfer case and minimal bodywork overhang which allowed approach and departure angles of 45 degrees.

Top speed:	62 mph (99 km/h)
0–60 mph (0–96 km/h):	30 sec
Engine type:	In-line four
Displacement:	134 ci (2,195 cc)
Transmission	3-speed manual
Max power:	60 bhp (45 kW) @ 3,600 rpm
Max torque:	105 lb ft (142 Nm) @ 2,000 rpm
Weight:	2,453 lb (1,115kg)
Economy:	13.8 mpg (4.88 km/l)

Mercury Sportsman (1946)

While the Sportsman didn't pack any new technology, nor a powerful engine (as the name suggested), it did have a beautifully designed body and a ride quality which belied its ancient underpinnings. The styling was brought about by Bob Gregorie, who had to create the feel of the upmarket Lincoln Continental without the cost, so he produced wood panelling in maple and mahogany which dovetailed exquisitely throughout the rear of the car. As mentioned, underneath the car had nothing revolutionary. There was a separate steel chassis with large centre tunnel to house the torque tube (like all Mercurys of the time), while the suspension was plain old solid axle with transverse leaf springs at both ends. Even using the biggest Flathead V8 of the time, the car's performance was still leisurely, though it did have good low speed torque, and the powerplant was very reliable.

Top speed:	82 mph (131 km/h)
0–60 mph (0–96 km/h):	21.2 sec
Engine type:	V8
Displacement:	239 ci (3,916 cc)
Transmission	3-speed manual
Max power:	100 bhp (74 kW) @ 3,800 rpm
Max torque:	N/A
Weight:	3,407 lb (1,548 kg)
Economy:	16 mpg (5.66 km/l)

Chrysler Town & Country (1947)

This car was so called because the coachbuilder once commented that the front end looked town, while the rear looked country. The wood was more than decoration though, because it formed part of the structure, using white ash and Honduras mahogany inserts. The car was direct competition to the Mercury Sportsman in this niche market, but had a number of advances over that car. Firstly, it used Chrysler fluid-drive semi-automatic transmission with two high and two low gears for ultra-smooth operation. It also had the power advantage with its extra displacement straight-eight which used twin carbs. The ride was also better thanks to a double wishbones front end with coils and telescopic shocks. Whilst somewhat heavier than the Mercury, the Town & Country did feel very well built, with doors that shut like a bank vault. The car continued in production for two years.

Top speed:	105 mph (168 km/h)
0–60 mph (0–96 km/h):	20.0 sec
Engine type:	In-line eight
Displacement:	324 ci (5,309 cc)
Transmission	4-speed semi-automatic
Max power:	135 bhp (101 kW) @ 3,400 rpm
Max torque:	N/A
Weight:	4,332 lb (1,969 kg)
Economy:	14 mpg (4.95 km/l)

Chevrolet Fleetmaster (1948)

Post-war Chevys were often regarded as too bulbous and weighty to make decent hot rods out of, but that all changed with the trend for 'fat fendered' cars among the custom and cruising fans. With naturally rounded lines, the cars could be further smoothed by de-badging and de-trimming, thus making them fuss-free externally, and very striking cars. This car not only has the smoothed lines, but its body has been channelled over the chassis for a low ride height, which is further enhanced on the Mustang II independent wishbone front end by 2-inch (50mm) drop spindles that effectively bring wheels up inside the arch without changing suspension geometry. The rear end is a basic live axle with leaf springs, built to be tough and durable to take the power from the Tri-Power (triple carburettors) small-block Chevy V8 with performance heads and a low restriction exhaust.

Top speed:	139 mph (222 km/h)
0–60 mph (0–96 km/h):	6.8 sec
Engine type:	V8
Displacement:	350 ci (5,735 cc)
Transmission	3-speed auto
Max power:	325 bhp (242 kW) @ 5,500 rpm
Max torque:	340 lb ft (461 Nm) @ 3,500 rpm
Weight:	3,450 lb (1,568 kg)
Economy:	14 mpg (4.95 km/l)

Ford F1 (1948)

Being one of the most popular workhorses of the time, the F1 had many fans as it was tough, reliable and could be ordered with the optional 239ci (3.9-litre) Flathead V8. The F1 was Ford's first new production vehicle following the war, and it had increased room over pre-war models, plus greater refinement, something that truck lovers were to demand more of in later models. As the trucks were built rugged in the first place, this one has needed little to cope with the extra power provided by a small-block Ford V8. A 9-inch (229mm) Ford rear axle puts down the torque well, but apart from that, just the gearbox has changed, with all fitting where they're supposed to without major modification. The original suspension remains, with lowering blocks on the front leaf springs to get the nose 'in the weeds' and the rear having the axle put above the leaf springs, instead of below, as standard.

Top speed:	105 mph (168 km/h)
0–60 mph (0–96 km/h):	8.7 sec
Engine type:	V8
Displacement:	351 ci (5,751 cc)
Transmission	3-speed auto
Max power:	275 bhp (205 kW) @ 4,800 rpm
Max torque:	380 lb ft (515 Nm) @ 3,400 rpm
Weight:	3,120 lb (1,418 kg)
Economy:	15 mpg (5.31 km/l)

Buick Roadmaster (1949)

Buick started to make cars again as soon as World War II was over in 1945. Their cars changed a little in style, going long and wider in looks thanks to subtle grille changes and new trim. The Roadmaster model first appeared in 1945 and was restyled for 1949 with the front fender tops extending all the way to the top of the rear fenders, thus finally ditching the sloping fender look which dated cars back to the 1930s. The looks were a big success with the public and Buick sales increased by 100,000. The Roadmaster kept a similar suspension set-up to the pre-war cars, with a separate chassis, double wishbone independent front suspension and a live axle rear on leaf springs. The big advance was Buick's Dynaflow auto gearbox, which was the first to use a torque converter. This sophisticated fluid coupling magnified the torque produced by the engine, making the Roadmaster smooth and powerful.

Top speed:	100 mph (160 km/h)
0–60 mph (0–96 km/h):	17.1 sec
Engine type:	In-line eight
Displacement:	320 ci (5,243 cc)
Transmission	2-speed auto
Max power:	150 bhp (112 kW) @ 3,600 rpm
Max torque:	260 lb ft (352 Nm) @ 2,400 rpm
Weight:	4,370 lb (1,986 kg)
Economy:	14 mpg (4.95 km/l)

Hudson Super Six (1949)

Hudson introduced their 'Step Down' range in the late '40s to much acclaim. They featured low-slung, sleek styling and slab sides, but were notable for other advances. They used unitary construction with the body and chassis as one, to provide better torsional control. They also had a powerful six-cylinder engine on the Super Six, which weighed less than the straight eight but still gave the car a low centre of gravity so it handled well. The cars were natural to turn into lead sleds because of their fared-in rear wheels and rounded styling. The owner of this car has 'shaved' all the trim off the bodywork, then blended in the front and rear lights plus a sun visor to make the body as smooth as possible. Under the hood lies a fuel-injected small-block Chevy, again fully smoothed, but colour-coded in white, like the full leather interior with some original and some modern digital instruments.

Top speed:	124 mph (198 km/h)
0–60 mph (0–96 km/h):	9.0 sec
Engine type:	V8
Displacement:	350 ci (5,735 cc)
Transmission	4-speed auto
Max power:	310 bhp (231 kW) @ 5,000 rpm
Max torque:	340 lb ft (461 Nm) @ 2,400 rpm
Weight:	3,554 lb (1,615 kg)
Economy:	14.7 mpg (5.2 km/l)

Mercury Lead Sled (1949)

In the late 1940s and 1950s, hot rodding became hugely popular with returning servicemen looking to hot up their cars. Styles started to develop and some guys improved their car's for looks more than performance, making customs the cars to be seen in. The 1949 Mercury was a very radical design, aerodynamic and flowing and looking custom chopped with its low roof. Within a few years it was available cheaply and hot rodders began using the Merc body so much that it quickly became the car for customizing. It's often referred to as a 'lead sled' because in the days before plastic bodyfiller, car refinishing experts used molten lead to fill seams or trim holes, which was then shaped before spraying. This particular Mercury is typical of the late 1950s/early 1960s, with custom wheel hubcaps, flame paint, 1954 DeSoto toothed grille and rear fenders skirts. It's fitted with a small-block Chevy.

Top speed:	120 mph (192 km/h)
0–60 mph (0–96 km/h):	7.8 sec
Engine type:	V8
Displacement:	350 ci (5,735 cc)
Transmission	3-speed auto
Max power:	380 bhp (283 kW) @ 5,100 rpm
Max torque:	380 lb ft (515 Nm) @ 3,200 rpm
Weight:	3,374 lb (1,533 kg)
Economy:	9 mpg (3.18 km/l)

Pontiac Chieftan (1949)

Pontiac was one of the last brands to offer new models following the war, but when it did, it gave them cleaner, more integrated styling with a handsome front fender line which continued down the side to flow into the rear fender. The Chieftan replaced the Torpedo and was lower-slung because of a new chassis design which incorporated an X-brace for improved rigidity. The front suspension featured double wishbones while the rear had leaf springs, but all were designed to be soft to give the Chieftan the best possible ride quality. The straight-eight engine had made its debut in 1933 so was old, but by 1949 it was up in displacement and, thanks to the long-stroke crankshaft, torquey at low revs. The convertible was the most expensive model in 1949, and continues to be the most 'in demand' Pontiac today, with values up to $30,000.

Top speed:	89 mph (142 km/h)
0–60 mph (0–96 km/h):	19.0 sec
Engine type:	In-line eight
Displacement:	249 ci (4,080 cc)
Transmission	4-speed auto
Max power:	104 bhp (76 kW) @ 3,800 rpm
Max torque:	188 lb ft (255 Nm) @ 2,000 rpm
Weight:	3,670 lb (1,668 kg)
Economy:	17 mpg (6.01 km/l)

Ford Custom Tudor (1950)

Known as one of the toughest on and off road races in the world, the Carrera Panamericana, has long been run and in the early 1950s Ford entered carssimilar to this one. The Tudor sedan was lightweight and rugged, and with a Flathead V8, which had proved reliable and durable, the car was ideal for the nlong distance event. Five decades later the same cars are still proving tough contenders, though this version has far more packed in than the original race machines. It has a similar chassis layout but is strengthened with a six-point roll cage. There are double wishbones up front and leaf springs at the rear, uprated and supplemented by anti-roll bars front and rear plus a Watts linkage on the beefy 9-inch (229mm) Ford axle. The Flathead has been bored out and stroked for extra displacement and power, and the gearbox is the ultra-tough Borg Warner T10 'Toploader'.

Top speed:	110 mph (176 km/h)
0–60 mph (0–96 km/h):	10.1 sec
Engine type:	V8
Displacement:	290 ci (4,752 cc)
Transmission	4-speed manual
Max power:	226 bhp (168 kW) @ 4,000 rpm
Max torque:	240 lb ft (325 Nm) @ 2,600 rpm
Weight:	3,112 lb (1,414 kg)
Economy:	15 mpg (5.31 km/l)

Ford Woody (1950)

Woodys were always regarded as the family station wagon with a country feel, until surfers found them useful for their long boards. They became firm favourites with both surfers and hot rodders, who had lifestyles that were very alike with a general disregard to conforming to the norm. Most surf wagons were kept stock mechanically but lowered and sometimes fitted with custom wheels. This 1950 Ford has taken the Woody to another level with late-model Mustang independent front suspension and a narrowed 9-inch (229mm) Ford axle located on a four-bar set-up. The power comes via a supercharged small-block Chevy with massive torque, and to put the power down, the owner has fitted 13-inch (330mm) wide Mickey Thompson Pro Street Radials at the rear. While inside the rear seat has been removed, it features air-conditioning and a modern multi-speaker sound system.

Top speed:	147 mph (235 km/h)
0–60 mph (0–96 km/h):	4.7 sec
Engine type:	V8
Displacement:	406 ci (6,653 cc)
Transmission	4-speed auto
Max power:	410 bhp (306 kW) @ 5,100 rpm
Max torque:	450 lb ft (610 Nm) @ 3,100 rpm
Weight:	3,402 lb (1,546kg)
Economy:	16.7 mpg (5.91 km/l)

GMC FC-101 Stepside (1951)

GMC introduced their new range of light-duty trucks in 1947, with smoother styling and a redesigned cab. The cab gave an extra inch headroom but, more importantly, an extra 7 inches (178mm) leg-room, which made all the difference to many buyers. It also had improved glassware, making visibility much better in this utility vehicle. Underneath it remained very much the same as the previous CC/EC series models, with solid axle front and rear supported on leaf springs, though the telescopic shocks were a big improvement for ride quality, and buyers could opt for an extra set on the rear if they carried heavy loads. The engine was given slightly more power for the 1951 model year, along with better electrics and optional twin tail lamps, and through a four-speed manual, while performance wasn't brisk, it was torquey at low rpm, which is exactly what most owners needed.

Top speed:	83 mph (132 km/h)
0–60 mph (0–96 km/h):	22.0 sec
Engine type:	In-line six
Displacement:	228 ci (3,736 cc)
Transmission	4-speed manual
Max power:	100 bhp (74 kW) @ 3,400 rpm
Max torque:	187 lb ft (253 Nm) @ 1,700 rpm
Weight:	3,275 lb (1,488 kg)
Economy:	17 mpg (6.01 km/l)

Nash Healey (1951)

Donald Healey is better known for his involvement with Austin throughout Europe, but he worked with American company Nash after a meeting with Nash-Kelvinator president George Mason aboard the *Queen Elizabeth* liner in 1949. The two found they had common ground and hatched a plan to build a Nash-Healey sportscar, which was built in the UK and shown in prototype form the following year. Racing that same year, it took a ninth at the Mille Miglia and a 4th at the Le Mans 24-hour. At first, the roadster looked unusual, with both headlights mounted in a narrow and fussy grille, but by 1951 Pininfarina had restyled the car into the style shown, making it far more handsome. The car used an Ambassador sedan motor with an aluminium cylinder head, hotter camshaft and higher compression ratio. In 1952 with revisions it received an extra 10bhp (7kW).

Top speed:	105 mph (168 km/h)
0–60 mph (0–96 km/h):	11.5 sec
Engine type:	In-line six
Displacement:	252 ci (4,140 cc)
Transmission:	3-speed manual with overdrive
Max power:	135 bhp (100 kW) @ 4,000 rpm
Max torque:	230 lb ft (312 Nm) @ 2,000 rpm
Weight:	2,950 lb (1,340 kg)
Economy:	22 mpg (7.78 km/l)

Studebaker Champion (1951)

Often described by people as the car which didn't know which way it was going – due to the wraparound rear screen which could have been the windshield – the Studebaker Champion was designed by famed stylist Raymond Loewy. He took a lot of his influence from the aircraft industry, and nowhere was this more evident than with the bullet nose which even carried a small spinning propeller early in production. This car has been substantially modified since those days, with a revised and strengthened chassis, Mustang II independent front suspension and a Chrysler rear axle on lowered leaf springs. A tuned Mopar 360 sits under the hood and is mated to a Chrysler Torqueflite gearbox with shift-improvement kit. The body has been treated to shaving off any superfluous trim, and the door handles now open on electric solenoid locks operated by remote control.

Top speed:	115 mph (184 km/h)
0–60 mph (0–96 km/h):	9.8 sec
Engine type:	V8
Displacement:	360 ci (5,899 cc)
Transmission	3-speed auto
Max power:	244 bhp (182 kW) @ 4,200 rpm
Max torque:	290 lb ft (393 Nm) @ 3,000 rpm
Weight:	2,690 lb (1,222 kg)
Economy:	17 mpg (6.01 km/l)

Chevrolet Sedan Delivery (1952)

Chevrolet first officially recognized its car-based Sedan Delivery models as separate to their other purpose-built trucks in 1934 by giving them different ID codes. However, they were built six years prior to that and remained very popular through to the late 1950s/early 1960s, after which the El Camino took over along with bigger trucks. The Sedan Delivery was a great concept for its time, however, because it combined the comfort and driveability of a regular production Sedan with the practicality of a delivery van. They also offered great promotion potential with their slab sides which were often adorned with signwriting and company decals. This model looks original but has a few tweaks to improve it, including dual carbs and a free-flowing exhaust, plus wider rims and radials, and finally a custom interior with two seats, where they left the factory with just one for the driver.

Top speed:	92 mph (147km/h)
0–60 mph (0–96 km/h):	14.0 sec
Engine type:	In-line six
Displacement:	217 ci (3,555 cc)
Transmission:	3-speed manual
Max power:	110 bhp (82 kW) @ 3,400 rpm
Max torque:	187 lb ft (253 Nm) @ 1,700 rpm
Weight:	3,100 lb (1,409 kg)
Economy:	16 mpg (5.66 km/l)

Ford Crestline Sunliner (1952)

Customising was always an art in which individual touches shone through. It's beauty was that virtually any body style could be chosen, though true customising started in the 1950s so that's where many people choose their base material from. The Ford Crestline Sunliner from '52 wasn't chosen as often as the early post–war Fords, but even so it lent itself well to the treatment as the general body shape was very similar to the new–for–'49 model. This car has a host of extras, and in customising the right type of extras are essential – things like upmarket hubcaps, whitewall tyres, grille teeth made from bumper overriders, A-pillar spotlamps and flames to give a real hot rod feel. The accessories inside are just as important, with fluffy dice hanging from the rear view mirror for luck, plus a tweaked dash with peaked switches. This car has also had a roof chop.

Top speed:	112 mph (179 km/h)
0–60 mph (0–96 km/h):	10.5 sec
Engine type:	V8
Displacement:	302 ci (4,948 cc)
Transmission	3-speed auto
Max power:	150 bhp (112 kW) @ 4,200 rpm
Max torque:	240 lb ft (325 Nm) @ 4,500 rpm
Weight:	3,415 lb (1,552 kg)
Economy:	16 mpg (5.66 km/l)

Hudson Hornet (1952)

The introduction of Hudson's Step Down range – which basically meant the chassis was stepped down for the main floor section so the body could be lower – made the cars great handlers because of the lower centre of gravity. While other cars would screech and understeer in corners, the Hudsons would offer handling cornering, which would turn into four-wheel drifts if pushed, thus making them far more predictable. They also had unconventional but very smooth styling so became a favourite with those wanting something different from the norm. Hudson stuck with their six-cylinder for the Hornet, enlarging it to 308ci (5 litres) to take on the V8 cars in NASCAR, which in 1953 it did, with many wins. This led to the production of the 7-X racing option engine, which featured a hotter cam, heavy duty crank, and revised cylinder head for 210bhp (157kW).

Top speed:	93 mph (149 km/h)
0–60 mph (0–96 km/h):	11.0 sec
Engine type:	In-line six
Displacement:	308 ci (5,047 cc)
Transmission:	4-speed manual
Max power:	145 bhp (108 kW) @ 3,800 rpm
Max torque:	257 lb ft (348 Nm) @ 1,800 rpm
Weight:	3,600 lb (1,636 kg)
Economy:	21 mpg (7.43 km/l)

Cadillac Eldorado (1953)

The first Eldorado came from Cadillac in 1953 and it was an expensive option over the regular Series 62 range, costing some $3,600 more. Just 532 were built, so in 1954 the company dropped the price to $4,438, just $300 above the regular range, and sales went up dramatically to over 2,000. The car was the epitome of luxury and featured such revolutionary touches as the wraparound screen which became an industry standard in the 1950s. It also had a signal-seeking radio, special cut down doors, wire wheels, white sidewall tyres, leather and cloth upholstery, fog lamps and a metal tonneau cover to fit over the roof when it was electrically retracted. The engine was the first new post-war V8 on the market and it was an excellent one. It weighed 200lb (107kg) less than the former unit, had 'slipper' pistons and a shorter stroke, plus a higher compression.

Top speed:	116 mph (186 km/h)
0–60 mph (0–96 km/h):	12.6 sec
Engine type:	V8
Displacement:	331 ci (5,424 cc)
Transmission	3-speed auto
Max power:	210 bhp (157 kW) @ 4,150 rpm
Max torque:	330 lb ft (447 Nm) @ 2,700 rpm
Weight:	4,799 lb (2,181 kg)
Economy:	14 mpg (4.95 km/l)

Buick Skylark (1954)

In 1954 Buick celebrated 50 years in car production with the introduction of the Skylark. Designed by Harley Earl, the car was built to be the top-level Buick and thus featured much chrome trim on its custom coachbuilt body, plus a wraparound windshield. The interior was luxurious and had such features as power steering, brakes, four-way adjustable front seat and a power convertible top, all as standard equipment. It was also fitted with a 'Selectronic' radio and 'Easy Eye' tinted glass. Underneath, the car was a Roadmaster and featured that car's double wishbone front with telescopic shocks, while the rear still had leaf springs and lever-arm shocks. It all made for a smooth, relaxing drive which the powerful engine and Dynaflow transmission only further enhanced. The Skylark was quick for its day, though most correctly labelled it as a fast cruiser rather than sportscar.

Top speed:	105 mph (168 km/h)
0–60 mph (0–96 km/h):	11.5 sec
Engine type:	V8
Displacement:	322 ci (5,276 cc)
Transmission	2-speed auto
Max power:	200 bhp (149 kW) @ 4,100 rpm
Max torque:	N/A
Weight:	4,260 lb (1,936 kg)
Economy:	14 mpg (4.95 km/l)

Chevrolet Corvette (1954)

The new Corvette debuted at the 1953 GM Motorama Show, and production began later that year, all cars being white. While it didn't do well in sales to start with, GM persevered. In 1954 several more colours were available and the car got a power increase. Being the world's first production car to be made out of glass-fibre was a daring move, but it worked. Underneath there was a separate steel chassis with X-brace for rigidity, along with the one-piece floor. Also new were leaf springs mounted outside the chassis rails to improve packaging. The straight-six engine came from the sedan range and as the performance 'Blue Flame Special' it used a high-lift cam, higher compression ratio, modified head, and double valve springs to withstand increased rpm. The car was almost shelved in 1954, and it was only the new, small-block V8 engine in 1955 which allowed it to survive.

Top speed:	107 mph (171 km/h)
0–60 mph (0–96 km/h):	11.0 sec
Engine type:	In-line six
Displacement:	235 ci (3,850 cc)
Transmission	2-speed auto
Max power:	150 bhp (112 kW) @ 4,200 rpm
Max torque:	223 lb ft (302 Nm) @ 2,400 rpm
Weight:	2,851 lb (1,295 kg)
Economy:	16 mpg (5.66 km/l)

Lincoln Capri (1954)

An all-new Lincoln was launched in 1952 and was built through '54, and it had the brand new engine to replace the dated Flathead V8. The new 317ci (5.2-litre) unit was extremely smooth, thanks to eight crankshaft counterbalances where most V8s had just six, plus it was easily tuned. The new car also had a very stiff chassis, with six crossmembers on the separate frame, making the car's new MacPherson strut suspension work well and improving the model's durability. In its inaugural year the Capri took the Carrera Panamericana in first, second, third and fourth places, then did the same the following year, but just first and second places in 1954. But the Capri boasted more than performance as it also has power-operated leather seats, power windows, power steering and brakes, and even a Hydramatic transmission. In 1956 the car was dramatically restyled; production fell by 50 percent.

Top speed:	108 mph (173 km/h)
0–60 mph (0–96 km/h):	13.4 sec
Engine type:	V8
Displacement:	317 ci (5,194 cc)
Transmission	3-speed auto
Max power:	205 bhp (153 kW) @ 4,200 rpm
Max torque:	280 lb ft (380 Nm) @ 1,800 rpm
Weight:	4,250 lb (1,931 kg)
Economy:	19 mpg (6.72 km/l)

Packard Caribbean (1954)

Packard were long considered a fairly conservative car manufacturer, but they wanted to change their image in the early 1950s so debuted a show car from the Henney Body Company. The following year it appeared again in show form as the Pan American, and reaction was so strong that Packard decided to go into production with a luxury convertible version, the range-topping Caribbean. The car used a fairly conventional chassis, with twin C-section rails supporting a double wishbone independent front arrangement and a leaf sprung rear axle. Even so, the 1954 had improved power from the Flathead straight-eight engine, plus body touches such as two-tone paint, partially enclosed rear wheels and new tail lights. Inside it featured a colour-coded interior and such luxuries as power steering and a power top which took just 30 seconds to lower.

Top speed:	101 mph (162 km/h)
0–60 mph (0–96 km/h):	15.8 sec
Engine type:	In-line eight
Displacement:	359 ci (5,882 cc)
Transmission	2-speed auto
Max power:	212 bhp (158 kW) @ 4,000 rpm
Max torque:	310 lb ft (420 Nm) @ 2,000 rpm
Weight:	4,400 lb (2,000 kg)
Economy:	17 mpg (6.01 km/l)

Chrysler C-300 (1955)

The Chrysler C-300 was one of the fastest and best-handling cars on the road at the time of launch. It was also one of the first true muscle cars thanks to the now legendary Hemi engine (which had arrived in 1951). Under the hood you'd find a motor which with hemispherical combustion chambers that placed the spark plug directly in the centre of the cylinder, thus ensuring the best burn and allowing the engine to run a slightly lower compression ratio than most of its contemporaries, whilst producing more power. The 300 was based on the Windsor two-door coupe and shared some of its components with the New Yorker and Imperial. It had a wishbone front and leaf rear, but all springs and shocks were uprated, making it a fine handler. The Hemi engine showed its potential even more the following year with 340bhp (227kW) in the 300B, making it as fast as most Ferraris of the era.

Top speed:	130 mph (208 km/h)
0–60 mph (0–96 km/h):	8.9 sec
Engine type:	V8
Displacement:	331 ci (5,424 cc)
Transmission	2-speed auto
Max power:	300 bhp (224 kW) @ 5,200 rpm
Max torque:	345 lb ft (467 Nm) @ 3,200 rpm
Weight:	4,005 lb (1,820 kg)
Economy:	14 mpg (4.95 km/l)

DeSoto Fireflite (1955)

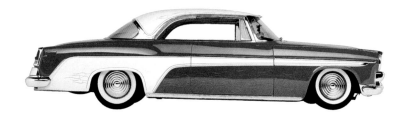

Being part of Chrysler, DeSoto got the technology from the parent company as soon as it was available. Hence, as early as the Fireflite had received the Hemi engine, which made it an incredible performer. A sign of how these new engines were is the fact that this customized version still uses its original 'Firedome' powerplant. Despite its near 2-ton weight, it can cover the quarter-mile in 16 seconds, helped by a custom performance exhaust. However, its real intention is as a cruiser, and for that reason it has lowered coils on the independent double wishbone front end and lowering blocks at the rear, which put the axle close to the body. While externally the car features little in the way of bodywork – aside from the obvious two-tone bright paint and pinstriping – inside it's been treated to a full tuck 'n' roll re-trim, which is indicative of 1950s customs.

Top speed:	118 mph (189 km/h)
0–60 mph (0–96 km/h):	8.2 sec
Engine type:	V8
Displacement:	331 ci (5,424 cc)
Transmission	3-speed auto
Max power:	255 bhp (190 kW) @ 5,200 rpm
Max torque:	340 lb ft (461 Nm) @ 2,800 rpm
Weight:	3,930 lb (1,786 kg)
Economy:	12 mpg (4.24 km/l)

Ford Thunderbird (1955)

At first the Thunderbird went head–to–head with the Corvette, and started off well, thanks to a V8 being put under the hood where the Corvette only had a feeble straight-six. The '55 T-bird made 16,000 sales, massively outselling the 'Vette and making the Blue Oval two-seater somewhat of a supercar. Decades later, the early model is still in demand as it's known as the purest form of the machine; later versions were larger, more bloated and not particularly sporty. This version retains a stock body but underneath the chassis has been designed for the best possible layout and packaging. It uses a Vortech supercharged V8 with NASCAR racing heads and custom engine management with fuel injection. A beefed-up Ford overdrive transmission sends torque to a strong 9-inch (229mm) Ford axle located on racing type four-bar suspension, to give 11-second quarter-mile times.

Top speed:	165 mph (264 km/h)
0–60 mph (0–96 km/h):	3.6 sec
Engine type:	V8
Displacement:	361 ci (5,915 cc)
Transmission	4-speed auto
Max power:	630 bhp (468 kW) @ 6,800 rpm
Max torque:	550 lb ft (746 Nm) @ 4,900 rpm
Weight:	2,980 lb (1,354 kg)
Economy:	8 mpg (2.83 km/l)

Ford Courier Custom Delivery (1955)

The 1955 Courier struck an ideal balance between luxury and practicality for small storekeepers and salesmen. It was restyled for the same year and looked sleeker and more purposeful than its previous incarnation, plus it had the new 272ci (4.4-litre) Y-block V8 with 162bhp (121kW) to replace the ageing Flathead. Years later the same vehicles offer the same practicality even as customs, though they're not favoured as much as two-door sedans because of their weight and heavy proportions. That didn't bother the owner of this vehicle, who has changed it by adding Camaro front wishbone suspension, a Ford 9-inch (229mm) rear on leaf springs, and Chevy engine with supercharger. Like many custom, the body has been fully smoothed and uses a remote key fob for entry to the doors and rear tailgate. Inside the rear is fitted with custom tweed upholstery.

Top speed:	128 mph (205 km/h)
0–60 mph (0–96 km/h):	6.3 sec
Engine type:	V8
Displacement:	350 ci (5,735 cc)
Transmission	3-speed auto
Max power:	365 bhp (272 kW) @ 5,800 rpm
Max torque:	410 lb ft (556 Nm) @ 3,600 rpm
Weight:	3,210 lb (1,459 kg)
Economy:	12 mpg (4.24 km/l)

Mercury Montclair (1955)

While overshadowed somewhat by its older brother, the 1949–1951 Mercury, the 1955 versions also offered custom potential, thanks to factory touches like the peaked headlamps, heavily chromed grille and fared-in rear arches. While sitting low as standard, this owner has gone further by fitting Camaro double wishbone front suspension and a live rear axle from the same car. However, instead of regular coil or leaf springs, a set of airbag springs have been installed. These can be controlled by an on-board compressor to raise or lower the suspension and give the car a ground-scraping look with the convenience of smooth driving, thanks to the whole body effectively riding on air. The original engine is long gone in favour of the cheapest and most tuneable engine, Chevy's 350ci (5.7-litre) V8. Other custom touches include a tuck x'n' roll interior, chopped roof, and extra grille teeth.

Top speed:	120 mph (192 km/h)
0–60 mph (0–96 km/h):	9.3 sec
Engine type:	V8
Displacement:	350 ci (5,735 cc)
Transmission	3-speed auto
Max power:	210 bhp (157 kW) @ 4,000 rpm
Max torque:	285 lb ft (386 Nm) @ 2,800 rpm
Weight:	3,558 lb (1,617 kg)
Economy:	16 mpg (5.66 km/l)

Chevrolet Nomad (1956)

Being top of the range exclusive does not save a car from the hands of a hot rodder, neither does rarity. Hence, the Nomad which was available from 1955 to 1957 often sees reworking. In 1955, the all-new small-block V8 was fitted which, displacing 265ci (4.3 litres), turned the sedans and station wagons into great performers. The Nomad was different too because it was a two-door body with tailgate. This car has gone some way further than the original and rather basic car, with 1986 Corvette front and rear suspension having been fitted for a lowered ride height and excellent handling, while the old 265 ci small-block has been replaced by a fully balanced 358ci (5.8-litre) small-block Chevy with ported heads and a B&M supercharger. So good are the Nomad's lines that little has been changed here except for the paint and a set of billet alloys with low–profile tyres.

Top speed:	131 mph (210 km/h)
0–60 mph (0–96 km/h):	5.5 sec
Engine type:	V8
Displacement:	358 ci (5,866 cc)
Transmission	3-speed auto
Max power:	400 bhp (298 kW) @ 4,800 rpm
Max torque:	420 lb ft (569 Nm) @ 3,000 rpm
Weight:	3,352 lb (1,523 kg)
Economy:	8.4 mpg (2.97 km/l)

DeSoto Pacesetter (1956)

Representing clean, stylish and classic-styled cars, DeSoto's were among the top models available on the market during the mid–1950s. They were almost amongst the most powerful cars available in the world, thanks to their version of Chrysler Hemi engine under the hood. Despite looking like a luxurious but sedate convertible, the Pacesetter nonetheless lived up to its name by being very rapid. In fact, one paced the Indy 500 in 1956, and all production cars paid homage to the race by having chequered flag badges on the rear fenders. While underneath it used the standard double wishbone front and leaf spring rear, it was inside where the Pacesetter was radically different, thanks to a split dash with twin pods and multiple gauges. It proved very quick against the competition, having a whole 100bhp (74kW) more than the V8 1957 Chevy, as an example.

Top speed:	115 mph (184 km/h)
0–60 mph (0–96 km/h):	10.2 sec
Engine type:	V8
Displacement:	341 ci (5,587 cc)
Transmission	2-speed auto
Max power:	320 bhp (239 kW) @ 5,200 rpm
Max torque:	365 lb ft (495 Nm) @ 2,800 rpm
Weight:	3,870 lb (1,759 kg)
Economy:	14 mpg (4.95 km/l)

Ford Fairlane Crown Victoria (1956)

Show cars had long used transparent roof sections to display their interior s and give the cars a light, airy feel, but few cars made it into production with such novelties. The Crown Victoria was different though, and used a similar Plexiglas section to the 1954 Ford Skyliner. It was a great idea for making the car feel less claustrophobic, but buyers were never really convinced enough and they preferred the safer option of the regular hardtop coupe. The underpinnings used a perimeter chassis with conventional suspension, consisting of double wishbones up front and leaf springs at the rear, all dampened by telescopic shock absorbers, thus making the ride very smooth. The engine was powerful, coming straight from the Thunderbird and giving plenty of straight line power low down in the rev range. Poor sales again in 1956 ensured the end of the Crown Victoria.

Top speed:	107 mph (171 km/h)
0–60 mph (0–96 km/h):	12.2 sec
Engine type:	V8
Displacement:	312 ci (5,112 cc)
Transmission	3-speed auto
Max power:	225 bhp (168 KW) @ 4,600 rpm
Max torque:	317 lb ft (430 Nm) @ 2,600 rpm
Weight:	3,299 lb (1,499 kg)
Economy:	15 mpg (5.31 km/l)

Ford F-100 (1956)

$\mathbf{A}$s far as classic trucks are concerned, the F-100 rates among the top models in most people's eyes. Its brutish styling won it fans right away, plus it was one of the most powerful, and therefore fastest, trucks in its day. It quickly achieved cult status in later years, because it was one of the best-looking Stepside trucks to be produced, and also one of the last, as the Fleetside styling was introduced just two years later (with the sides flush with the cab). This custom version uses suspension kits front and rear to lower the truck as far as it can practically go, but doesn't use modern trickery anywhere else. The engine is a tuned version of the Ford Y-block from the 1950s with triple two-barrel carbs, and the truck still drives through a three-speed manual transmission which makes performance lively. In order to stop it, the owner has fitted power disc brakes.

Top speed:	110 mph (176 km/h)
0–60 mph (0–96 km/h):	8.1 sec
Engine type:	V8
Displacement:	296 ci (4,850 cc)
Transmission	3-speed manual
Max power:	300 bhp (224 kW) @ 4,500 rpm
Max torque:	270 lb ft (366 Nm) @ 2,300 rpm
Weight:	3,175 lb (1,443 kg)
Economy:	14 mpg (4.95 km/l)

Continental Mark II (1956)

Lincoln was Ford's premium brand, but oddly the name wasn't used on the Continental Mark II, despite it being built by the company. The car was Ford's attempt at outdoing Cadillac and oozed opulence everywhere. Inside it was swathed in Scottish leather and it had classy separate gauges, electric everything and just one optional extra: air-conditioning. The car was tailor made, with the body's trail fitted to the 'cow belly' chassis (it dropped down between each end) before being painted, sanded and polished by hand. Also, the engines were hand picked off the production line to ensure the best possible performance from each car. Once finished, all went through a 12-mile (19km) road test followed by an in-depth inspection with tuning where necessary. Ford is reputed to have lost $1,000 on each one sold, even though they were priced at $9,695, some $2,300 more than a Cadillac.

Top speed:	112 mph (179 km/h)
0–60 mph (0–96 km/h):	10.5 sec
Engine type:	V8
Displacement:	368 ci (6,030 cc)
Transmission	3-speed auto
Max power:	285 bhp (213 kW) @ 4,800 rpm
Max torque:	401 lb ft (543 Nm) @ 2,800 rpm
Weight:	4,825 lb (2,193 kg)
Economy:	12 mpg (4.24 km/l)

Olds 88 Holiday Coupe (1956)

One of the best-looking cars of the decade, the Olds Holiday Hardtop Coupe had very clean lines and the popular panoramic windshield which was duplicated at the rear. The 88 model sold close to 400,000 models during 1956 and this has ensured the car's longevity and use even today, albeit often in modified form. The owner of this example has rightly chosen to avoid spoiling the car's original lines, but has made significant changes elsewhere. Modifications such as lowered and uprated suspension help to lower the centre of gravity and improve the handling dramatically, and all is not standard in the drive train either. The owner has swapped in a Rocket J-2 engine with its triple carb set-up, which provides the sort of performance you'd expect more from a modern V8 sedan. The colour is straight from a 1990's Ford Thunderbird and finishes the overall look perfectly.

Top speed:	121 mph (194 km/h)
0–60 mph (0–96 km/h):	8.7 sec
Engine type:	V8
Displacement:	371 ci (6,079 cc)
Transmission:	3-speed manual
Max power:	312 bhp (233 kW) @ 4,600 rpm
Max torque:	410 lb ft (556 Nm) @ 2,800 rpm
Weight:	3,771 lb (1,714 kg)
Economy:	11.8 mpg (4.17 km/l)

Studebaker Golden Hawk (1956)

The Golden Hawk, like its Studebaker sister models the Sky Hawk and Flight Hawk, was based on the original 1953 Starlight body, and so retained its single-piece rear window as opposed to the '52 model's four-piece panoramic item. The '56 Golden Hawk could be identified by its small upright glass-fibre fins on the top of the rear fenders and, being a top model, it shared the glitzy President Classic's wide grooved horizontal aluminium trim mouldings above the rocker panels. It was the most powerful of all Studebakers this year by some margin, so featured power brakes and 7-inch (178mm) wide tyres to make full use of the V8's torque. The car came as a two-door hardtop coupe only to emphasis its sporting nature, but came only with the Twin Drive automatic gearbox from Packard, who'd been in control since '53. In 1957 the Golden Hawk was supercharged and made over 300bhp (223kW).

Top speed:	109 mph (174 km/h)
0-60 mph (0–96 km/h):	9.5 sec
Engine type:	V8
Displacement:	352 ci (5,768 cc)
Transmission	3-speed auto
Max power:	275 bhp (205 kW) @ 4,600 rpm
Max torque:	300 lb ft (406 Nm) @ 2,800 rpm
Weight:	3,360 lb (1,527 kg)
Economy:	15 mpg (5.31 km/l)

Cadillac Eldorado Brougham (1957)

Making its mark as the most expensive Cadillac of the 1950s, the Eldorado Brougham featured every conceivable extra, and then some. Each car was hand built, and it was incredibly smooth and quiet to ride in thanks to the airbag suspension and precise automatic transmission. The car used the now familiar panoramic windshields front and rear, but unusually returned to suicide-style opening doors for the rear. Cadillac made sure the chassis was immensely strong to allow both side doors to top open without a central pillar. There were 44 interior and exterior colour options, but the car came standard with toys such as electric memory seats, cruise control, air-conditioning, and power windows, brakes and steering. The extras weighed down the car considerably hence, despite the power, the Brougham was sufficiently fast, as opposed to rapid.

Top speed:	110 mph (176 km/h)
0–60 mph (0–96 km/h):	11.4 sec
Engine type:	V8
Displacement:	365 ci (5,981 cc)
Transmission	3-speed auto
Max power:	325 bhp (242 kW) @ 4,800 rpm
Max torque:	435 lb ft (590 Nm) @ 3,400 rpm
Weight:	5,315 lb (2,415 kg)
Economy:	10 mpg (3.54 km/l)

Chevrolet Bel Air (1957)

The man repsonsible for the '57 chevy was stylist Harley Earl, and he created a car which became an American classic. Earl's philosophy was to make cars lower, wider and longer, with the large rear fins, hood fins and large side spears to embellish the looks. The grille was huge, gaping for air into the engine, which actually sat way back from the car's front. The most famous V8 ever, the small-block Chevy, was used under the hood and bu this time had grown to displace 283ci (4.6 litres), from the original 265ci (4.3-litre) in '55. This engine gave the Bel Air very good performance for the day, and even the handling was ahead of the competition, despite a basic chassis with a double wishbone front and leaf sprung live rear axle. While there were many options, one popular one was the exotic continental kit, which extended the rear deck and added chrome.

Top speed:	115 mph (184 km/h)
0–60 mph (0–96 km/h):	8.5 sec
Engine type:	V8
Displacement:	283 ci (4,637 cc)
Transmission	3-speed manual
Max power:	220 bhp (164 kW) @ 4,800 rpm
Max torque:	270 lb ft (366 Nm) @ 2,800 rpm
Weight:	3,409 lb (1,549 kg)
Economy:	20 mpg (7.08 km/l)

Chevrolet Bel Air modified (1957)

Being a performance model from the off, and being tuner friendly, the 1957 Chevy received modifications from the day it was produced. However, the timeless design means that few choose to radically alter the bodywork, instead concentrating on improving the car's chassis and drivetrain. This street/strip racer retains the original frame but has new suspension arms, 2-inch (50mm) drop spindles and lowering springs. Custom semi-elliptical leaf springs lower the rear to match while dropping the centre of gravity to improve handling. The powerplant is a small-block Chevy, though it's heavily modified with a B&M supercharger and large carburettor. To help traction, a narrowed 9-inch (229mm) Ford axle with Posi-traction limited-slip differential sits out back, along with 13-inch (330mm) wide Mickey Thompson street/strip tyres.

Top speed:	147 mph (235 km/h)
0–60 mph (0–96 km/h):	3.9 sec
Engine type:	V8
Displacement:	350 ci (5,735 cc)
Transmission:	3-speed auto
Max power:	420 bhp (313 kW) @ 5,400 rpm
Max torque:	435 lb ft (590 Nm) @ 2,500 rpm
Weight:	3,197 lb (1,453 kg)
Economy:	9.4 mpg (3.32 km/l)

Chevrolet Corvette (1957)

Almost shelved in 1955, the Corvette fortunately had the Chevrolet sedan come to it rescue which gave it a new lease of life thanks to the new small-block V8 engine. At first it came in 265ci (4.5 litres) form, though had grown to 283ci (4.6 litres) by 1957. This put it among the best-selling models that year, and while the motor was powerful, the best option was the Zora Arkus Duntov-inspired 'Ramjet' fuel injection. This was expensive, and just 1,040 were sold, but it did make the '57 Corvette the quickest sportscar in the world, with an almost unheard of 0–60mph (0–96km/h) time that neither Ford nor the big cats from Jaguar could come anywhere close to. The suspension was basic, and on the whietwall-equipped skinny bias ply tyres, the car demanded driver attention, though for straight line speed the Corvette was king.

Top speed:	132 mph (211 km/h)
0–60 mph (0–96 km/h):	5.7 sec
Engine type:	V8
Displacement:	283 ci (4,637 cc)
Transmission	3-speed manual
Max power:	283 bhp (211 kW) @ 6,200 rpm
Max torque:	270 lb ft (366 Nm) @ 3,600 rpm
Weight:	2,730 lb (1,240 kg)
Economy:	13 mpg (4.60 km/l)

Chevrolet 3100 Stepside (1957)

What made Chevrolet's trucks of the 1950s so liked in later decades was the ease at which they took modifications. The huge engine bays swallowed a small-block V8 with ease and in fact could take a big-block without major work. Being of wide track meant they could also handle suspension swaps from larger sedans without the need to narrow either axles or front crossmembers. The scope has produced numerous reworked examples, but many stick with the truck's original utilitarian lines as they appear aggressive in factory form. This truck has gone through the mildest of changes, featuring a tuned small-block V8 with Tri-Power three carb set-up, and uprated brakes with front discs to cope with the performance. Apart from that and the modern radials on alloy rims, the truck is just exceptionally clean and straight, with superb chrome work.

Top speed:	115 mph (184 km/h)
0–60 mph (0–96 km/h):	7.2 sec
Engine type:	V8
Displacement:	350 ci (5,735 cc)
Transmission	3-speed auto
Max power:	330 bhp (246 kW) @ 5,200 rpm
Max torque:	360 lb ft (488 Nm) @ 3,400 rpm
Weight:	3,230 lb (1,468 kg)
Economy:	14 mpg (4.95 km/l)

Chrysler 300C (1957)

No other car could match the dramatic Virgil Exner styled 300C of 1957. The huge tail fins pre-dated the Series 62 Cadillac's similar examples by two years, but the car wasn't all about style, because it also performed so amazingly that Chrysler had to tame the car down for drivers. They deliberately gave the throttle a stepped action so that the pedal had to be forcefully depressed for all eight carburettors mouths to open, thus unleashing full power. When it did the car leapt into action and made it easily one of the fastest production four-seaters in the USA. Other developments included torsion bar suspension which continued on Chrysler group cars well into the 1980s, and the Torqueflite transmission with push-button gear selection on the dashboard. To pull the car down, huge brake drums were fitted and the fronts had cooling vents fed from intakes just below the headlamps.

Top speed:	149 mph (238 km/h)
0-60 mph (0–96 km/h):	8.3 sec
Engine type:	V8
Displacement:	392 ci (6,423 cc)
Transmission	3-speed auto
Max power:	375 bhp (280 kW) @ 5,200 rpm
Max torque:	435 lb ft (590 Nm) @ 3,600 rpm
Weight:	4,389 lb (1,995 kg)
Economy:	10 mpg (3.54 km/l)

Ford Fairlane (1957)

Widely regard as one of the most stylish cars of the time, the 1957 Ford didn't excel in ostentatious chrome and fins like other manufacturers, though neither did it abstain completely. It had little wing peaks at the rear highlighted with chrome trim which ran along the side to break up the bodywork. The headlamps were peaked, like many other models of the era, but the grille and fender were surprisingly plain, and the fuss-free appearance made the car look both wider and lower. This car features much of the original running gear, though the suspension has been lowered by fitting shorted coils in the front and axle blocks at the rear, and at each corner there now sits low-profile tyres on new 15-inch (381mm) chrome wheels to improve handling. The engine is the top option 1957 Thunderbird engine, but with an extra 10bhp (7kW) out through a better exhaust.

Top speed:	120 mph (192 km/h)
0–60 mph (0–96 km/h):	10.2 sec
Engine type:	V8
Displacement:	312 ci (5,112 cc)
Transmission	3-speed auto
Max power:	255 bhp (190 kW) @ 4,600 rpm
Max torque:	354 lb ft (480 Nm) @ 2,800 rpm
Weight:	3,400 lb (1,545 kg)
Economy:	12.4 mpg (4.38 km/l)

Ford Thunderbird (1957)

The Thunderbird appeared a year after the Corvette and was direct competition. Ford's new two-seater had the same simple layout of a separate chassis with live rear axle on leaf springs, but with the important difference of a V8 up front. The 265ci (4.3-litre) engine gave the performance people expected, and a year later a larger, 312ci (5.1-litre) unit became available. The T-bird also had other advanced features such as power brakes and steering, making them better cars to drive. The car came with a glass-fibre bolt-on hardtop, but had the option of a convertible roof for an extra $290. At first the T-Bird carried its spare wheel above the fender, but Ford extended the rear for 1957, which meant it could be carried in the trunk. The extra weight put into the rear of the car also helped ride quality. This was the best-selling of all early Thunderbirds.

Top speed:	122 mph (195 km/h)
0–60 mph (0–96 km/h):	9.5 sec
Engine type:	V8
Displacement:	292 ci (4,785 cc)
Transmission	3-speed manual
Max power:	212 bhp (158 kW) @ 4,400 rpm
Max torque:	297 lb ft (402 Nm) @ 2,700 rpm
Weight:	3,050 lb (1,386 kg)
Economy:	13 mpg (4.60 km/l)

Ford Thunderbird Phase I/II (1957)

Most desirable of all Thunderbirds was the rare 300bhp (223kW) supercharged 1957 F-Bird, of which just 208 were made. The car came about through Ford wanting to compete in a flying-mile competition at Daytona Beach, Florida. NASCAR ran the event and stipulated that in order to compete, the car must be homologated, so Ford made the necessary amount of 200 and fitted each one with a Paxton-McCulloch centrifugal supercharger which gave an extra 75bhp (56kW) and 40lb ft (54Nm) torque, enough to propel the car to a flying mile of 93.312mph (150.13km/h), beating the record held by a Duntov Corvette. The car went through very few changes other then the addition of a blower, but because of its rarity, an unrestored clean model can now command a price upwards of $60,000. Few are left, but Ford fans who grew up at the time of the two-seater Thunderbirds pay for good examples.

Top speed:	130 mph (208 km/h)
0–60 mph (0–96 km/h):	9.2 sec
Engine type:	V8
Displacement:	312 ci (5,112 cc)
Transmission:	3-speed manual
Max power:	300 bhp (224 kW) @ 4,800 rpm
Max torque:	336 lb ft (455 Nm) @ 3,400 rpm
Weight:	3,145 lb (1,429 kg)
Economy:	15 mpg (5.31 km/l)

Nash Metropolitan (1957)

While looking as glitzy and typically 1950s as any other American car, in fact the Metropolitan was produced for the US market in England. Its body was built by Ludlow and Fisher in Birmingham, and this was based on an Austin chassis which came from the factory just a short distance away. With its tiny four-cylinder engine, it was a long way from the powerful cruisers that were abundant on American highways, but it was quite lively, thanks to low gearing. It did at least look like an American convertible, albeit one which had shrunk in the wash, thanks to a continental kit, two-tone paint and whitewall tyres. The car could seat just two in comfort and a third at a squeeze for short journeys. Remarkably, it went over 104,000 in sales in seven years, no doubt due to its cuteness, as well as its economical engine.

Top speed:	75 mph (120 km/h)
0–60 mph (0–96 km/h):	24.1 sec
Engine type:	In-line four
Displacement:	91 ci (1,489 cc)
Transmission	3-speed manual
Max power:	52 bhp (39 kW) @ 4,500 rpm
Max torque:	69 lb ft (94 Nm) @ 2,100 rpm
Weight:	1,885 lb (856 kg)
Economy:	38 mpg (13.4 km/l)

Plymouth Fury modified (1957)

Pro Street cars were really a street offshoot of the late 1970s Pro Stock drag-racing class. Pro Stock cars had to use the standard body of a street-going car, but apart from this many alterations were allowed to make them go quicker. In reality, the standard body was the only part of the race car which made the transition from the street, the rest of the car featuring a full tubular spaceframe in lightweight steel, plus lightweight suspension and a stripped interior with aluminium panels replacing steel wherever possible. This Plymouth is typical of later Pro Street cars, where the emphasis came back to them being streetable, hence it has a stock interior and even stock front suspension, although the powerplant is anything but stock. It's a drag motor barely tamed for street use, but it can catapult this Fury down the quarter-mile in just 7.5 seconds at over 190mph (306km/h).

Top speed:	197 mph (315 km/h)
0–60 mph (0–96 km/h):	2.6 sec
Engine type:	V8
Displacement:	511 ci (8,373 cc)
Transmission	3-speed auto
Max power:	1,485 bhp (1,107 kW) @ 7,200 rpm
Max torque:	1,250 lb ft (1,695 Nm) @ 4,200 rpm
Weight:	3,520 lb (1,600 kg)
Economy:	N/A

Pontiac Bonneville (1957)

Performance was fast becoming a major selling point in the 1950s and Pontiac were likely to be left behind if they didn't release a vehicle to capture the public's imagination. In 1956 the company brought in Bunkie Knudson as new General Manager, and he quickly announced the availability of a new model called the Pontiac Bonneville, so called after the Pontiac which made a record-breaking run of 118mph (88km/h) for 24 hours at the Bonneville Salt Flats. The car was launched in 1957 at a NASCAR meeting, where the company showcased its new fuel-injection system. It was only ever a limited edition, with 630 supplied at a very high price, but the customer got a lot for their money. Displacement was up from 316ci (5.2 litres) with a new stroker crank, and the compression ratio was raised. It gave seamless acceleration through the 1956 Hydramatic transmission.

Top speed:	114 mph (182 km/h)
0–60 mph (0–96 km/h):	8.5 sec
Engine type:	V8
Displacement:	370 ci (6,063 cc)
Transmission	3-speed auto
Max power:	315 bhp (235 kW) @ 4,800 rpm
Max torque:	N/A
Weight:	4,285 lb (1,947 kg)
Economy:	14 mpg (4.95 km/l)

Buick Limited (1958)

Like many companies of the era, Buick decided bigger was better for 1958 and they added the lengthened Limited to their range. The car had such innovative extras as air suspension for an ultra smooth ride, plus alloy brake drums to speed heat dispersal and hence create better braking. Also new was the Flight-Pitch Dynaflow, a version of Buick's Dynaflow, which had three rather than two turbines inside to give a smoother transition through the gears. What all this actually created was an overly soft ride which would pitch the car over in corners, and an unresponsive gearbox. The brakes were the saving grace. This car was most about showing off Buick style, however, and nowhere was this more evident than on the over-fussy rear end, which had an overhang of over 60 inches or 5ft (1.5 m). Despite this, rear leg-room was atrocious. The car lasted until 1959.

Top speed:	110 mph (176 km/h)
0–60 mph (0–96 km/h):	11.2 sec
Engine type:	V8
Displacement:	364 ci (5,964 cc)
Transmission	3–speed auto
Max power:	300 bhp (224 kW) @ 4,600 rpm
Max torque:	400 lb ft (542 Nm) @ 3,200 rpm
Weight:	4,691 lb (2,132 kg)
Economy:	13 mpg (4.60 km/l)

Chevrolet Impala (1958)

Making a successful model after a trio of successes from 1955 to 1957 was no easy task, but Chevrolet were up to it with their 1958 Impala. This was the first time any Chevy had used the Impala name, and it supplemented the regular Bel Air, Biscayne and Delray models. Designers gave the new car a longer, lower look which required a new chassis of X-frame design, with the main rails joined in the middle. Because of the lack of connection to the body sides, more mounting points were needed to the body elsewhere, and this improved structural rigidity. The car ran a new W-Series small-block which was initially designed for light truck duty. It was compact and at first made 250bhp (186kW), though when fitted with theTri-Power option could acheive 315bhp (235kW). Optional was air suspension with rubber bellows replacing the springs, plus an on-board air compressor.

Top speed:	115 mph (184 km/h)
0–60 mph (0–96 km/h):	10.5 sec
Engine type:	V8
Displacement:	348 ci (5,702 cc)
Transmission	3-speed manual
Max power:	250 bhp (186 kW) @ 4,400 rpm
Max torque:	355 lb ft (481 Nm) @ 2,800 rpm
Weight:	3,459 lb (1,572 kg)
Economy:	14 mpg (4.95 km/l)

Chevrolet Impala modified (1958)

The 1958 Impala was the last of Chevrolet's 'tri-Chevys' because of the 1955 to 1958 cars all looking very similar and being an almost identical size. All three were favourites for modifying as they could be ordered with the small-block V8 as standard, and if they had the base straight-six, the larger engine could easily be found second-hand and slotted in. What made the 1958 model most famous was a custom version in the movie *American Graffiti*, driven by then actor but now famous movie director, Ron Howard. The car shown is typical of the 1960s customs, with the original chrome, a new tube grille, scallop paint work, reversed steel wheels, triple 1959 Cadillac tail lights and a tuck 'n' roll interior. The powerplant is a stroked small-block Chevy with triple carbs which helps the car to 14-second quarter-miles. The Impala gets its low ride through adjustable hydraulic suspension.

Top speed:	102 mph (163 km/h)
0–60 mph (0–96 km/h):	6.5 sec
Engine type:	V8
Displacement:	383 ci (6,276 cc)
Transmission:	3-speed auto
Max power:	430 bhp (321 kW) @ 6,700 rpm
Max torque:	420 lb ft (570 Nm) @ 3,400 rpm
Weight:	3,447 lb (1,566 kg)
Economy:	9 mpg (3.19 km/l)

Edsel Bermuda (1958)

While the Edsel was long regarded as a flop – embarrassing for parent company Ford, as the brand was named after Henry Ford's only son – its unique looks have ensured its collectability. And the rarer a model is, the more collectable it becomes, which is why the Bermuda is probably one of the most sought-after in the range. When it arrived, the Bermuda was available in either six- or nine-seater configuration, the latter costing just $57 more for the extra seats. The car truly was a family vehicle, with such convenient extras as Tele Touch auto transmission, where the gear-selection buttons were in a circular pattern in the centre of the steering wheel, and air-conditioning, power windows, and even power lubrication, which greased all the steering and front suspension points at the touch of a button. The car was a very smooth drive and had plenty of power for long hauls too.

Top speed:	108 mph (173 km/h)
0-60 mph (0–96 km/h):	11.8 sec
Engine type:	V8
Displacement:	361 ci (5,915 cc)
Transmission	3-speed auto
Max power:	303 bhp (226 kW) @ 4,600 rpm
Max torque:	400 lb ft (542 Nm) @ 2,600 rpm
Weight:	3,853 lb (1,751 kg)
Economy:	18 mpg (6.37 km/l)

Edsel Citation (1958)

Hurried into production, the Edsel was beset by production problems and quality control. But it wasn't all bad. Once the problems had been overcome it represented a premium brand with a lot going for it, Unfortunately by then most buyers had turned to other cars! What the Citation offered was power everything including the hood and front bench seat. Unusual extras inside included the 'cyclops' style rotating speedo placed centrally in the dash, and the station-seeking radio. Underneath there was nothing radical with wishbones and leaf springs front and rear, though the powerplant was extremely torquey to make the Edsel quite a performer for its day. With hindsight it's easy to see that the car was doomed from the very start, and it now represents one of the biggest flops in motoring history. Which, ironically, is also what makes it highly collectable.

Top speed:	105 mph (168 km/h)
0–60 mph (0–96 km/h):	9.7 sec
Engine type:	V8
Displacement:	410 ci (6,718 cc)
Transmission	3-speed auto
Max power:	345 bhp (257 kW) @ 4,600 rpm
Max torque:	475 lb ft (644 Nm) @ 2,900 rpm
Weight:	4,311 lb (1,959 kg)
Economy:	10 mpg (3.54 km/l)

Ford Fairlane modified (1958)

While 1958 isn't considered a landmark year for cars out of Detroit, Ford were at least top of what was out there. Their cars had stylish lines and seemed blend all the trends of the time together the best. Their Fairlane hardtop coupes had pillarless styling, glitzy yet stylish front and rear ends, and looked very well proportioned. In recent decades, when people have become tired of seeing the same Chevys getting modified, they've turned straight to Ford as they offer striking potential for customizing. This example uses little more than 2-inch (50mm) drop spindles at the front and 3-inch (76mm) lowering blocks at the rear, but its effect is dramatic, along with flame paint and whitewall-equipped chromed steels. It uses Ford's underrated engine from the 1960s, the torquey 390ci (6.4-litre) big-block, which easily puts the Fairlane 500 among the early muscle machines.

Top speed:	115 mph (184 km/h)
0–60 mph (0–96 km/h):	8.4 sec
Engine type:	V8
Displacement:	390 ci (6,390 cc)
Transmission	3-speed auto
Max power:	340 bhp (254 kW) @ 5,000 rpm
Max torque:	430 lb ft (583 Nm) @ 3,200 rpm
Weight:	3,485 lb (1,584 kg)
Economy:	15 mpg (5.31 km/l)

Plymouth Fury (1958)

The 'Fury' name couldn't have been more apt with the launch of the 1958 two-door from Plymouth. While it looked like a car that had more style than substance, it was quicker than most from Detroit. Furys had always received Chrysler's biggest engines, since their launch in 1956, and the 1957 cars' 318ci (5.2-litre) engine disappeared after a year to be replaced by a more potent 350ci (5.7-litre) V8. The Fury deserved its reputation for being the best-handling car in its class too, which was down to Chrysler's new-for-1957 'Torsion Air Ride' suspension which had longitudinal torsion bar springs up front. The design was so good it lasted through until 1980 in the Volaire. The car also handled well thanks to a low centre of gravity, possibly due to the low stance. Styling was typical for the era, with tall fins, wraparound front and rear windshields and pillarless side windows.

Top speed:	122 mph (195 km/h)
0–60 mph (0–96 km/h):	8.0 sec
Engine type:	V8
Displacement:	350 ci (5,735 cc)
Transmission	3-speed auto
Max power:	305 bhp (227 kW) @ 5,000 rpm
Max torque:	370 lb ft (502 Nm) @ 3,600 rpm
Weight:	3,510 lb (1,595 kg)
Economy:	13 mpg (4.60 km/l)

Cadillac Series 62 (1959)

Chrysler's ever-growing fins on its late-1950s cars caused some concern at GM, as the competition was getting all the attention. So they hired stylist Harley Earl to come up with some wild ideas for their new Cadillac model – the Series 62. Earl was influenced by aeroplanes, and it showed. Large tail fins, in fact the biggest to appear on any car ever, stood tall and housed bullet tail-light lenses, while the front fender and grille looked like a reflection of itself with four shotgun lenses, the upper two of which automatically came on at dusk and dipped from high- to low beam when oncoming traffic was detected. Underneath were coil springs and telescopic shocks, but the top Eldorado models could be ordered with luxurious air suspension. The cast-iron big block was enlarged for 1959 and came in two tunes, either a 325bhp (242kW) single carb version, or 345bhp (257kW) triple-carb motor.

Top speed:	121 mph (193 km/h)
0–60 mph (0–96 km/h):	11.0 sec
Engine type:	V8
Displacement:	390 ci (6,390 cc)
Transmission	3-speed auto
Max power:	325 bhp (242 kW) @ 4,800 rpm
Max torque:	435 lb ft (590 Nm) @ 3,400 rpm
Weight:	4,885 lb (2,220 kg)
Economy:	13 mpg (4.60 km/l)

Chevrolet Corvette modified (1959)

Corvettes were fast cars for their day; in fact, most would be fast among modern sportscars today, if a little behind in the technology to harness the power. But being quick cars as standard didn't mean they weren't subject to modification, in fact, because of the performance-biased hardware from the factory, it made many people keener to upgrade theirs, so it was faster than their neighbour's. This 1959 example uses one of Chevrolet's most famous engines of the early 1960s, the 409 from the larger Impala. This one has been bored out, tuned with a higher compression ratio, and fitted with dual four-barrel Carter carbs. An aftermarket Richmond gearbox hands the power back to a live axle, as the Corvette didn't go independent at the rear until 1963. The car uses a custom tube chassis cleverly mated to the stock front suspension, while the rear has a four-bar link.

Top speed:	164 mph (262 km/h)
0–60 mph (0–96 km/h):	4.6 sec
Engine type:	V8
Displacement:	416 ci (6,816 cc)
Transmission	6-speed manual
Max power:	454 bhp (338 kW) @ 5,500 rpm
Max torque:	460 lb ft (624 Nm) @ 5,500 rpm
Weight:	2,620 lb (1,190 kg)
Economy:	11 mpg (3.89 km/l)

Chevrolet Impala (1959)

Chevrolet's top-of-the-range Impala had everything in 1959. The outrageous fins, plenty of horsepower and luxurious extras. It didn't matter so much about the handling of the car to designers - the Impala was more about style so it only had a basic separate chassis with double wishbones up front and a coil sprung live rear axle. It was available with a number of powerplants, from a straight-six right up to the 348ci (5.7-litre). Stylists worked hard to get the car long and low and lose the earlier Chevys' upright stance, then gave owners an options list with which to personalise their vehicles. The car shown came with every one it seems, having side skirts, spot lights, continental kit, fender guards, remote trunk release, cruise control, air-conditioning and power everything. Inside it can carry six and due to its custom–friendly nature, it's been the model of choice for many lowrider fans.

Top speed:	134 mph (214 km/h)
0–60 mph (0–96 km/h):	9.0 sec
Engine type:	V8
Displacement:	348 ci (5,702 cc)
Transmission	3-speed auto
Max power:	315 bhp (235 kW) @ 5,600 rpm
Max torque:	357 lb ft (484 Nm) @ 3,600 rpm
Weight:	3,649 lb (1,658 kg)
Economy:	11.8 mpg (4.17 km/l)

Ford Fairlane Skyliner (1959)

Revolutionary at the time, the Skyliner offered a practical hardtop coupe plus the style of a drop top. The retractable hardtop roof was a masterpiece in engineering and required 7 electric motors, 13 switches, 10 solenoids, 8 circuit breakers and over 600ft (182m) of wiring to make it function. The car was fairly conventional underneath with a separate chassis and double wishbones up front with leaf springs at the rear, though the frame did have an X-brace to give it extra strength as the roof was not part of the structure. On the body, one of the best changes for the 1959 model year was the switch to large, round tail lights, which became a trademark feature of early 1960s Fords. Standard was the Mercury's 292ci (4.78-litre) Flathead V8, though with fuel at 20 cents a gallon, the big-blocks were favoured, and this has the 352ci (5.3-litre) Police Interceptor special.

Top speed:	112 mph (179 km/h)
0–60 mph (0–96 km/h):	10.5 sec
Engine type:	V8
Displacement:	352 ci (5,768 cc)
Transmission	3-speed auto
Max power:	300 bhp (224 kW) @ 4,600 rpm
Max torque:	381 lb ft (517 Nm) @ 2,800 rpm
Weight:	4,064 lb (1,847 kg)
Economy:	14 mpg (4.95 km/l)

Lincoln Continental Mk IV (1959)

Everything about the Mk IV was big. It was one of the largest cars ever to come out of Detroit, and had the biggest-capacity engine ever available in a passenger car up until the 1960s. Like the Skyline which had arrived just two years before, the Lincoln used a retractable hardtop which neatly stowed away in the trunk, but when up, the rear screen raked inwards and offered an opening window for rear-passenger ventilation. Given the ostentatious time, the Mk IV was one of the least fussy cars from Detroit, but it was immensely stylish with its wide, canted headlight grille and work-of-art fenders both ends. Suspension was conventional for the time, with wishbones and leaf springs front and rear, while the all cast-iron engine thumped out enormous torque to make the Mk IV a great cruiser and, significantly, quicker than the Cadillacs.

Top speed:	118 mph (188 km/h)
0–60 mph (0–96 km/h):	10.4 sec
Engine type:	V8
Displacement:	430 ci (7,046 cc)
Transmission	3-speed auto
Max power:	350 bhp (261 kW) @ 4,400 rpm
Max torque:	490 lb ft (664 Nm) @ 2,800 rpm
Weight:	5,192 lb (2,360 kg)
Economy:	7 mpg (2.47 km/l)

Pontiac Bonneville (1959)

Anew style of longer and lower Pontiacs arrived in 1959, and they picked up the brand name from its lacklustre image. The Bonneville felt more sporty to drive compared to older models, thank to its lower seating position and ultra powerful engine. To enhance the car's low stance, the wheels were down in size to 14 inches (355mm) and other styling touches included the now-famous Pontiac split grille, which has been virtually every model from the company since. While the main concentration at the time was on engine power and outward style, Pontiac did have one advance on the suspension and that was the use of coil springs at the rear instead of semi-elliptical units, which improved the ride significantly. While this car had the powerful 389ci (6.3-litre) unit, there was a Tri-Power set-up with three carbs to boost output to 345bhp (257kW), for a sub 7-second 0–60mph (0–96km/h) sprint.

Top speed:	120 mph (192 km/h)
0–60 mph (0–96 km/h):	8.1 sec
Engine type:	V8
Displacement:	389 ci (6,374 cc)
Transmission	3-speed auto
Max power:	300 bhp (224 kW) @ 4,600 rpm
Max torque:	450 lb ft (610 Nm) @ 2,800 rpm
Weight:	4,233 lb (1,924 kg)
Economy:	10 mpg (3.54 km/l)

Chevrolet El Camino (1959)

What did you get if you mixed a car with a truck back in the 1950s? Well, usually a compromise of both, but it wasn't as simple as that with the El Camino. It was launched by Chevrolet in response to Ford's car-based Ranchero and was beautifully styled inside and out, so it felt more like the glamorous cars of the era. Yet it had a huge loading bed, which meant that it found favour with many image-conscious small businesses. The car was based on the station wagon but had obvious traits straight from the sedans too, with the huge fins, cat eye tail lights, and headlamp eyebrows. Underneath the live axle had extra location with both a Panhard rod and torque arm, therefore reducing wheel hop while accelerating. And the car could do that in abundance, thanks to the top-option 348ci (5.7-litre) V8, which put it ahead of many performance sedans of the time.

Top speed:	131 mph (210 km/h)
0–60 mph (0–96 km/h):	8.7 sec
Engine type:	V8
Displacement:	348 ci (5,702 cc)
Transmission	3-speed auto
Max power:	315 bhp (235 kW) @ 5,600 rpm
Max torque:	357 lb ft (484 Nm) @ 3,600 rpm
Weight:	3,881 lb (1,764 kg)
Economy:	11.8 mpg (4.17 km/l)

Ford Thunderbird (1960)

It seems odd now that Ford changed the direction of the Thunderbird from its two-seater origins, when it was launched as direct competition to the Corvette. But sales dictate direction, and as evidence of how much the public liked the 1960 T-bird, it sold over twice as many cars as the 1958 model. Unitary construction was adopted in 1958 to make the car handle better, but it also featured a dropped floorpan to lower the ride height and, thus, the centre of gravity. Coil springs all around gave an excellent ride quality, and although the car wasn't as sporty as the original T-birds, it was quieter and more refined. This model was the top option in its year, having the Lincoln 430ci (7-litre) cast-iron engine up front, which made the car very heavy. However, it was one of the most rapid machines of its day, which was one reason it sold well in those horsepower-hungry times.

Top speed:	121 mph (194 km/h)
0–60 mph (0–96 km/h):	8.2 sec
Engine type:	V8
Displacement:	430 ci (7,046 cc)
Transmission:	3-speed auto
Max power:	350 bhp (261 kW) @ 4,800 rpm
Max torque:	490 lb ft (664 Nm) @ 3,100 rpm
Weight:	4,381 lb (1,991 kg)
Economy:	15.7 mpg (5.55 km/l)

Oldsmobile Super 88 (1960)

The Super 88 was Oldsmobile's factory hot rod, and over 16,000 were sold in 1960. All GM cars featured a new chassis for 1959 and the Super 88 ran an X-braced steel frame with independent front and live axle rear, all on coil springs. This custom version has been changed by adding lowered and uprated springs from a 1969 Chevy and air shocks at the rear. While the Super 88 left the factory with a torquey 394ci (6.5-litre) V8, this car's has since been replaced by a small-block Chevy for cost and ease of tuning, and the new unit is both lighter and more powerful in addition. Body modifications include the hood being extended and peaked by 2 inches (50mm), the tail lights frenched (sunken) into the body, and the side trim being shaved for a smooth look. The rims are 8 inches (203mm) wide and carry low profiles to bring the handling up to modern standards.

Top speed:	120 mph (192 km/h)
0–60 mph (0–96 km/h):	8.3 sec
Engine type:	V8
Displacement:	350 ci (5,735 cc)
Transmission	3-speed auto
Max power:	345 bhp (257 kW) @ 5,800 rpm
Max torque:	370 lb ft (502 Nm) @ 3,000 rpm
Weight:	3,860 lb (1,754 kg)
Economy:	14 mpg (4.95 km/l)

Pontiac Bonneville (1960)

The new long and lower Bonnevilles had been introduced in 1959 and were acclaimed for their slender, sporty looks and good road-holding. They carried on in similar mechanical guise for 1960, but this was the only year that, styling-wise, the Pontiacs didn't have the split grille. Underneath, the car used a X-braced chassis with unequal-length wishbone front suspension and a live rear axle. Changes were made to the rear suspension with the attachments points of the upper-control arms raised and given stiffer bushings to better locate the axle. Other changes to the drive train included a redesign of the bellhousing to lower the transmission tunnel and give an inch extra room inside the car. The standard engine was again the 389ci (6.3-litre) as in 1959, but the top option was the 10.5:1 compression unit which ran with a high-lift camshaft, less restrictive heads and a Tri-Power intake.

Top speed:	113 mph (181 km/h)
0–60 mph (0–96 km/h):	9.7 sec
Engine type:	V8
Displacement:	389 ci (6,374 cc)
Transmission:	3-speed auto
Max power:	318 bhp (237 kW) @ 4,600 rpm
Max torque:	420 lb ft (569 Nm) @ 2,800 rpm
Weight:	4,070 lb (1,850 kg)
Economy:	12 mpg (4.24 km/l)

Watson Roadster (1960)

Indy racing is part of the US culture, and in the early 1960s A.J. Watson dominated the manufacturing of the cars, at a time when Formula One machines were just starting to influence design. Watson's history goes back to 1950 when, as a mechanic, he built his own car for the Indy 500 which Dick Rathmann drove. In 1954 Watson got his break with the John Zink Jnr team, and a year later his modified version of the Frank Kurtis-built roadster won the Indy 500. This 1960 example is typical of his racers, with a basic chassis with front/rear solid axles but torsion bar suspension that could be tweaked by the driver whilst going along. The Offenhauser Sprint and Champ car engine was offset to the left to make the car turn naturally in that direction, and gearbox only needed two speeds due to the massive torque available low down, plus the car's light weight.

Top speed:	175 mph (280 km/h)
0–60 mph (0–96 km/h):	3.3 sec
Engine type:	In-line four
Displacement:	252 ci (4,129 cc)
Transmission	2-speed manual
Max power:	400 bhp (298 kW) @ 6,600 rpm
Max torque:	N/A
Weight:	1,600 lb (727 kg)
Economy:	N/A

Chevrolet Corvette (1961)

Introduced in 1955 in V8 form, the Corvette established Chevrolet as kings of the US automotive world with a range of cars to suit every taste and pocket. By 1958 the car had been restyled more aggressively, and was both wider and longer. The famous small-block Chevy engine, which started out at 265ci (4.5 litres) V8, grew to 283ci (4.6 litres) by 1958 and by 1962 it was bored and stroked to 327ci (5.4 litres). The significance of this V8 engine can't be underestimated as, in fuel injected form at least, it made the Corvette one of the most powerful sportscars in the world and certainly one of the quickest at the time. Unfortunately the brakes and handling didn't match, though the steering was precise enough to catch the sudden oversteer the Corvette suffered from when pushed. But the 1956–1962 car was more about style, being inspired by fighter planes of the time.

Top speed:	135 mph (216 km/h)
0–60 mph (0–96 km/h):	6.1 sec
Engine type:	V8
Displacement:	327 ci (5,358 cc)
Transmission:	4-speed manual
Max power:	360 bhp (268 kW) @ 6,000 rpm
Max torque:	352 lb ft (477 Nm) @ 4,000 rpm
Weight:	2,942 lb (1,337 kg)
Economy:	12.4 mpg (4.39 km/l)

Chrysler 300G (1961)

Continuing the well respected 'letter' cars from Chrysler which had started with the 1955 C-300, the 300G was a muscle car with much to offer. On getting in, you could swivel the front seats, which was a first, then once inside you had push-button transmission and stylish aluminium dashboard, plus optional air-conditioning, electric mirrors, and a self-seeking Music Master radio. Stiffer suspension was fitted underneath to make the heavyweight a much better-handling car than its predecessors, and a tough Dana rear axle was fitted to cope with the massive power. New was Chrysler's 'Cross Ram' intake manifold, which put the dual four-barrel carbs either side of the Max Wedge V8 motor, with very long intake runners. It worked for torque production, nearing the magic 500lb ft (677Nm) mark and making the 'G' extremely quick off the line. Just 337 were built as convertibles.

Top speed:	130 mph (208 km/h)
0–60 mph (0–96 km/h):	8.4 sec
Engine type:	V8
Displacement:	413 ci (6,767 cc)
Transmission	3-speed auto
Max power:	305 bhp (227 kW) @ 5,000 rpm
Max torque:	495 lb ft (671 Nm) @ 2,800 rpm
Weight:	4,315 lb (1,961 kg)
Economy:	12 mpg (4.24 km/l)

Ford Galaxie Starliner (1961)

This Galaxie hot rod carries the now legendary SOHC Ford engine which was developed in order to compete with Chrysler's Hemi-engined NASCAR racers. It made an impressive 675bhp (503kW) on Ford dyno, but it was outlawed immediately because it was too good. The engines did make it on several factory-sponsored A/FX drag racers, which subsequently won their class in 1965. Even so, it never made it into a production car, though some de-tuned engines were sold over the counter. One of those made its way into this modified Galaxie, which has had to have the hood reshaped to fit the induction system. Elsewhere the car features stiffer front suspension to cope with the weight, plus there's a Top Loader gearbox and 4.30:1 geared rear end with Detroit Locker differential. Quarter-miles zip by in just 13 seconds for this Starliner, but it looks like a period factory racer.

Top speed:	130 mph (208 km/h)
0–60 mph (0–96 km/h):	5.4 sec
Engine type:	V8
Displacement:	427 ci (6,997 cc)
Transmission:	4-speed manual
Max power:	625 bhp (466 kW) @ 7,000 rpm
Max torque:	515 lb ft (698 Nm) @ 3,800 rpm
Weight:	3,660 lb (1,663 kg)
Economy:	7 mpg (2.47 km/l)

Ford Galaxie Sunliner (1961)

Wider than any other Ford produced in the 1960s, the 1961 Galaxie range was huge in every respect. The Sunliner topped the range and was over 79 inches (2m) wide. It ran nothing radical on the separate chassis, but it did use ideas developed during NASCAR racing to transform the suspension and handling of the car. The body has a minor facelift for this use with a concave grille and stylish single side crease which developed into horizontal fins at the rear. There was a detachable hardtop roof available for the Sunliner, but most opted for the electric folding top. Even in base form the Sunliner had a 300bhp (224kW) V8, but buyers could opt for the Police Interceptor tune which had 401bhp (299kW) and pushed the car under seven seconds in the 0–60mph (0–96km/h) sprint. In the rapidly changing motor world of the early 1960s, the new car lasted but a year before getting a redesign.

Top speed:	122 mph (195 km/h)
0–60 mph (0–96 km/h):	9.5 sec
Engine type:	V8
Displacement:	390 ci (6,390 cc)
Transmission	3-speed auto
Max power:	300 bhp (224kW) @ 4,600 rpm
Max torque:	427 lb ft (579 Nm) @ 2,800 rpm
Weight:	3,792 lb (1,723 kg)
Economy:	12 mpg (4.24 km/l)

Imperial Crown (1961)

Chrysler made Imperial a marque in its own right in 1955 and aimed it squarely at the luxurious Cadillacs and Lincolns. The spectacular-looking 1957 Imperials, deigned by stylist Virgil Exner, had ideas which were continued into the early 1960s. His quad headlights continued, but this time he put them in small body coves to make the car stand out from the prevalent integrated look. The car continued the tradition of a separate chassis which helped reduce noise intrusion and vibration, important for such a luxury car. Chrysler's torsion bar suspension was also fitted up front, which was a big improvement over coil springs, to make Imperials one of the best-riding premium cars. The tooling costs of the Hemi meant a new engine was designed, called the 'Wedge Head'. Not only was this cheaper, but it also required less tune-ups and was more flexible throughout the rev range.

Top speed:	120 mph (192 km/h)
0–60 mph (0–96 km/h):	10.0 sec
Engine type:	V8
Displacement:	413 ci (6,767 cc)
Transmission	3-speed auto
Max power:	350 bhp (261 kW) @ 4,600 rpm
Max torque:	470 lb ft (637 Nm) @ 2,800 rpm
Weight:	4,790 lb (2,177 kg)
Economy:	15 mpg (5.31 km/l)

Lincoln Continental (1961)

Lincoln worked hard to make their 1961 Continental one of the best ever, and it won praise for its high construction standards. It had a new, streamlined body with slab sides and a flush-fitting grille, plus 'clap-hand' doors which opened away from each other for excellent access. It was advanced, and because of the emphasis on quality, had no concessions towards weight-saving. The huge chassis was on a 123-inch (3.12m) wheelbase and ran self-adjusting brakes, along with coil springs and leaf springs front and rear. It was inside where the innovations were, with power-assisted features such as the windows, door locks, hydraulic wipers, steering, six-way seats, plus there was air-conditioning and cruise control. The car was very subtle in its styling, too, compared to what was available just to previous years. New, small lights and conservative use of chrome made it a favourite for stately owners.

Top speed:	117 mph (187 km/h)
0–60 mph (0–96 km/h):	11.2 sec
Engine type:	V8
Displacement:	430 ci (7,046 cc)
Transmission	3-speed auto
Max power:	300 bhp (224 kW) @ 4,100 rpm
Max torque:	465 lb ft (630 Nm) @ 2,000 rpm
Weight:	5,220 lb (2,372 kg)
Economy:	12 mpg (4.24 km/l)

Oldsmobile Starfire (1961)

Like many cars of the time, the 1961 Oldsmobile Starfire had a bargelike feel thanks to light steering, soft suspension and wallowing ride. But this was exactly how people liked it, as they associated these attributes with quality and prestige. Yet the Starfire was intended to be sporting amongst its rivals and so had a torquey big-block engine. The chassis was stronger than most, featuring a separate frame with four steel triangulated crossmembers to promote torsional rigidity. This worked most noticeably on the convertible, which was particularly solid in construction. Dual exhaust gave away the engine's sporting prowess, which had an improved induction system and hotter camshaft, as well as the Skyrocket's four-barrel carb and high-compression pistons. Through the smooth Hydramatic gearbox, it performed extremely well, making the Starfire very quick for its size and bulk.

Top speed:	120 mph (192 km/h)
0–60 mph (0–96 km/h):	9.0 sec
Engine type:	V8
Displacement:	394 ci (6,456 cc)
Transmission	3-speed auto
Max power:	330 bhp (246 kW) @ 4,600 rpm
Max torque:	440 lb ft (596 Nm) @ 2,800 rpm
Weight:	4,305 lb (1,956 kg)
Economy:	12 mpg (4.24 km/l)

Pontiac Ventura (1961)

Pontiac were at the forefront of muscle-car production, and nowhere was this more evident than with models such as the Ventura. And being one of the good-looking 'bubble top' cars produced at the time – so called because of their thin pillars and large glass area – the car is in demand as a classic today. It also has Pontiac's famous split grille, which is still used to the present day. This example is barely different from stock, with simple but effective changes to the rolling stock to improve handling and looks. Where it has seen dramatic change is under the hood, with a 1969 400ci (298kW) GTO engine fitted and tuned up for more power. The Ram Air option motor has been fitted with a free-flowing exhaust and the heads have been ported. This puts it in the 14-second range for the quarter-mile, enough to surprise, thanks to the car's sneakily stock appearance.

Top speed:	124 mph (198 km/h)
0–60 mph (0–96 km/h):	6.5 sec
Engine type:	V8
Displacement:	400 ci (6,554 cc)
Transmission	3-speed auto
Max power:	380 bhp (283 kW) @ 5,500 rpm
Max torque:	450 lb ft (610 Nm) @ 3,900 rpm
Weight:	3,687 lb (1,676 kg)
Economy:	11.8 mpg (4.17 km/l)

Chevrolet Bel Air 409 (1962)

The 1962 Chevy Bel Air was deceptive. On the outside it was ordinary, but underneath it was potent. Chevrolet released it out as the muiscle car wars were getting hotter in the early 1960s, and fit the 409ci (6.7-litre) big-block V8 which could chirp the tyres through each gear. In 1962 the engine was rated at 380bhp (283kW), but with twin four-barrel carbs, this went to 409bhp (305kW). Though the 409 could be had in any body style, most chose the coupe because of its handsome looks. Weight could be shed by ordering aluminium front panels from the factory, and Chevy even made 12 cars like this themselves, for drag racers only. Inside the car was spartan, because most buyers were interested only in its performance, and as a sign of this a small steering column-mounted 7000rpm rev counter was part of the dash. The car won the NHRA S/S (Super Stock) championship in its debut year.

Top speed:	115 mph (184 km/h)
0–60 mph (0–96 km/h):	7.3 sec
Engine type:	V8
Displacement:	409 ci (6,702 cc)
Transmission	4-speed manual
Max power:	380 bhp (283 kW) @ 6,000 rpm
Max torque:	420 lb ft (570 Nm) @ 3,200 rpm
Weight:	3,480 lb (1,581 kg)
Economy:	14 mpg (4.95 km/l)

Chevrolet Impala SS (1962)

Lowriding's origins can be traced back to the 1950s when the customizing craze was going full swing. Car modifiers would take their machines and lower them as far as possible for maximum visual impact. While amongst the regular family cars, these lowered rides looked aggressive and ultra cool, but they had one problem: their height. The cars couldn't be driven over anything without scraping the underneath of the car. Inventive modifiers used the hydraulic rams off of commercial vehicles to help them raise and lower their cars as required, thus the current craze of hydraulic cars began. Due to availability, bargain price and their good looks when dropped to the ground, the Chevy Impalas became very popular. This one has a full custom paint job, deep buttoned velour interior and hydraulic rams at each corner with pumps for each chromed and mounted in the trunk.

Top speed:	107 mph (171 km/h)
0–60 mph (0–96 km/h):	12.1 sec
Engine type:	V8
Displacement:	283 ci (4,637 cc)
Transmission	3-speed auto
Max power:	170 bhp (127 kW) @ 4,200 rpm
Max torque:	270 lb ft (366 Nm) @ 2,800 rpm
Weight:	3,512 lb (1,596 kg)
Economy:	15 mpg (5.31 km/l)

Ford Thunderbird (1962)

The square lines were abandoned for 1961 in the third-generation Thunderbird, but the car remained as popular as ever, with over 73,000 built in that year alone. The new cigar shape was powered by just the one engine option: the 390 ci (6.4-litre) big-block. It was a heavy engine, but by now the Thunderbird wasn't so much a sportscar as a luxury cruiser. For that same reason, it was softly sprung and hence didn't corner very well, though it was better than initial impressions would lead you to believe, and once at a reasonable speed, the handling turned more neutral. The styling has turned this era T-bird into a classic, and cars like the Sports Roadster shown remain much in demand, partly because of the enclosed tonneau rear. Also available that year was the Coupe, Landau and convertible. The car was restyled in 1964.

Top speed:	118 mph (188 km/h)
0–60 mph (0–96 km/h):	9.3 sec
Engine type:	V8
Displacement:	390 ci (6,390 cc)
Transmission	3-speed auto
Max power:	300 bhp (224 kW) @ 4,600 rpm
Max torque:	427 lb ft (579 Nm) @ 2,800 rpm
Weight:	4,471 lb (2,032 kg)
Economy:	10 mpg (3.54 km/l)

Greer-Black-Prudhomme rail (1962)

This dragster hails from a time before massive sponsorship and multi-million dollar championships. It also represents drag racing in its purest form, being a Top Fuel dragster. This class evolved from stripped-down Model T racers of the early 1930s, which were little more than a chassis and engine. As these cars developed, they grew longer wheelbases to make them more stable at speed, but retained the front engine format into the late 1960s, before switching to rear engines for safety reasons. The Greer, Black & Prudhomme car was backed by Tom Greer, the engine was by Keith Black, and the driving was handled by Don Prudhomme, who later went on to become World NHRA Top Fuel Champion. The car features a chrome-moly tubular chassis and a Chrysler Hemi with modified 6/71 GMC supercharger. It did the quarter in 7.7 seconds at 270mph (434km/h).

Top speed:	270 mph (432 km/h)
0–60 mph (0–96 km/h):	N/A
Engine type:	V8
Displacement:	398 ci (6,522 cc)
Transmission	None, direct drive to axle
Max power:	830 bhp (619 kW) @ 7,000 rpm
Max torque:	795 lb ft (1,078 Nm) @ 4,000 rpm
Weight:	N/A
Economy:	N/A

Pontiac Tempest Le Mans (1962)

Of the three compact cars GM introduced in 1960, the Tempest was the most radical, with its all-independent suspension. It used a rear mounted transaxle for near-perfect weight distribution, which produced exceptional handling for great driver reward. The other advantage with the Tempest was its weight. Although in standard form it came with a 194ci (3.2-litre) slant four engine, it was best with Buick's all-aluminium V8 (later sold to Rover in the UK) which was virtually the same weight as the four-cylinder unit and helped put the Tempest's overall weight under 3000lb (130kg), almost unheard of for a muscle car of that era. The Tempest used Pontiac's famous split grille, albeit in a slightly subdued fashion for this 1962 year, and inside was roomy for a compact, thanks to the flat floor through the lack of a transmission tunnel.

Top speed:	115 mph (184 km/h)
0–60 mph (0–96 km/h):	9.9 sec
Engine type:	V8
Displacement:	215 ci (3,523 cc)
Transmission	3-speed auto
Max power:	190 bhp (142 kW) @ 4,800 rpm
Max torque:	240 lb ft (325 Nm) @ 2,600 rpm
Weight:	2,955 lb (1,343 kg)
Economy:	17 mpg (6.01 km/l)

Buick Riviera (1963)

Combining power and luxury, the 1963 Riviera was one of Buick's landmark cars. It was the company's first true luxury coupe and reflected styling supremo Bill Mitchell's ideals of having a clean, European-looking car. The grille, as an example, was styled on Ferrari's 250GT, while inside the long centre console was very similar to Ferrari's finest too. Buick used many parts from the corporate parts bin for the Riviera's underpinnings, with a separate chassis, wishbone suspension up front, and a live axle on coil springs at the rear. The ride was very soft and the steering over-light, but in those days that's exactly what luxury meant. It was having all the comfort of a big car in something relatively small, compared to a Cadillac or Lincoln, that made the Riviera popular. It was also quick for a top-brand machine, thanks to the Wildcat 445 engine (named after the torque figure).

Top speed:	125 mph (200 km/h)
0–60 mph (0–96 km/h):	8.0 sec
Engine type:	V8
Displacement:	401 ci (6,571 cc)
Transmission:	2-speed auto
Max power:	325 bhp (242 kW) @ 4,400 rpm
Max torque:	445 lb ft (603 Nm) @ 2,800 rpm
Weight:	4,367 lb (1,985 kg)
Economy:	12 mpg (4.24 km/l)

Chevrolet Corvette Sting Ray (1963)

Using a chassis from the cancelled Corvette SS racing programme, GM Chief stylist Bill Mitchell and designer Larry Shinoda styled their own body, called it the Stingray, then campaigned it with their own money. It was to be the shape that defined the 1963 second-generation Corvette, right down to the split rear window which Mitchell fought hard to keep. The Sting Ray came in both hardtop or open top form, and was the first Corvette to use fully independent suspension which dramatically improved the handling, allowing it to complete with the Jaguar XKE race cars. The rear used a single transverse leaf spring which ran either side of the differential, which itself could be ordered with anything from 3.08:1 to 4.56:1 gearing. The base engine was the 327ci (244kW), but potential racers could order the 'Fuelie' fuel-injected 360bhp (268kW) with four-speed manual and Posi rear.

Top speed:	118 mph (189 km/h)
0–60 mph (0–96 km/h):	6.1 sec
Engine type:	V8
Displacement:	327 ci (5,358 cc)
Transmission:	4-speed manual
Max power:	300 bhp (224 kW) @ 5,000 rpm
Max torque:	360 lb ft (488 Nm) @ 3,200 rpm
Weight:	3,160 lb (1,436 kg)
Economy:	18 mpg (6.37 km/l)

Chrysler Turbine (1963)

While Chrysler weren't the inventors of the gas-turbine engine, they were its greatest exponents, and started by fitting one to a Plymouth Belvedere as early as 1955, developing a seventh-generation engine even in the late 1970s, which was fitted in a 1977 Dodge Aspen. The advantages with the turbine were that it could run on all kinds of fuel, including diesel and kerosene, its huge torque was available from zero rpm, it could rev to very high speeds (up to nearly 45,000rpm) very quietly, and it warmed up instantaneously. Unfortunately, it boasted little power, did precious little miles per gallon, and was heavy. For evaluation, Chrysler gave 45 gas-turbine cars to member of the public to try out, but of the 55 built, in total 46 were destroyed simply to avoid paying import duty on the Italian-built cars. Just 9 machines remain, in museums and private collections, across America.

Top speed:	115 mph (184 km/h)
0–60 mph (0–96 km/h):	10.0 sec
Engine type:	Gas-turbine
Displacement:	N/A
Transmission	3-speed auto
Max power:	130 bhp (97 kW) @ 44,600 rpm
Max torque:	425 lb ft (576 Nm) at zero output
Weight:	3,900 lb (1,772 kg)
Economy:	12 mpg (4.24 km/l)

Ford Falcon Racer (1963)

This Ford Falcon actually uses very little in the way of Ford parts. While it looks like a hardtop coupe, it is actually a convertible body and has had the roof from another Falcon welded on. All that remains of the steel body is the roof, rear three-quarters and doors, while the rest are glass-fibre moulded items in order to save weight. For the same reason, and for improved safety, the glass has also made way for Lexan, reinforced plastic. The frame has been built to the NHRA's (National Hot Rod Association) drag-racing standards for the class of Super Gas, to which the cars run an index of 9.90 seconds on the quarter-mile. The chassis is tubular steel and the front and rear suspension uses lightweight coilover damper units with tubular locating arms. The engine is based on a Ford 460ci (7.5-litre) big-block, but with a stroker crankshaft and a race-spec build.

Top speed:	160 mph (256 km/h)
0–60 mph (0–96 km/h):	2.8 sec
Engine type:	V8
Displacement:	500 ci (8,193 cc)
Transmission	2-speed auto
Max power:	710 bhp (529 kW) @ 7,000 rpm
Max torque:	685 lb ft (929 Nm) @ 5,200 rpm
Weight:	2,015 lb (916 kg)
Economy:	6 mpg (2.12 km/l)

Ford Galaxie 500XL (1963)

The slogan 'Win on Sunday, sell on Monday' was boasted by Ford as they heated up the competition in NASCAR, the Galaxie XL being their star machine. The XL stood for 'extra light' and the trunk lid, doors, hood and front fenders were all moulded in glass-fibre, while the fenders were made in aluminium. Even the rest of the body panels were made from lighter-gauge steel, all of which helped save 700lb (318kg) in weight. The front suspension was kept as double wishbone, while the rear was a live axle with semi-elliptical springs and telescopic shocks, In order to get the best acceleration, 4.56:1 gears were fitted in the axle. The engine was built for racing with a 12.2 compression high-lift cam and dual Holley four-barrel carbs. Inside, the car used low back van seats, while all sound-deadening plus the heater, radio and clock had been removed to further reduce weight.

Top speed:	115 mph (184 km/h)
0–60 mph (0–96 km/h):	4.7 sec
Engine type:	V8
Displacement:	427ci (6,997 cc)
Transmission	4-speed manual
Max power:	425 bhp (317 kW) @ 6,000 rpm
Max torque:	480 lb ft (650 Nm) @ 3,700 rpm
Weight:	3,772 lb (1,714 kg)
Economy:	6 mpg (2.12 km/l)

Plymouth Savoy 426 (1963)

The early 1960s saw Chrysler, GM and Ford doing battle on both the race tracks and drag strips across America. Chrysler's 1963 weapon of choice was the Super Stock Savoy, a lightweight, race-prepped car with their most powerful engine. Chrysler cleverly did as much to make the Savoy as suitable a drag racer as possible, things like mounting the battery in the trunk to help weight-distribution, and deliberately leaving the torsion bar front suspension set in a high position to aid weight transfer to the rear wheels during acceleration. The engine was tuned to the max, with the wedge-designed chamber taking 13.5:1 compression, and massive valves allowing flow up to 7,500rpm. Dual four-barrel carbs fed the engine, and a free-flowing exhaust was designed to further improve output. The Super Stock was regularly on the winner's podium during its inaugural year.

Top speed:	125 mph (200 km/h)
0–60 mph (0–96 km/h):	5.0 sec
Engine type:	V8
Displacement:	426 ci (6,980 cc)
Transmission	3-speed auto
Max power:	425 bhp (317 kW) @ 5,600 rpm
Max torque:	470 lb ft (637 Nm) @ 4,400 rpm
Weight:	3,400 lb (1,545 kg)
Economy:	7 mpg (2.47 km/l)

Ford Falcon GT racer (1963)

A successful beginning in Falcon sales of 1960 led Ford to develop the car in the following years. Although they'd managed to sell over 410,000 cars in '60, the next year they produced a Falcon Sprint model with V8 to increase power and its appeal, then in 1962 they sent race cars to Europe for use in rallying events. In 1964 the car was restyled with squarer, neater lines, but faced tough competition from the new Mustang which, ironically, was a Falcon underneath. This race Falcon is today used in historic circuit competition in the UK. It has lowered and stiffened suspension and in order to shed weight its hood, trunk and front fenders have been moulded in glass-fibre. The engine is a High Performance V8, which means slightly more compression, a high-lift camshaft and free-flowing exhaust. It works through the brutally strong Borg Warner T10 'Top Loader' gearbox.

Top speed:	135 mph (216 km/h)
0–60 mph (0–96 km/h):	6.4 sec
Engine type:	V8
Displacement:	289 ci (4,735 cc)
Transmission	4-speed manual
Max power:	271 bhp (202 kW) @ 6,000 rpm
Max torque:	312 lb ft (423 Nm) @ 3,400 rpm
Weight:	2,811 lb (1,277 kg)
Economy:	12.4 mpg (4.38 km/l)

Shelby/Cooper King Cobra (1963)

In 1963 Carroll Shelby, in his search for an ideal race car, chose British racer John Cooper's mid-engined design and shoehorned in an American V8. The chassis was rigid yet lightweight, being tubular steel and with the engine and transmission forming part of the structure. Double A-arms, anti-roll bars and disc brakes sat fore and aft, and the aluminium body was hand-formed. The engine was race tuned and a full balancing and blueprinting job made sure it was durable and reliable. The compression was raised to 10.5:1 for a power increase, and four twin Weber carburettors gave great response and acceleration, even from low rpm. In the space of two racing seasons, only 12 cars were constructed and just three of those are still around, hence they're incredibly valuable – a sort of car collectors' version of the Holy Grail.

Top speed:	176 mph (282 km/h)
0–60 mph (0–96 km/h):	3.5 sec
Engine type:	V8
Displacement:	289 ci (4,735 cc)
Transmission	4-speed manual
Max power:	400 bhp (298 kW) @ 6,800 rpm
Max torque:	345 lb ft (467 Nm) @ 4,000 rpm
Weight:	1,400 lb (636 kg)
Economy:	10 mpg (3.54 km/l)

Ford Fairlane Thunderbolt (1964)

Aﬀter getting beat by Pontiac and Chrysler in the NHRA's Super Stock class of 1963, Ford went all out for the following season and created the Thunderbolt. It didn't pretend to be anything but a full-blown drag machine, available through Ford only to racers. To fit the huge 427 engine, an outside company, Dearborn Steel Tubing, had to widen the shock towers, plus move the A-arm pivot point out by an inch. The car's high beam headlights were replaced with air intakes to feed the engine, and simple steel wheels were fitted as many got replaced by lightweight racing alloys. The leaf sprung rear end had a torque arm locating the axle to help launch the car, and the battery was mounted in the trunk for improved weight distribution. The body featured lightweight glass-fibre panels where possible, but it was the race-tuned engine which helped push the car to 11.7-second quarters.

Top speed:	130 mph (208 km/h)
0–60 mph (0–96 km/h):	4.7 sec
Engine type:	V8
Displacement:	427 ci (6,997 cc)
Transmission	4-speed manual
Max power:	425 bhp (317 kW) @ 6,000 rpm
Max torque:	480 lb ft (650 Nm) @ 3,700 rpm
Weight:	3,225 lb (1,465 kg)
Economy:	7 mpg (2.47 km/l)

Pontiac GTO (1964)

Often thought of as the sedan which started the muscle car wars, the 1964 GTO used a Tempest body with a 389ci (6.3-litre) V8 engine shoehorned in the front. Designers found a loophole in the GM ruling which limited its intermediate cars to a maximum engine size of 330ci (5.4-litre), and as such the trend for putting big engines into medium cars began, developing still further until the fuel crisis of 1973. The GTO had a thicker anti-roll bar, stiffer springs, uprated shocks and higher-speed rated tyres compared to the stock Tempest. The best gearbox was the four-speed 'Muncie' that made the most of the huge power output. Drum brakes weren't great, but they could be ordered with sintered linings which helped stopping power. The biggest advantage was the weight, some 300lb (136kg) lighter than most later muscle cars, thus making it very quick in acceleration.

Top speed:	120 mph (192 km/h)
0–60 mph (0–96 km/h):	6.6 sec
Engine type:	V8
Displacement:	389 ci (5,735 cc)
Transmission	4-speed manual
Max power:	348 bhp (260 kW) @ 4,900 rpm
Max torque:	428 lb ft (580 Nm) @ 3,600 rpm
Weight:	3,126 lb (1,420 kg)
Economy:	14 mpg (4.95 km/l)

Pontiac Le Mans (1964)

Without the original factory-backed race cars' class constraints, modern drag racers have been able to develop muscle cars further still, and this Le Mans is a prime example. It uses some of the original frame but with the rear rails narrowed in order to fit in the huge racing slicks and custom-fabricated coilover damper suspension and adjustable four-bar locating arms. At the front all unnecessary steel has been stripped out which means no inner fenders. The interior too has been stripped completely, with painted metal left for the floor and door panels. Two lightweight racing bucket seats stand alone inside. The engine comprises a 400ci (6.6-litre) block with 455ci (7.5-litre) crank and Super Duty con-rods, plus 12.5:1 pistons and a huge carburettor that can flow 1150 cubic feet (32 cubic metres) of air per minute. Nitrous oxide adds 150bhp (112kW) while racing.

Top speed:	159 mph (254 km/h)
0–60 mph (0–96 km/h):	3.8 sec
Engine type:	V8
Displacement:	449 ci (7,357 cc)
Transmission	3-speed auto
Max power:	520 bhp (388 kW) @ 5,500 rpm
Max torque:	524 lb ft (710 Nm) @ 4,000 rpm
Weight:	2,501 lb (1,137 kg)
Economy:	5.9 mpg (2.08 km/l)

Corvette BP Racer (1965)

Chevrolet launched its radical new Corvette in 1962, based on the Sting Ray race car. The road cars had a huge number of performance options, and it is this, plus the car's very quick pace, which made many successful race machines. This roadster is typical of the breed, with the original frame reinforced with a multi-point roll cage that stiffens up the structure and helps to make the suspension work better. The springs and shocks have all been uprated to the sort of standard that would usually rattle fillings loose on the road, though they make this roadster into the ultimate corner carver. This car uses the highest factory-rated engine, the 327ci (5.4 litre) 'Fuelie', so called because it had Rochester mechanical fuel injection. It also had specially designed aluminium cylinders heads, 11:1 compression, and a modified distributor to promote power.

Top speed:	148 mph (237 km/h)
0–60 mph (0–96 km/h):	5.4 sec
Engine type:	V8
Displacement:	327 ci (5,358 cc)
Transmission	4-speed manual
Max power:	375 bhp (280 kW) @ 6,000 rpm
Max torque	352 lb ft (477 Nm) @ 4,000 rpm
Weight:	3,150 lb (1,431 kg)
Economy:	12 mpg (4.24 km/l)

Dodge A100 (1965)

Ford and GM virtually dominated the truck market in the 1960s, and while their trucks have long been modified, it takes a little more work to modify a Dodge pick-up. The A100 was ideal for the modification, however, as it featured an optional 273ci (4.5-litre) V8 small-block for 1965. This rev-happy engine made an ideal candidate for tuning, as this example shows. The added benefit was the motor being mounted well behind the front wheels, which improved weight-distribution even though this truck can still light up the rears at a touch of the throttle. The truck features the original suspension, albeit lowered, and Cragar chromed five-spoke rims with modern radials to improve both traction and handling. While intended mostly for work use as standard, this updated example has a reworked interior with full Sony sound system and custom-built console, plus leather seats.

Top speed:	115 mph (184 km/h)
0-60 mph (0–96 km/h):	8.4 sec
Engine type:	V8
Displacement:	273 ci (4,473 cc)
Transmission	3-speed manual
Max power:	235 bhp (175 kW) @ 5,200 rpm
Max torque:	280 lb ft (380 Nm) @ 4,000 rpm
Weight:	3,010 lb (1,368 kg)
Economy:	17 mpg (6.01 km/l)

Ford Falcon Ranchero (1965)

Ford introduced the Ranchero as 'America's lowest price pick-up' in 1960, priced at just $1,882. It was based on the Falcon platform and power came from a 144ci (2.6-litre), 90bhp (67kW) engine, though its saloon counterpart was fitted with a V8 and hence the ranchero could swallow one with ease. This made them popular with modifiers, who liked the lightweight, no-frills approach that could get them very quick cars for relatively little money. This example uses a 302ci (4.9-litre) V8 tuned with aftermarket intake, heads and camshaft from Edelbrock, plus a free-flowing dual exhaust. As the Ranchero shares its underpinnings with the Mustang, the owner of this car has used 1969 Mustang front disc s and traction bars. The rims are aftermarket alloys in 8x15 (203x381mm) and 10x15-inch (251x381mm) with BF Goodrich tyres, giving improved handling and better traction.

Top speed:	120 mph (192 km/h)
0–60 mph (0–96 km/h):	7.4 sec
Engine type:	V8
Displacement:	302 ci (4,948 cc)
Transmission:	4-speed manual
Max power:	200 bhp (149 kW) @ 4,400 rpm
Max torque:	285 lb ft (386 Nm) @ 3,200 rpm
Weight:	2,820 lb (1,281 kg)
Economy:	16 mpg (5.66 km/l)

Ford Mustang GT (1965)

A huge reaction garnered Ford impressive Mustang sales in its first year,so the model was developed further with the debut of a performance GT 2+2 in 1965. It had fastback stayling and sporting touches, such as the louvers on the rear pillars. As costs had to be kept down, little was changed on the stock chassis which had subframes and a double wishbone front plus leaf spring rear. A special handling package came with the GT, however, which included heavy-duty springs and shocks plus quicker ratio steering and fade-resistant front disc brakes. Although three gearboxes were available, the one to get most power through was the Borg Warner 'Top Loader' manual, while the engine to order was the 'K-code' which had 10.5:1 compression, four-barrel carb, a solid lifter camshaft and high-flow air filter. Testers were impressed and called it 'a four-passenger Cobra'.

Top speed:	123 mph (197 km/h)
0–60 mph (0–96 km/h):	7.3 sec
Engine type:	V8
Displacement:	289 ci (4,735 cc)
Transmission	4-speed manual
Max power:	271 bhp (202 kW) @ 6,000 rpm
Max torque:	312 lb ft (423 Nm) @ 3,400 rpm
Weight:	3,100 lb (1,409 kg)
Economy:	15 mpg (5.31 km/l)

Mercury Comet Cyclone (1965)

The Comet was seen by most to be granny's grocer-getter, but that changed when the Cyclone GT option came in 1965. The car was essentially an upmarket Ford Falcon, being stretched in the wheelbase but retaining the wishbone front end and leaf spring rear. What made it better was the revised spring and shock rates to improve handling. The engine was Ford's 289ci (4.7-litre) Falcon/Mustang V8, but in the Cyclone fitted with a higher-lift camshaft, 10.5:1 compression pistons, and a four-barrel carb. Through the Top Loader manual the car did 15-second quarters. Externally the styling took cues from Pontiac's best-selling GTO, with square ends, stacked headlights and slim roof pillars. At a cost of $346 more than the Falcon, it was only natural that the Cyclone had a plusher interior, so featured tinted glass, bucket seats, power windows and even seat belts!

Top speed:	124 mph (198 km/h)
0–60 mph (0–96 km/h):	7.4 sec
Engine type:	V8
Displacement:	289 ci (4,735 cc)
Transmission	4-speed manual
Max power:	271 bhp (202 kW) @ 6,000 rpm
Max torque:	312 lb ft (423 Nm) @ 3,400 rpm
Weight:	2,994 lb (1,360 kg)
Economy:	15 mpg (5.31 km/l)

Pontiac Catalina 2+2 (1965)

As the 1960s went on, mid-sized cars became increasingly popular as they were lighter and therefore responded better to modifications. However, the full-sized machines still had their fans, and that's why Pontiac persevered with their Catalina. The 2+2 performance package included uprated suspension comprising stiffer springs and shocks and thicker front anti-roll bar, a Safe-T-Track differential, and an uprated 421ci (6.8-litre) engine available in three states of tune. The first, rated at 338bhp (252kW), had a single four-barrel carb, while the other two had three-two barrel 'Tri-Power' carb manifolds. These gave out 356bhp (265kW) and 376bhp (280kW), the latter higher due to a less restrictive exhaust system. Though most people regard the GTO as Pontiac's ultimate muscle car, the Catalina remains one of the finest and most in demand.

Top speed:	125 mph (200 km/h)
0–60 mph (0–96 km/h):	7.0 sec
Engine type:	V8
Displacement:	421 ci (6,898 cc)
Transmission	4-speed manual
Max power:	376 bhp (280 kW) @ 5,500 rpm
Max torque:	461 lb ft (625 Nm) @ 3,600 rpm
Weight:	3,748 lb (1,703 kg)
Economy:	12 mpg (4.24 km/l)

Chevrolet Chevelle SS396 (1966)

Launched in response to the Pontiac GTO and Oldsmobile 4-4-2, the Chevelle SS396 quickly gained a formidable reputation. GM had agreed to cap its cars to 400ci (6.6 litres) or under, hence the SS396 which featured the Mark IV L78 big-block, a detuned version of the engine available in the 1965 Corvette. The unit had 11:1 compression, a steel crank high-lift long duration camshaft for high-rpm use, plus an aluminium high-rise intake manifold which also responded best at high engine speeds. In order to best put down the power, the rear axle was located on four bars and used coil springs and telescopic dampers, while the front had wishbones and an anti-roll bar. While steel wheels were the standard with bias-ply tyres, Torque-Thrust D rims from American Racing were dealer options. This has them with modern radial tyres for optimum handling, without sacrificing looks.

Top speed:	130 mph (208 km/h)
0–60 mph (0–96 km/h):	6.0 sec
Engine type:	V8
Displacement:	396 ci (6,489 cc)
Transmission:	4-speed manual
Max power:	375 bhp (280 kW) @ 5,600 rpm
Max torque:	415 lb ft (562 Nm) @ 3,600 rpm
Weight:	3,700 lb (1,681 kg)
Economy:	13 mpg (4.60 km/l)

Chevrolet II SS (1966)

With plain styling, the Chevy II was more often regarded as a leisurely old people's car. That all changed when Chevrolet installed their L79 Corvette 350ci (5.7-litre) V8 into the 1966 SS model. Having a lightweight body, the SS could easily mix it up with the best muscle cars, though looked more sedate than any, with just the badges giving it away. Underneath it relied on drum brakes, which could get frightening, given the performance which was on tap, and wheel hop was a problem under acceleration because of the simple leaf spring rear end. The transmission to have was the close-ratio four-speed manual which could get it easily into the 14-second range on the quarter mile, though the auto wasn't far behind. There was a base L-30 275bhp (205kW) engine too, which had double the production run of the L-29, though the latter is more collectable.

Top speed:	123 mph (196 km/h)
0–60 mph (0–96 km/h):	6.5 sec
Engine type:	V8
Displacement:	327 ci (5,358 cc)
Transmission	4-speed manual
Max power:	350 bhp (262 kW) @ 5,800 rpm
Max torque:	360 lb ft (488 Nm) @ 3,600 rpm
Weight:	3,140 lb (1,427 kg)
Economy:	14 mpg (4.95 km/l)

Chevrolet II SS modified (1966)

Due to its light weight and powerful small-block V8, the Chevy II was popular with modifiers. It remains so today, with a healthy aftermarket of parts suppliers. As the SS cars were built so well and with performance in mind as standard, the modifications don't need to be drastic in order to make the cars quicker as street- and strip racers. This one simply features the stock suspension which has been fitted with lowering springs and uprated shocks, though it retains the stock anti-roll bar up front. Most of the work has been done in the drive train, with the original motor having much race tuning. It now has reworked heads, a high-rpm camshaft, new intake, and a huge 105cfm carburettor, plus fenderwell full-length headers to optimize mid- and top end power. The car is easily capable of 12-second quarters, thanks to the Hoosier semi-slick street tyres on the rear.

Top speed:	129 mph (206 km/h)
0–60 mph (0–96 km/h):	5.7 sec
Engine type:	V8
Displacement:	327 ci (5,358 cc)
Transmission	3-speed auto
Max power:	393 bhp (293 kW) @ 6,000 rpm
Max torque:	366 lb ft (496 Nm) @ 3,600 rpm
Weight:	2,899 lb (1,317 kg)
Economy:	12 mpg (4.24 km/l)

Chevrolet Corvair (1966)

While being cutting edge, the first Corvair had a nasty trait which gained it a bad reputation. Its swing-axle suspension at the rear made it revolutionary, but with the rear-mounted engine over the top of it, the outside wheel would fold under the car in corners, and in some instances, the car rolled. The car had received full independent suspension in '65 and from then on the problem was solved, making following cars fine-handlers. The engine was good too, being an all-aluminium air-cooled flat six which, in turbocharged form as in the Corsa model shown, could produce exceptional performance for a compact car. The multi-dial interior and high-back seats also made the Corsa a sporty model, and Chevrolet thought they had a winner, but the damage had been done with earlier models, and production was ended in 1969, having seen 1,659,012 models produced in 10 years.

Top speed:	115 mph (184 km/h)
0–60 mph (0–96 km/h):	10.8 sec
Engine type:	Flat six
Displacement:	164 ci (2,687 cc)
Transmission	4-speed manual
Max power:	180 bhp (134 kW) @ 4,000 rpm
Max torque:	232 lb ft (314 Nm) @ 3,200 rpm
Weight:	2,720 lb (1,236 kg)
Economy:	28 mpg (9.91 km/l)

Chevy Corvette Sting Ray ('63–'67)

The Corvette has been called 'America's favourite sportscar' and for good reason: it works as a road car, a fast GT tourer, a streets/strip racer and a circuit car. The Sting Ray which came along in 1963 made the car formidable around the world, taking on the likes of Jaguar and Ferrari and, in many cases, being successful. It was developed from a one-off race car originally built by Bill Mitchell and styled by Larry Shinoda, and by 1966 the car had developed into a formidable machine. The chassis was a steel ladder frame design with independent suspension front and rear, and the car had vented disc brakes all around. The engine was set well back in the frame to give near-perfect 50:50 weight distribution, making it handle well. The 427ci (6.9-litre) big-block was the biggest engine offered in the Corvette, the L88 version the most powerful at 435bhp (324kW).

Top speed:	135 mph (216 km/h)
0–60 mph (0–96 km/h):	5.6 sec
Engine type:	V8
Displacement:	427 ci (6,997 cc)
Transmission:	4-speed manual
Max power:	435 bhp (324 kW) @ 6,200 rpm
Max torque:	460 lb ft (623 Nm) @ 4,000 rpm
Weight:	3,150 lb (1,431 kg)
Economy:	10.8 mpg (3.82 km/l)

Chevrolet Suburban (1966)

Launched in 1935, the Suburban is one of Chevy's best-loved name tags, and is still in production today. It has always been based on a truck chassis, but as the owner of this vehicle wanted something different, he decided to use the front and rear axles off a 1980 GMC Jimmy, for four-wheel drive. Up front a powerful small-block Chevy provides all the power needed for either off-roading or towing, though it's something of a road performer too, with a sub-11 second time to 60mph (96km/h). To adjust the height, a set of Airlift shocks are used at each corner, but the biggest changes are inside, with a full custom interior, supportive buckets eats, digital gauges mounted inside the original housings, plus air-conditioning and a powerful sound system. It all adds up to a vehicle which can accomplish virtually everything a late-model Suburban can, but in the style of a classic body.

Top speed:	114 mph (182 km/h)
0–60 mph (0–96 km/h):	10.4 sec
Engine type:	V8
Displacement:	350 ci (5,735 cc)
Transmission	4-speed auto
Max power:	300 bhp (224 kW) @ 4,800 rpm
Max torque:	380 lb ft (515 Nm) @ 3,200 rpm
Weight:	3,850 lb (1,750 kg)
Economy:	14 mpg (4.95 km/l)

Dodge Charger (1966)

Creating a sensation when it arrived in 1966, the first-generation Charger used fastback styling, which was quickly becoming popular. It also had engine options from 318ci (5.2-litre) right up to the legendary 426 Hemi, making it suitable for many pockets. The car was based on the new-for-1965 intermediate B-body chassis which it shared with the Coronet, and as such used Chrysler's ever-present torsion bar front end with a conventional leaf spring rear. Hemi-powered Chargers such as the model shown got stiffer front torsion bars and an anti-roll bar in an effort to handle the extra weight up front. The Hemi came at an extra cost of $900, but it combined incredible power with reasonable driveability. Power was put down through either a 3-speed Torqueflite automatic or 4-speed manual. This Charger was the car that thrust Dodge into the spotlight for the rest of that decade.

Top speed:	134 mph (214 km/h)
0–60 mph (0–96 km/h):	5.3 sec
Engine type:	V8
Displacement:	426 ci (6,980 cc)
Transmission:	4-speed manual
Max power:	425 bhp (317 kW) @ 5,000 rpm
Max torque:	490 lb ft (664 Nm) @ 4,000 rpm
Weight:	3,990 lb (1,813 kg)
Economy:	9 mpg (3.18 km/l)

Dodge Charger modified (1966)

The 1966 Charger was successful, but rarely did it get modified. For one thing, its production of just 37,344 models has made it far less easy to track one down, compared to the later restyled 1968 model. However, early versions like this can get more attention when given the right treatment. This one's torsion bar front suspension has been lowered one spline, and the rear springs have been reshaped for a 2- and 1.5-inch (50- and 38-mm) drop respectively. The stock engine has long gone, and now in its place sits a 1978 Dodge Ram truck 360ci (5.9-litre), which has been upgraded with Mopar parts (Plymouth, Dodge and Chrysler's performance arm), including a high-lift camshaft, four-barrel carburettor and an Edelbrock. The wheels used are 17-inch (432mm) Center Line billets, with 215/45s and 255/45 BF Goodrich Comp ZR radials to maximize the handling ability.

Top speed:	135 mph (216 km/h)
0–60 mph (0–96 km/h):	8.0 sec
Engine type:	V8
Displacement:	360 ci (5,899 cc)
Transmission	3-speed auto
Max power:	365 bhp (272 kW) @ 4,700 rpm
Max torque:	400 lb ft (542 Nm) @ 2,800 rpm
Weight:	3,900 lb (1,772 kg)
Economy:	14 mpg (4.95 km/l)

Ford Galaxie 500 7-litre (1966)

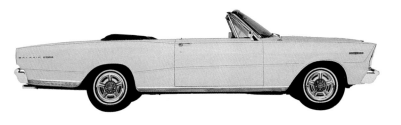

Like many muscle cars, the 1966 Galaxie 500 used the simple formula of a massive engine up front driving the rear wheels. It had stacked headlamps, all new suspension, and the emphasis was more on comfort, despite obviously being a muscle machine. The A-arm suspension was very good and went on to be used in NASCAR competition, while at the rear, coil springs and control arms replaced the former leaf spring set-up. It all added up to a refined ride but the big-block up front could soon change that. Up to 1965 the biggest engine in the Galaxie had been the 427ci (6.9-litre), but the 428ci (7-litre), also part of the FE range of big-block Fords, was built mainly to produce torque. It was a more streetable engine than the 427 engine, but still had plenty of power and incredible torque at low rpm. Inside, being a top-of-the-range car, the 500 featured leather seats and wood trim.

Top speed:	105 mph (168 km/h)
0–60 mph (0–96 km/h):	8.2 sec
Engine type:	V8
Displacement:	428 ci (7,013 cc)
Transmission:	3-speed auto
Max power:	345 bhp (257 kW) @ 4,600 rpm
Max torque:	462 lb ft (626 Nm) @ 2,800 rpm
Weight:	4,059 lb (1,845 kg)
Economy:	9 mpg (3.18 km/l)

Ford Mustang (1966)

Such huge popularity has produced an equally massive aftermarket for the Mustang, so owners can pick from a large range of components to produce very individual cars when they choose to modify them. The owner of this coupe example has left nothing untouched, although the looks tell you exactly what the car is. What's obvious from the outside is the 17-inch (432mm) diameter wheels and billet grilles front and rear, the latter of which houses 900 LEDs for the tail lights. Inside the car has leather and billet aluminium which is matched in the trunk too, where the battery and stereo equipment is mounted. The suspension has been upgraded to Mustang II on the front and to a 9-inch (229mm) Ford rear axle on stiffened leaf springs out back. The motor is a late-model Mustang 32 Modular V8, with Kenne Bell supercharger and multipoint fuel injection.

Top speed:	141 mph (226 km/h)
0–60 mph (0–96 km/h):	4.3 sec
Engine type:	V8
Displacement:	281 ci (4,604 cc)
Transmission	3-speed auto
Max power:	392 bhp (292 kW) @ 5,800 rpm
Max torque:	405 lb ft (549 Nm) @ 4,500 rpm
Weight:	3,358 lb (1,526 kg)
Economy:	12 mpg (4.24 km/l)

Oldsmobile 4-4-2 W-30 (1966)

Most people associate the 4-4-2 package with the later model Oldsmobiles, but it actually started life in 1964 as an option on the F-85 intermediate model. In the following year, GM limited its engines to 400ci (6.55 litres) in intermediate-sized cars, and as such, the 425 Olds engine had to be destroked to 400ci, and this motor became part of the 4-4-2 package. The F-85 for 1966 was restyled and the 4-4-2 was again available as an option. This car came about in an increased effort to promote the company's presence on the drag strip. For $279 the W-30 package gave the engine a high-lift camshaft, bigger valves and a pair of hoses that gave fresh air to the triple two-barrel Rochester carburettors. Most W-30 models in 1966 were the stripped-out two-door pillared coupes, and as 4-4-2s, featured stiffer rate springs and shocks, plus front and rear anti-roll bars.

Top speed:	130 mph (208 km/h)
0–60 mph (0–96 km/h):	6.0 sec
Engine type:	V8
Displacement:	400 ci (6,554 cc)
Transmission	4-speed manual
Max power:	360 bhp (268 kW) @ 5,000 rpm
Max torque:	440 lb ft (596 Nm) @ 3,600 rpm
Weight:	3,197 lb (1,453 kg)
Economy:	10 mpg (3.54 km/l)

Oldsmobile Tornado (1966)

Normally conservative in its car production, Oldsmobile shocked everyone with the launch of the radical Tornado in 1966. The main reason for the shock was the fact that the car was the first to use front-wheel drive in nearly 30 years, since the 1930s Cord. But the layout set the tone for GM cars for the next two decades. The engine was mounted conventionally and even had the torque converter on the rear, but from there a 2-inch (50mm) Morse chain sent drive to the transmission which went forward to the front differential. At the rear in place of the live axle was a single beam, supported on leaf springs but with four shocks, two mounted conventionally and two sitting horizontally. The layout produced an excellent handling vehicle. Top engine option was the W-34 package which gave out 400bhp (298kW), thanks to a high-lift cam and twin free-flowing exhausts.

Top speed:	124 mph (198 km/h)
0–60 mph (0–96 km/h):	9.9 sec
Engine type:	V8
Displacement:	425 ci (6,964 cc)
Transmission	3-speed auto
Max power:	385 bhp (287 kW) @ 4,800 rpm
Max torque:	475 lb ft (644 Nm) @ 3,200 rpm
Weight:	4,655 lb (2,115 kg)
Economy:	12 mpg (4.25 km/l)

Pontiac GTO (1966)

Borrowing a Ferrari name, Pontiac created the GTO (Grand Turismo Omologato) and by 1966 it had more power than anything Italian. The 389ci (6.4-litre) engine gave enough torque to overpower the rear tyres with a mere touch of the throttle, even when fitted with the optional Safe-T-Track limited-slip differential. For 1966 the GTO, having been available since 1964 as a high-performance option, had a new larger and more curvy 'Coke bottle' body style, which improved looks while retaining an aggressive stance. The 389ci (6.4-litre) was standard issue on all GTOs from 1964 to 1967, and to start with the package even had an optional Tri-Power set-up, though multi-carbs were outlawed by GM in mid–1966. Performance parts like the 4.33:1 optional gears and a four-speed Muncie transmission were the things to have, and this model has them all, plus the style of a convertible.

Top speed:	125 mph (200 km/h)
0–60 mph (0–96 km/h):	6.2 sec
Engine type:	V8
Displacement:	389 ci (6,374 cc)
Transmission	4-speed manual
Max power:	360 bhp (268 kW) @ 5,200 rpm
Max torque:	424 lb ft (575 Nm) @ 3,600 rpm
Weight:	3,555 lb (1,615 kg)
Economy:	14 mpg (4.96 km/l)

Shelby Mustang GT350 (1966)

Carroll Shelby turned his tuning skills to the Mustang in 1965. Using the 271bhp (202kW) Mustang as a base, he created the GT350. It had to beat the Corvette in all areas, and so Shelby relocated the front suspension control arms, fitted stiffer springs and Koni shocks for the handling, then put traction control arms at the rear. For better braking he fitted Kelsey-Hayes front discs, and cooled the rear drums with air ducts on the car's side. The 289ci (4.7-litre) V8 engine went through alterations to improve the power, with higher compression, a high-lift camshaft, larger valves in the heads and a bigger carburettor. The higher-spec'd Shelby R was even more powerful, but only 37 were built for racing, though they did win Sports Car Club of America's B-production class against Corvettes, Cobras, Ferraris, Cobras, Lotuses and Jaguar E-Types.

Top speed:	135 mph (216 km/h)
0–60 mph (0–96 km/h):	5.7 sec
Engine type:	V8
Displacement:	289 ci (4,735 cc)
Transmission	4-speed manual
Max power:	350 bhp (261 kW) @ 6,750 rpm
Max torque:	312 lb ft (423 Nm) @ 3,800 rpm
Weight:	2,600 lb (1,181 kg)
Economy:	13.8 mpg (4.89 km/l)

Corvette Sting Ray 427 (1967)

Hitting the market at just over $5,000, the '67 Corvette Sting Ray was a performance sensation. While in 1965 the car had been available with the 396ci big-block Chevy, the 427 ci (6,997 cc) took power and torque up and made the Sting Ray a serious rival to the Shelby Cobra 427 which used Ford's big–block, though the 'Vette was less expensive. Production was just shy of 23,000 for the '67 model year, which could be an indication of buyers taking the handsome split-window shape while they could get it, because the following year the car restyled to mixed reviews. The chassis still featured Zora Arkus Duntov's excellent independent rear suspension, but in order to cope with the extra weight and power, the 427 also received stiffer suspension, a heavy-duty clutch, larger radiator and fan, and dealers recommended everyone take the four-wheel brake discs option for the obvious reason.

Top speed:	141 mph (226 km/h)
0–60 mph (0–96 km/h):	5.5 sec
Engine type:	V8
Displacement:	427 ci (6,997 cc)
Transmission:	4-speed manual
Max power:	435 bhp (324kW) @ 5,800 rpm
Max torque:	460 lb ft (624 Nm) @ 4,000 rpm
Weight:	3,000 lb (1,363 kg)
Economy:	12 mpg (4.25 km/l)

Ford Fairlane 427 (1967)

Amidst the fierce muscle-car wars, Ford debuted the Fairlane 427. To fit the big-block engine, they widened the shock towers and added larger front coil springs to cope. Output was a 'mere' 410bhp (306kW) with single carburettor, but on the Fairlane most were ordered with twin carbs and, therefore, 425bhp (317kW). The body and chassis were monocoque in design and the car could be ordered with a handling package which consisted of longer leaf springs on the live rear axle, front disc brakes and larger 15-inch (381mm) wheels fitted with blackwall tyres. Only one transmission, Borg-Warner's 'Top Loader' T10, could handle the engine's torque, so every Fairlane 427 got it. Because the Fairlane was a thinly disguised race car, it meant potential purchasers were carefully screened by dealers to make sure that only racers who could handle the car's power would get to own one.

Top speed:	121 mph (194 km/h)
0–60 mph (0–96 km/h):	6.0 sec
Engine type:	V8
Displacement:	427 ci (6,997 cc)
Transmission	4-speed manual
Max power:	425 bhp (317 kW) @ 6,000 rpm
Max torque:	480 lb ft (650 Nm) @ 3,700 rpm
Weight:	4,100 lb (1,863 kg)
Economy:	16 mpg (5.66 km/l)

Ford GT40 (1967)

Ford wanted to buy Ferrari in 1963, and when they failed, they directed their might towards the race track. In conjunction with Lola, they turned the Lola GT into a prototype Ford GT, then in 1964 came out with the GT40, so called because it stood just 40 inches (1016mm) tall. The cars weren't successful and failed to finish in any races. But with huge resources, the GT40 programme continued with Carroll Shelby at the helm, and in 1965 production of the road-going car started for homologation, and a GT40 won its first race. In 1966 three GT40s fitted with 427ci (6.9-litre) big-block engines took Le Mans with a 1-2-3 win, beating Ferrari, to the delight of Ford bosses. After this, the cars used the smaller 289ci (4.7-litre) V8s, and a sheet steel semi-monocoque with separate subframes for the rear engine and gearbox. Deep sills (for fuel cells) meant the whole chassis was extremely stiff.

Top speed:	165 mph (264 km/h)
0–60 mph (0–96 km/h):	5.5 sec
Engine type:	V8
Displacement:	289 ci (4,735 cc)
Transmission:	4-speed manual
Max power:	306 bhp (228 kW) @ 6,000 rpm
Max torque:	328 lb ft (445 Nm) @ 4,200 rpm
Weight:	2,200 lb (1,000 kg)
Economy:	14.7 mpg (5.20 km/l)

Plymouth Barracuda (1967)

Chrysler's pony car was launched two weeks before Ford's Mustang in 1965, and was as good a car to drive, had as many options, but to many eyes didn't quite have the looks. The base engine was the 145bhp (108kW) slant-six 225ci (3,687cc), while the base V8 was a 273ci (4,473cc). The only other choice was the 383ci (6,276cc) which, while nowhere near the Hemi in power, still pumped out a very strong 400lb ft (542Nm) torque. In the sub-3,000lb (1,361kg) Barracuda this gave performance aplenty. It started out on Chrysler's Valiant platform to keep costs down, which meant a torsion bar front and live rear axle on leaf springs. Optional were the Sure Grip limited-slip differential, racing stripes and bucket seats. The following year options got even better with the Formula S package, which added a 4-speed manual transmission, anti-roll bars, dual exhaust and wider tyres.

Top speed:	120 mph (192 km/h)
0–60 mph (0–96 km/h):	7.0 sec
Engine type:	V8
Displacement:	383 ci (6,276 cc)
Transmission	4-speed manual
Max power:	280 bhp (209 kW) @ 4,200 rpm
Max torque:	400 lb ft (542 Nm) @ 2,400 rpm
Weight:	2,940 lb (1,336 kg)
Economy:	12 mpg (4.25 km/l)

Plymouth GTX 426 Hemi (1967)

Plymouth brought out the big gun in 1967 to compete with Pontiac's GTO. The Hemi-powered GTX was more a luxury vehicle with huge engine than a racer, with the Hemi engine being de-tuned with a new cam and lower compression (10.25:1) to improve it at low rpm. Chrysler's torsion bar front end provided a smooth ride and was assisted by tubular shocks and an anti-roll bar. The brakes came stock as heavy-duty drums, though 11-inch (279mm) front disc upgrades were sensible. The Torqueflite three-speed auto had its shift points altered to better suit the Hemi's power, but if you wanted manual there was a four-speed. Inside, the seats were very comfortable and the dash hinted of what could be achieved with its 150mph (241km/h) speedometer. The GTX was all about speed, because it could easily do the standing quarter-mile in 13 seconds (12 seconds with racing slicks).

Top speed:	127 mph (203 km/h)
0–60 mph (0–96 km/h):	4.8 sec
Engine type:	V8
Displacement:	426 ci (6,980 cc)
Transmission:	4-speed manual
Max power:	425 bhp (317 kW) @ 5,000 rpm
Max torque:	490 lb ft (664 Nm) @ 4,000 rpm
Weight:	3,535 lb (1,606 kg)
Economy:	12 mpg (4.25 km/l)

Pontiac Firebird H.O. (1968)

Pontiac's Firebird was somewhat overshadowed by the Camaro from which it was derived. The car arrived in 1967 and offered an attractive shape with the classic muscle layout of a front engine driving the rear wheels. Base models came with manual steering and brakes, but many buyers opted for power versions of both, which transformed the car. Inside were buckets seats and deep-set gauges. The H.O. 350ci (5.7-litre) wasn't the most powerful engine, but it did have a long duration camshaft, 10.25:1 compression and big valves to achieve its impressive power. While it was barely slower than the bigger-engined car, it was much cheaper, so was a good seller. The four-speed manual was the gearbox to have, while at the rear the 10-bolt, leaf-sprung axle could be ordered with the Safe-T-Track limited-slip differential and a variety of gear ratios.

Top speed:	114 mph (182 km/h)
0–60 mph (0–96 km/h):	6.9 sec
Engine type:	V8
Displacement:	350 ci (5,735 cc)
Transmission	4-speed manual
Max power:	320 bhp (239 kW) @ 5,000 rpm
Max torque:	380 lb ft (515 Nm) @ 3,400 rpm
Weight:	3,740 lb (1,700 kg)
Economy:	12 mpg (4.25 km/l)

Pontiac Grand Prix (1967)

The Grand Prix was Pontiac's top-of-the-line car, and was a sales sensation for the company. While they already had a strong muscle image from the GTO, they built the big Grand Prix more for luxury, but it accelerated like a muscle car, thanks to the tuned 400ci (6,554cc) motor under the hood. The luxury was emphasized further with the ride quality, which was possible through coil springs at each corner and a separate chassis. The drum brakes were self-adjusting, but there was also an option of discs up front to stop the 400lb (181kg) leviathan. Externally the car was smoothly styled with a 'Coke bottle' rear which set the fashion that lasted into the 1970s, plus concealed headlights in the trademark Pontiac split grille. Inside there was the choice of three-speed auto or four-speed fully synchronized manual transmission and a luxury leather bench seat, plus wood dash trim.

Top speed:	110 mph (176 km/h)
0–60 mph (0–96 km/h):	9.4 sec
Engine type:	V8
Displacement:	400 ci (6,554 cc)
Transmission:	3-speed auto
Max power:	350 bhp (261 kW) @ 5,000 rpm
Max torque:	440 lb ft (596 Nm) @ 3,200 rpm
Weight:	4,005 lb (1,820 kg)
Economy:	15 mpg (5.34 km/l)

Shelby Mustang GT500 (1967)

The Shelby GT500 joined its GT350 brethren in 1967 and was a sales success, outselling the smaller-engined car two to one. The car was based on the Mach 1 Mustang visually but differed with a new grille, tail lights, Shelby stripes and a pair of square tailpipes. Like the Mach 1, the Shelby used the same 428 Cobra jet big-block V8 engine, but the biggest difference was on the vastly superior handling. Heavy-duty springs and shocks, wider tyres, thicker anti-roll bars and an in-built roll cage to stiffen the shell meant the Shelby was well balanced. The handling was its biggest attraction alongside exclusivity, for which you had to pay dearly at three times the cost of Ford's regular Mach 1. Although Ford rated the Cobra Jet motor at 335bhp (250kW) to reassure insurance companies who were charging $1,000 for guys to drive it, the output was closer to 400bhp (298kW).

Top speed:	132 mph (211 km/h)
0–60 mph (0–96 km/h):	7.0 sec
Engine type:	V8
Displacement:	428 ci (7,013 cc)
Transmission	4-speed manual
Max power:	355 bhp (265 kW) @ 5,400 rpm
Max torque:	420 lb ft (569 Nm) @ 3,200 rpm
Weight:	3,520 lb (1,600 kg)
Economy:	8.4 mpg (2.97 km/l)

Chevrolet Camaro RS/SS (1968)

The SS badge donated a performance package on the Camaro, while the RS was a luxury package. Together, they made a formidable machine, and in 396ci (6.4-litre) form, as in this example, it was about as good as the Camaro could get. The 1968 model had changed little in the looks from the first version, but had styling differences such as the loss of the window vents in favour of GM's new Astro ventilation system, plus hidden headlights in the front grille. Mechanically it had staggered shocks and multi-leaf rear springs to control wheel hop. Ordering the SS option gave your car heavy-duty suspension, a 285bhp (213kW) 350ci (5.7-litre) V8, a nose striped and hood emblems. The 396ci (6.4-litre) big-block V8 was a separate option. Also a good idea were the 7x14 inch (178x356mm) rims which aided traction. The 325bhp (242kW) output was just one of three options with the 396.

Top speed:	130 mph (208 km/h)
0–60 mph (0–96 km/h):	6.6 sec
Engine type:	V8
Displacement:	396 ci (6,489 cc)
Transmission	3-speed auto
Max power:	325 bhp (242 kW) @ 4,800 rpm
Max torque:	410 lb ft (556 Nm) @ 3,200 rpm
Weight:	3,860 lb (1,754 kg)
Economy:	12 mpg (4.25 km/l)

Chevrolet Camaro Pro Street (1968)

While muscle cars were indeed fast for their day and indeed still are, in the fastest accelerating motorsport, they look pretty tame. But as soon as the 1960s cars made it out of the showroom, they were put on to drag strips, then stripped and tuned for speed. During the late 1970s the cars took cues from the Pro Stocks classes, which used a stock bodyshell with huge drag tyres fitted underneath to get traction. It developed further, and in the late 19870s and 1990s, these street cars started turning in times that a Top Fuel dragster would have been proud of two decades earlier. This Camaro is typical of the most recent street-racing machines, with a full tube chassis lightweight front and rear racing suspension, 21-inch (533mm) wide slicks on the rear and a huge horsepower engine barely useable on the street. The Jerico gearbox has a lever per gear to aid rapid full-throttle changes.

Top speed:	175 mph (280 km/h)
0–60 mph (0–96 km/h):	2.6 sec
Engine type:	V8
Displacement:	540 ci (8,848 cc)
Transmission	4-speed clutchless manual
Max power:	735 bhp (548 kW) @ 6,200 rpm
Max torque:	695 lb ft (942 Nm) @ 4,000 rpm
Weight:	3,674 lb (1,670 kg)
Economy:	4 mpg (1.42 km/l)

Chevrolet Camaro Z28 (1968)

General Motors designed the Camaro to compete with Ford's Mustang, but with the likes of the Shelbys around, GM needed more power in their car. Also, in order to race in the Trams Am series, GM had to build 1,000 road models, though at the end of 1968, the new Z28 had gone well past 7,000 sales. The car needed a high-rpm race-type engine with less than 305ci (5-litres) so Chevrolet combined their 4-inch (102mm) bore 327 block with a short-stroke 3-inch (76.2mm) forged crank similar to the one in their 283. With a high compression of 11:1, large valve heads and high-lift cam, it revved well, and though rated at 290bhp (216kW) output was closer to 350bhp (262kW). Handling was improved by quickening the steering, fitting harder brake linings, stiffening the rear leaf springs and uprating the shocks. The car had a three-speed auto, but the Muncie four-speed manual was often fitted.

Top speed:	123 mph (197 km/h)
0–60 mph (0–96 km/h):	6.5 sec
Engine type:	V8
Displacement:	302 ci (4,948 cc)
Transmission:	4-speed manual
Max power:	290 bhp (216 kW) @ 5,800 rpm
Max torque:	290 lb ft (393 Nm) @ 4,200 rpm
Weight:	3,528 lb (1,603 kg)
Economy:	15.7 mpg (5.56 km/l)

Chevrolet Camaro Z28 Racer (1968)

The 1967 Z28 track car had been fairly unsuccessful, so the following year it received changes in the hands of various teams, but none were more famous for their race victory than the Roger Penske organization. Their Sunaco-backed car was fitted stiffer springs, Koni shocks and a rear anti-roll bar which gave the car more neutral handling. The rear had multi-leaf springs, and a Panhard rod was also fitted for maximum location of the 12-bolt live axle. To save weight, the body was acid-dipped and also given extra rigidity with more tubes in the multi-point roll cage. The steering was given a higher ratio for better response and under the nose an air dam was fitted to redirect air and minimize front end lift. The engine's displacement, actually 302.4ci (4,955cc), could be revved through to 7,000rpm, thanks to 11.5:1 compression, tubular headers and a Holley four-barrel carb.

Top speed:	140 mph (224 km/h)
0–60 mph (0–96 km/h):	5.5 sec
Engine type:	V8
Displacement:	302.4 ci (4,955 cc)
Transmission	4-speed manual
Max power:	402 bhp (299 kW) @ 6,800 rpm
Max torque:	340 lb ft (461 Nm) @ 5,500 rpm
Weight:	2,875 lb (1,306 kg)
Economy:	10 mpg (3.54 km/l)

Chevrolet Chevelle Pro Street (1968)

The Chevelle was restyled for 1968, becoming shorter and sportier, yet retaining its muscular status. While it may never have been as popular as the Camaro, it used a similar coupe shape and therefore had the necessary wide haunches suitable for the Pro Street treatment. This meant the biggest tyres out back, and here the owner has fitted Mickey Thompson racing slicks with over 3ft (0.91m) of contact patch across their width. At the front are the complete opposite skinny rims and tyres for minimum weight and thus the best weight transfer on to the rear treads. Horsepower is what it's all about in Pro Street, and this mainly strip-racing car has a massive big-block engine which is aided by the nitrous oxide injection for an extra 500bhp (373kW) on top of the standard 832bhp (620kW). A Lenco clutchless transmission makes gear-shifting as fast, as the five levers can be pulled back.

Top speed:	188 mph (300 km/h)
0–60 mph (0–96 km/h):	2.0 sec
Engine type:	V8
Displacement:	632 ci (10,356 cc)
Transmission	5-speed clutchless manual
Max power:	870 bhp (649 kW) @ 7,000 rpm
Max torque:	720 lb ft (976 Nm) @ 4,400 rpm
Weight:	3,420 lb (1,554 kg)
Economy:	2 mpg (0.71 km/l)

Chevrolet Impala SS427 (1968)

The new-for-1967 Impala 427 was marketed with the slogan 'For the man who'd buy a sports car if it had this much room'. By slotting in the big-block engine from the Corvette, the result was impressive. The engine had been released the year before and from the outset the 'Rat' motor was engineered to produce much power. Staggered valves in the heads created better flow (at the cost of size and weight), while the impressive torque made hauling along the Impala easy. The new car used a wider front track than early 1960s Chevrolets and, because of the fastback coupe shape, the bodyshell was required to be very strong, which aided handling. The SS also had superior rear axle location with four rather than three links, making it one of the best-handling large muscle cars of the era. The SS427 reverted to an option package in 1968, then was retired the following year.

Top speed:	130 mph (208 km/h)
0-60 mph (0–96 km/h):	6.0 sec
Engine type:	V8
Displacement:	400 ci (6,554 cc)
Transmission:	4-speed manual
Max power:	360 bhp (268 kW) @ 5,000 rpm
Max torque:	440 lb ft (596 Nm) @ 3,600 rpm
Weight:	3,197 lb (1,453 kg)
Economy:	10 mpg (3.54 km/l)

Dodge Charger modified (1968)

The Charger was one of the biggest two-door coupes ever built, but its size didn't mean it was slow. Its most popular big-block engine option for 1968 wasn't the Hemi but the 440ci (7.2-litre), which gave plenty of power plus good street manners. Because of the handsome lines and muscular 'Coke bottle' styling, the Chargers of 1968 and 1969 rarely see major modification. Items like the door sculpted 'vents', concealed headlamps and Ferrari-like double tail lamps make it a favourite for muscle-car fans even in stock form, and knowing that they have the full support of Chrysler's Mopar performance division for spares makes all the difference. The amount of money they are worth now also makes it sensible to keep mods to a minimum. The owner of this vehicle has made minor changes to the engine for extra power, and the car runs in the 13s in the trim used on the street.

Top speed:	140 mph (224 km/h)
0–60 mph (0–96 km/h):	7.5 sec
Engine type:	V8
Displacement:	440 ci (7,210 cc)
Transmission:	3-speed auto
Max power:	400 bhp (298 kW) @ 4,800 rpm
Max torque:	4,100 lb ft (556 Nm) @ 3,600 rpm
Weight:	3,574 lb (1,624 kg)
Economy:	10.7 mpg (3.79 km/l)

Dodge Hurst Hemi Dart (1968)

Drag racing of 1960s was used to test products, and it worked extremely well in some cases, especially cars. The 1968 Hurst Hemi Dart was very successful in the NHRA Super Stock class, with Hurst Performance and Chrysler producing 72 cars as stripped-out racers. They had the radio, heater, rear seats, sound-deadening and windows winders removed, had the battery mounted in the trunk, and came in flat grey primer ready for racing paint schemes. The fenders and hood were glass-fibre, while the steel doors and fenders were acid dipped to thin them and thus lose more weight. Bigger rear arches were fitted to cater for the large slick tyres and a Dana axle was fitted with 4.88:1 race gears. With 12.5:1 compression, a forged crank, solid lifter cam and twin Holley carbs, the engine was highly tuned and was eventually rated at a more truthful 500bhp (373kW) by the NHRA.

Top speed:	140 mph (224 km/h)
0–60 mph (0–96 km/h):	3.6 sec
Engine type:	V8
Displacement:	426 ci (6,980 cc)
Transmission	4-speed manual
Max power:	425 bhp (317 kW) @ 6,000 rpm
Max torque:	480 lb ft (650 Nm) @ 4,600 rpm
Weight:	3,000 lb (1,363 kg)
Economy:	6 mpg (2.12 km/l)

Ford Galaxie 500 (1968)

During the 1960s the Galaxie turned from a muscle car into something more subtle and formal, though it remained a good seller for Ford. The car had lost its ground-breaking lines in favour of the fastback style, which was fast becoming the norm later that decade, though Dodge and Plymouth had the edge on shape. This custom version has taken the stock look and colour-coded everything to help bring the shape up to date, also helped by the addition of modern billet alloy rims with low-profile tyres. Three-inch drop spindles have been fitted to lower the front, while the rear does the same through lowering blocks between the leaf springs and live axle. The body has been seam welded to make it torsionally stiffer, and to take advantage of the extra handling available, there's a modified 390ci (6.3-litre) big-block engine with new headers, an Edelbrock intake and a bigger carb.

Top speed:	110 mph (176 km/h)
0-60 mph (0–96 km/h):	7.9 sec
Engine type:	V8
Displacement:	390 ci (6,390 cc)
Transmission:	3-speed auto
Max power:	365 bhp (272 kW) @ 5,800 rpm
Max torque:	370 lb ft (501 Nm) @ 3,400 rpm
Weight:	3,554 lb (1,615 kg)
Economy:	12 mpg (4.25 km/l)

Ford Mustang GT/CS (1968)

The Mustang was extremely popular during its first few years of production, but competition from other manufacturers saw a drop in sales for 1968, so Ford released a number of limited-edition models to rectify the situation. The GT/SC was one, and it stood for Grand Turismo California Special. As a GT, it got heavy-duty springs and shocks, dual exhaust with special double protruding tips (for this year only) and a thicker front anti-roll bar. The CA part of the deal added special side scoops, Shelby-style rear lights, a plain grille and special emblems all over. Under the hood of this special was the mighty 390ci (6.3-litre) big-block, which had huge torque throughout the rev range. It could easily accelerate the car to 14-second quarter-mile times in stock form, but it was most impressive on the street once the Goodyear Polyglas bias-ply tyres had found grip.

Top speed:	120 mph (192 km/h)
0–60 mph (0–96 km/h):	7.5 sec
Engine type:	V8
Displacement:	390 ci (6,390 cc)
Transmission	3-speed auto
Max power:	280 bhp (209 kW) @ 4,400 rpm
Max torque:	403 lb ft (546 Nm) @ 2,600 rpm
Weight:	3,635 lb (1,652 kg)
Economy:	14 mpg (4.96 km/l)

Mercury Cougar GT-E (1968)

To start with, the Cougar was more of a refined cruiser, a sort of upmarket Mustang. But just a year on in 1968 Ford went with the flow of demand and shoehorned in their 427ci (6.9-litre) big-block to create the GT-E. Inside it retained its luxury with overhead map lights, a long centre console and wood grained dash. Underneath it was beefed up with traction bars, heavy-duty suspension, Traction Lock limited-slip differential and 3.91:1 gears. The engine ran at 10.9:1 compression and had the option of two four-barrel carbs to feed its huge thirst. This made the Cougar a fearsome street racer, with 14 seconds possible at the strip once a 'super tune' of adjusting the timing and removing the air filter had been carried out. The GT-E was replaced by the Eliminator in 1969 and 1970, showing how much the public liked what Ford were doing.

Top speed:	128 mph (204 km/h)
0–60 mph (0–96 km/h):	7.0 sec
Engine type:	V8
Displacement:	427 ci (6,997 cc)
Transmission	3-speed auto
Max power:	390 bhp (291 kW) @ 5,600 rpm
Max torque:	460 lb ft (623 Nm) @ 3,200 rpm
Weight:	3,174 lb (1,442 kg)
Economy:	8 mpg (2.83 km/l)

Oldsmobile 4-4-2 modified (1968)

Oldsmobile's 4-4-2 cars demanded respect on the street. They made so much torque even in stock form that they could chirp the tyres in all three gears as they accelerated. But GM's self-imposed limit of 400ci (6.5 litres) on its cars in the 1960s meant that none could use over that amount of cubic inches, at a time when both Ford and Chrysler was going well over that displacement. What the owner of this hot-rodded Oldsmobile has done is get one of the 1970 455ci (7.4-litre) Rocket engines, which came about as restrictions were lifted. It's the biggest and most powerful engine Oldsmobile ever offered, and with a few special mods it makes enough power to push this near 2-ton car to 13-second quarter miles. The rest of the car is pretty much how Oldsmobile intended, with uprated anti-roll bars and stiffer springs for improved handling. Special features include a 1970 Oldsmobile dash.

Top speed:	134 mph (214 km/h)
0–60 mph (0–96 km/h):	6.2 sec
Engine type:	V8
Displacement:	455 ci (7,456 cc)
Transmission	3-speed auto
Max power:	410 bhp (306 kW) @ 5,500 rpm
Max torque:	517 lb ft (701 Nm) @ 3,500 rpm
Weight:	3,890 lb (1,768 kg)
Economy:	9.4 mpg (3.33 km/l)

Plymouth Road Runner (1968)

Chrysler realized in the late 1960s that muscle-car enthusiasts wanted high power and no frills, in a car at reasonable price, so they responded and launched the Road Runner. Warner Bros were paid $50,000 for the use of the cartoon name and logo, and although the forecast was sales of 2,500, the Road Runner was such a success that it sold 44,589. Chrysler torsion bars were uprated or the front and the live axle was on leaf springs with 3.23:1 gears, though higher gearing for better acceleration was available. The engine was the basic cast-iron big-block which had been in production since the 1950s, in this form displacing 383ci (6.3 litres) but putting out tremendous torque. The heads, camshaft, exhaust were all from the bigger 440ci (7.2-litre) motor. Despite its size, the Road Runner in basic form was relatively lightweight and performed very well.

Top speed:	130 mph (208 km/h)
0–60 mph (0–96 km/h):	6.7 sec
Engine type:	V8
Displacement:	383 ci (6,276 cc)
Transmission	4-speed manual
Max power:	335 bhp (249 kW) @ 5,200 rpm
Max torque:	425 lb ft (576 Nm) @ 3,400 rpm
Weight:	3,400 lb (1,545 kg)
Economy:	12 mpg (4.25 km/l)

Pontiac GTO (1968)

The GTO's huge 400ci (6.6-litre) engine provided so much torque that the car could overpower the rear tyres with the slightest blip of the throttle, even with the Safe-T-Track limited-slip differential. For 1968 the GTO, having been out since 1964 as a high-performance option, had a new body style which improved looks while retaining an aggressive look and the trademark Pontiac split grille. It was also slighter shorter in the wheelbase than its predecessor, but kept the separate chassis and body. At the front it used unequal-length A-arms, while the live rear axle used trailing arms and coil springs with separate shocks. Three versions of the engine were available in 1968, the base having 350bhp (261kW), the second featuring a higher lift cam and 360bhp (268kW), and the third the Ram Air II option with improved heads and hood cold-air feed, giving 366bhp (273kW).

Top speed:	120 mph (192 km/h)
0–60 mph (0–96 km/h):	6.4 sec
Engine type:	V8
Displacement:	400 ci (6,554 cc)
Transmission	4-speed manual
Max power:	360 bhp (268 kW) @ 5,400 rpm
Max torque:	445 lb ft (603 Nm) @ 3,800 rpm
Weight:	3,506 lb (1,593 kg)
Economy:	11 mpg (3.89 km/l)

Shelby GT 350 (1968)

While the original Shelby Mustangs of 1965 and 1966 had been fast and furious machines designed for the committed driver, by 1968 they'd been tamed somewhat and were more refined. However, performance was still the key, and in an effort to pep up the GT 350, Shelby offered a Paxton centrifugal supercharger to its 302ci (4,949cc) V8, which gave exceptional power across the rev range. The car used the same double wishbone suspension up front and live axle rear with leaf springs as regular Mustangs, but with stiffer spring and shock rates to improve the handling. The brakes had optional 11.4-inch (290mm) front discs which the supercharged version really cried out for. Externally the car had a restyle with 1965 Thunderbird rear lights, a new grille, and wide Shelby alloys. Just 1,657 cars were made, and in 1968 Ford took over the Shelby operation.

Top speed:	131 mph (210 km/h)
0–60 mph (0–96 km/h):	6.2 sec
Engine type:	V8
Displacement:	302 ci (4,948 cc)
Transmission:	4-speed manual
Max power:	335 bhp (250 kW) @ 5,200 rpm
Max torque:	325 lb ft (440 Nm) @ 3,200 rpm
Weight:	3,340 lb (1,518 kg)
Economy:	14 mpg (4.96 km/l)

Buick GS 400 Stage 1 (1969)

Buick loaded its GS model with luxuries, but also gave it a powerful engine with the Stage 1. The drive was leisurely, and the handling would turn to understeer when pushed, but in a straight line it was incredible. Its 400ci (6.6-litre) 'Nailhead' engine is a bored and stroked version of the 340. The Stage 1 got 11:1 compression ratio, a four-barrel carb, low-restriction exhaust and the Cold Air package twin snorkel hood induction, which was claimed to an 8 percent increase in power. An uprated GM Turbo-Hydramatic three-speed auto was aided by a Positraction limited-slip differential to help put the power down through skinny bias-ply tyres. The fastback coupe was the most body style, though the convertible has remained the most desirable, as just 1,776 were made. In 1970, the GS 400 was replaced by the GS 455 as Oldsmobile continued to uprate their car's performance.

Top speed:	125 mph (200 km/h)
0–60 mph (0–96 km/h):	5.8 sec
Engine type:	V8
Displacement:	400 ci (6,554 cc)
Transmission	3-speed auto
Max power:	345 bhp (257 kW) @ 4,800 rpm
Max torque:	440 lb ft (596 Nm) @ 3,200 rpm
Weight:	3,594 lb (1,633 kg)
Economy:	14 mpg (4.96 km/l)

Buick Riviera (1969)

Rarely are Buicks used as customized cars, as their luxury street-fighter status has often meant they belong to muscle-car enthusiasts. In the right hands, however, they can be made to look good in any style, and this smoothed-out Riviera is a prime example. Externally the body has gone through a 'shave' which means all the superfluous trim and badging has been removed and the resulting holes filled in. To complement the style, concentric ring smooth hubcaps have been fitted, which blend well with the stock front and rear deep fenders. The suspension is all coil spring and even in stock form they're firm, but this owner has taken more coils out of the springs which has stiffened up the ride still further. The interior is an immaculate mix of white leather tuck 'n' roll and the stock dash equipment, plus some custom-fit stereo equipment.

Top speed:	125 mph (200 km/h)
0–60 mph (0–96 km/h):	7.2 sec
Engine type:	V8
Displacement:	430 ci (7,046 cc)
Transmission:	3-speed auto
Max power:	360 bhp (268 kW) @ 5,000 rpm
Max torque:	475 lb ft (644 Nm) @ 3,200 rpm
Weight:	4,199 lb (1,908 kg)
Economy:	7 mpg (2.48 km/l)

Chevrolet Blazer (1969)

Long at the forefront of US 4x4s, the Blazer was one of the first of what is now known as an SUV (Sport Utility Vehicle). It has become an icon and its name is still used by GM. The K5-code vehicle started out in 1969, offered by Chevrolet as a roomy on/off road vehicle with a 120bhp (89kW) base engine or 307ci (5-litre) and 350ci (5.7-litre) V8. It was utilitarian in design, but made a formidable off-roader. Because it was stiffly sprung to cope with any terrain, on the road it tended to bounce around on anything but smooth roads, but it could cruise effortlessly at 70mph (113km/h), so was ideal for US roads. The Blazer's chassis was separate and very strong, and it mounted the engine well back for perfect 50:50 weight distribution. The 350ci (5,735cc) V8 was the most popular engine choice and it was driven through an automatic with two-speed transfer case with high and low ratios.

Top speed:	98 mph (157 km/h)
0–60 mph (0–96 km/h):	15.0 sec
Engine type:	V8
Displacement:	350 ci (5,735 cc)
Transmission	3-speed auto
Max power:	165 bhp (123 kW) @ 3,800 rpm
Max torque:	255 lb ft (345 Nm) @ 2,800 rpm
Weight:	5,157 lb (2,344 kg)
Economy:	8.7 mpg (3.08 km/l)

Chevrolet Camaro Pace Car (1969)

When the first Camaro appeared in 1967 it was rolled out to pace the famous Indianapolis 500, and two years later it was back once again in convertible form to do the same. The limited edition – just 3,675 were made – was available by ticking the Z11 option which, priced at $37, got you the racing stripes and door decals. To make a replica pace car you also had to tick the SS package, which meant a cowl induction hood and rear spoiler, plus order the hidden headlight RS grille. The actual machine which paced the event had a 375bhp (280kW) 396ci (6,489cc) V8, but in the interests of driveability, most of the replicas came with small-block 350ci (5,735cc) V8s, which still thumped out plenty of power. Chevy Rallye wheels at 7 inches (178mm) wide improved handling and a Posi-traction live rear axle ensured maximum grip from a standing start.

Top speed:	124 mph (198 km/h)
0–60 mph (0–96 km/h):	6.8 sec
Engine type:	V8
Displacement:	350 ci (5,735 cc)
Transmission:	3-speed auto
Max power:	300 bhp (224 kW) @ 4,800 rpm
Max torque:	380 lb ft (515 Nm) @ 3,200 rpm
Weight:	3,395 lb (1,543 kg)
Economy:	15 mpg (5.31 km/l)

Chevrolet Camaro Z28 (1969)

For 1969 the Camaro got all-new sheet metal with more aggressive styling. In Z28 form it was designed to compete against the Mustang in the Transmission-Am racing series, and it even stole two championships from Ford's pony car in the late 1960s. What made it most legendary, however, was the road-going versions, which were barely tamed race cars. The chassis got uprated springs and shocks, while the rear live axle also had staggered positioning on the shocks to help control wheel hop, which earlier Z28s had suffered from badly. Four-wheel disc brakes were an option too and were straight from the Corvette. From the same car were the Rallye steel rims with 6 inches (152mm) of width to improve handling. The engine was a short stroke 302ci (4.9-litre) so could rev very well, though it was best over 3,000rpm for manners. This car has the rare dual carb option for more power.

Top speed:	132 mph (211 km/h)
0–60 mph (0–96 km/h):	6.9 sec
Engine type:	V8
Displacement:	302 ci (4,948 cc)
Transmission	4-speed manual
Max power:	290 bhp (216 kW) @ 5,800 rpm
Max torque:	310 lb ft @ 4,200 rpm (420 Nm)
Weight:	3,050 lb (1,386 kg)
Economy:	13 mpg (4.60 km/l)

Chevrolet Camaro ZL1 (1969)

This was Chevy's most uncompromised machines and the most powerful Camaro too. It was also very exclusive with a production numbering just 69. In the 1960s Chevrolet supported the Automotive Manufacturers Association's ban by using any engine over 400ci (6.9 litres) only in Corvettes or large sedans. That was until one of their employees, Vince Piggins, found a loophole in the ban and conceived the ZL1. The car started as an SS396 model, with F41 uprated suspension, front discs, a cowl induction hood and unique engine unlike anything Chevrolet had. It was an all-aluminium 427ci (7.2-litre) V8 which weighed the same as a small-block, hence the ZL1's handling remained sharp. However, the awesome power meant the car could run 11-second quarter-miles with racing tyres. Serious muscle-car collectors will pay up to $250,000 for a ZL1.

Top speed:	125 mph (200 km/h)
0–60 mph (0–96 km/h):	5.3 sec
Engine type:	V8
Displacement:	427 ci (6,997 cc)
Transmission	4-speed manual
Max power:	430 bhp (321 kW) @ 5,200 rpm
Max torque:	450 lb ft (610 Nm) @ 4,400 rpm
Weight:	3,300 lb (1,500 kg)
Economy:	7 mpg (2.48 km/l)

Chevrolet Corvette Stingray (1969)

The Corvette underwent a controversial restyle in 1968, and while the press reviews were mixed, the public voted with their wallets and bought 28,566 in one year. Over 15,000 of those were built with the big-block 427ci (6.9-litre) engine which shows just how performance-hungry buyers were. Even the lowest-powered 427, code L36, made 390bhp (291kW), then came the L68 with 400bhp (298kW), the L71 with 435bhp (324kW), and the over-the-top engine was the L88 with an underrated figure of 430bhp (321kW) though output was closer to 500bhp (373kW). Underneath the car was virtually the same as previous models, with an independent front and rear and disc brakes all around. This car has the mandatory four-speed Muncie 22 close-ratio gearbox which is required to take the torque and spread the power well, and with the right driver, the car could do low-13-second quarter miles.

Top speed:	135 mph (216 km/h)
0–60 mph (0–96 km/h):	5.5 sec
Engine type:	V8
Displacement:	427ci (6,997 cc)
Transmission	4-speed manual
Max power:	435 bhp (324kW) @ 5,600 rpm
Max torque:	460 lb ft (623 Nm) @ 4,000 rpm
Weight:	3,145 lb (1,429 kg)
Economy:	10 mpg (3.54 km/l)

Chevrolet Yenko Chevelle (1969)

Don Yenko tuned Camaros, but during 1969 also turned his hand to the Chevelle, the result being an incredible performer on the street. He replaced the 375bhp (280kW) 390ci (6.6-litre) big-block engine with a 427ci (7.2-litre) Rat motor. To cope with the new-found performance, the car was fitted with disc brakes as standard, plus a Muncie four-speed close-ratio manual, or GM TH400 if buyers preferred an auto. At the rear end the car came with a strengthened GM 12-bolt live axle with 4.10:1 gearing as standard for the best possible acceleration. The Chevelle was kitted out with uprated suspension on the coil spring rear and independent wishbone front. Externally the cars were identified with 'Yenko SC' (Super Car) logos and black stripes, but they were rare on the street, as just 99 were built in 1969, being replaced by the Yenko Chevelle SS454 in 1970.

Top speed:	110 mph (176 km/h)
0-60 mph (0–96 km/h):	5.7 sec
Engine type:	V8
Displacement:	427 ci (6,997 cc)
Transmission	3-speed auto
Max power:	450 bhp (336 kW) @ 5,000 rpm
Max torque:	460 lb ft (623 Nm) @ 4,000 rpm
Weight:	3,800 lb (1,727 kg)
Economy:	8 mpg (2.83 km/l)

Dodge Charger 500 (1969)

Ford were having it all their own way on the super speedways of NASCAR in the late 1960s, so Chrysler fought back with the launch of their Charger 500. Most notable about the bodywork was the flush grille where previously there had been sunken headlamps. Dodge found the flush look helped significantly with aerodynamics so the rear window was also mounted as such. Underneath, the 500 had a unitary body/chassis with torsion bar front end and anti-roll bar, while the rear was conventional leaf springs. Disc brakes came as standard at 11 inches (280mm) diameter and were needed with the big-block powerplants. The two options were the 375bhp (280kW) 440ci (7.2-litre) Magnum engine or the Hemi which was rated at 425bhp (317kW), even though it was closer to 500bhp (373kW) in reality. The 500s won 15 races in 1969, but alas, Ford's victories numbered 30.

Top speed:	138 mph (220 km/h)
0-60 mph (0–96 km/h):	6.1 sec
Engine type:	V8
Displacement:	426 ci (6,980 cc)
Transmission:	4-speed manual
Max power:	425 bhp (317 kW) @ 5,000 rpm
Max torque:	490 lb ft (664 Nm) @ 4,000 rpm
Weight:	4,100 lb (1,863 kg)
Economy:	8 mpg (2.83 km/l)

Dodge Charger Daytona (1969)

To qualify for NASCAR racing, Dodge had to build a certain number of Charger Daytonas for the street. They looked extremely radical for the time; in fact, they were too radical for most and many even had their wings and spoilers removed to be sold as regular Chargers, just to get them off the showroom floor. The Chargers were some 200lb (91kg) lighter than their Plymouth Superbird cousins, hence were fastest away from a standing start. Their aerodynamic aids didn't really come into effect until over 100mph (169km/h), which made them more visual aids than helpful in the real sense, but the visual part is something which sells the car well on the second-hand market today. The engines it used were either the 440ci (7.2-litre) Magnum or Street Hemi, a detuned version of the race engine with hydraulic lifters to quieten it down and, ultimately, limit its rpm potential.

Top speed:	135 mph (216 km/h)
0–60 mph (0–96 km/h):	5.0 sec
Engine type:	V8
Displacement:	426 ci (6,997 cc)
Transmission	4-speed manual
Max power:	425 bhp (317 kW) @ 5,600 rpm
Max torque:	490 lb ft (664 Nm) @ 4,000 rpm
Weight:	3,671 lb (1,668 kg)
Economy:	11 mpg (3.89 km/l)

Dodge Charger Daytona (1969)

Appearing in 1969, the Charger Daytonas impressed the NASCAR ranks with lap speeds of nearly 200mph (322km/h). A Daytona took the chequered flag at the debut race that year and during the season, Daytonas won another 21 victories. The following season they were joined by their similar-looking cousins, the Plymouth Superbirds, but 1971 was to be both their last year, as a ruling on their rear spoiler meant a drastic reduction in engine size, so they could no longer compete. The NASCARS from this era were still relatively stock, hence the Daytona used torsion bar front and leaf spring rear suspension, all uprated. The doors were welded shut to increase body stiffness and parts were riveted in place to withstand the speeds, plus inside a full roll cage was added. The Hemi engines under the hood had raised compression to 13.3:1 and used single plane racing manifolds with single carb.

Top speed:	200 mph (320 km/h)
0–60 mph (0–96 km/h):	4.3 sec
Engine type:	V8
Displacement:	426 ci (6,997 cc)
Transmission	4-speed manual
Max power:	556 bhp (415 kW) @ 6,000 rpm
Max torque:	497 lb ft (674 Nm) @ 5,400 rpm
Weight:	3,100 lb (1,409 kg)
Economy:	N/A

Dodge Dart GTS (1969)

Dodge first introduced the compact Dart in 1963 and, far from being a performance model, it came that year with a six-cylinder engine only. But as the mid-
60s turned to the late-'60s the Dart developed much like the rest of the Dodge line–up,
hence it got a small-block V8 in '64, though with just 180 bhp (134 kW) performance
was brisk rather than exciting. It was certainly a long way from the larger, hemi cars
which had 425 bhp (316 kW) under their hoods. Even so, the Dart grew in popularity
and had increasingly bigger displacement engines. By 1969 the top sport model was
the GTS, which came with the company's new 340 ci (5571 cc) small-block, firmer
shocks, 'Rallye' uprated springs, Red Tread wider tyres and bumble bee stripes over
the trunk and sides. Optional on the engine was the 'Six Pack' consisting of three two-
barrel carburettors which gave 15bhp (11kW increase in power.

Top speed:	118 mph (189 km/h)
0–60 mph (0–96 km/h):	6.8 sec
Engine type:	V8
Displacement:	340 ci (5,571 cc)
Transmission	4-speed manual
Max power:	290 bhp (216 kW) @ 5,200 rpm
Max torque:	360 lb ft (624 Nm) @ 3,800 rpm
Weight:	3,097 lb (1,407 kg)
Economy:	15 mpg (5.31 km/l)

Ford Mustang Boss 302 (1969)

While the Boss 302 was a rare machine that went to driving enthusiasts or, more often, racers, enough made it into the hands of modifiers, and the car provided a great base on which to start work. The owner of this Boss has further lowered the suspension with different coil springs up front and reverse-eye leaf springs at the rear. Relocated arms ensure correct geometry on the front double wishbones, as this car is made to handle and has virtually zero body roll through corners, thanks to the anti-roll bars front and rear. The 302 engine has been fitted with the race-type injection stacks that poke through the hood, for extended rpm use through the Borg Warner T10 manual gearbox and 4.11:1 geared Ford 9-inch (229mm) rear end. Magnesium rims at 8 inches (203mm) wide with modern Goodyear 225/50ZR15 low-profile tyres complete the style.

Top speed:	149 mph (238 km/h)
0–60 mph (0–96 km/h):	4.8 sec
Engine type:	V8
Displacement:	302 ci (4,948 cc)
Transmission	4-speed manual
Max power:	400 bhp (298 kW) @ 6,500 rpm
Max torque:	343 lb ft (465 Nm) @ 4,300 rpm
Weight:	3,209 lb (1,458 kg)
Economy:	18 mpg (6.37 km/l)

Ford Torino Talladega (1969)

The late 1960s held some of the fiercest NASCAR battles, with Ford and Chrysler slugging it out. In response to the Dodge Charger 500, Ford came up with the Torino Talladega which did well in this debut year with 30 wins. The car was based on the Fairlane Torino which appeared in 1968. Underneath it used a double wishbone front and a leaf spring rear, though the back had staggered shocks to prevent wheel hop. All Talladegas came with the 428ci (7-litre) Cobra Jet big-block V8 engine, rated at 335bhp (250kW), even though output was close to 450bhp (336kW). The motor had 10.6:1 compression, a steel crank, stronger con rods and a 735cfm Holley carb. The suspension used stiffer springs and shocks plus a thicker anti-roll bar up front, while at the rear a Traction Lok diff and 3.25:1 gears were stock. For aerodynamics the nose was stretched by 5 inches (127mm) and tapered.

Top speed:	130 mph (208 km/h)
0–60 mph (0–96 km/h):	5.8 sec
Engine type:	V8
Displacement:	428 ci (7,013 cc)
Transmission:	4-speed manual
Max power:	335 bhp (250 kW) @ 5,200 rpm
Max torque:	440 lb ft (596 Nm) @ 3,400 rpm
Weight:	3,536 lb (1,607 kg)
Economy:	14 mpg (4.96 km/l)

Pontiac GTO Judge (1969)

The Judge carried on a Pontiac tradition of being the quintessential muscle car. It debuted in the Carousel Red paint with 'The Judge' decals on the hood and front wings, so you couldn't miss Pontiac's new high-performance version GTO. The looks were backed with performance too, as Judges got the 366bhp (251kW) Ram Air III engine. Also fitted to the car were stiffer springs and shocks to improve cornering and ride. The standard gear ratio in the rear axle was 3.90:1 with a Safe-T-Track differential, though steeper gears for better acceleration could be ordered. Externally the car was one of the first to use energy-absorbing bumpers which would cope with up to 4mph (6.3km/h) impact. Inside the car was praised for its style, with a clear dash layout and the hood-mounted rev counter. The buckets seats gave good support and the floor-mounted Hurst shifter stirred a Muncie gearbox.

Top speed:	123 mph (197 km/h)
0–60 mph (0–96 km/h):	6.2 sec
Engine type:	V8
Displacement:	400 ci (6,554 cc)
Transmission	4-speed manual
Max power:	366 bhp (251 kW) @ 5,400 rpm
Max torque:	445 lb ft (603 Nm) @ 3,600 rpm
Weight:	3,503 lb (1,592 kg)
Economy:	11 mpg (3.89 km/l)

Pontiac Trans Am (1969)

The Trans Am was Pontiac's sporty answer to the Camaro, and was the most sought-after of the all the Firebirds. The sheet metal was based on the Camaro, but a new nose with split grille and double headlamps either side ensured the looks remained pure Pontiac. The car was named after the American race series, so came with all the right components fitted to make it a street racer, uprated springs and shocks and more powerful brakes being just a some of the parts. The owner of this car has gone one step further by fitting rear discs brakes from a 1979 model Trans Am, and there are wide 7x15 inch (178x381mm) rims with 235/60 tyres to take full advantage of the new powertrain. Long gone is the original small-block, in favour of a late-model Tuned Port Injection small-block, which gives as much power but with more miles per gallon and better manners.

Top speed:	140 mph (224 km/h)
0–60 mph (0–96 km/h):	6.8 sec
Engine type:	V8
Displacement:	350 ci (5,735 cc)
Transmission:	3-speed auto
Max power:	250 bhp (186 kW) @ 5,000 rpm
Max torque:	295 lb ft (400 Nm) @ 3,650 rpm
Weight:	3,649 lb (1,658 kg)
Economy:	15.7 mpg (5.56 km/l)

Dodge Super Bee (1969)

The muscle-car wars were about being ahead of the competition, and that's what prompted Chrysler to create the Super Bee in 1968. It was a bare-bones Coronet, achieved by stuffing the monster 440ci (7.2-litre) into the lightest intermediate bodyshell. The huge amount of power came from extras such as a free-flow twin exhaust system, but mostly it was though the 'Six Pack' carb set-up. This consisted of three two-barrel Holley carbs, on which the centre one only would work at part throttle, but when the throttle was pushed further, the other two carbs would open up for more fuel and full power that could propel the car down the quarter-mile in 13 seconds. Power wasn't the whole picture; the car could handle, thanks to heavy-duty torsion bar front suspension. The Super Bee had a tough Dana axle with 4.1:1 gearing from the factory, plus black steel wheels.

Top speed:	130 mph (208 km/h)
0–60 mph (0–96 km/h):	6.0 sec
Engine type:	V8
Displacement:	440 ci (7,210 cc)
Transmission	4-speed manual
Max power:	390 bhp (291 kW) @ 4,700 rpm
Max torque:	490 lb ft (664 Nm) @ 3,200 rpm
Weight:	4,100 lb (1,863 kg)
Economy:	7 mpg (2.48 km/l)

Ford Mustang Boss 302 (1969)

Winning the sales war of the 1960s with the Mustang wasn't everything for Ford, because Chevrolet's Camaro Z28 was taking blue oval scalps out on the street. Ford answered the call for cavalry with the Boss 302. It mated the larger 351ci (5.7-litre) Cleveland heads to the small Windsor 302ci (5.0-litre) block, with increased 10.6:1 compression and a larger carb with high-lift camshaft. The result was a revvy V8 which, though rated at 290bhp (216kW), was closer to 350bhp (261kW). Styling guru Larry Shinoda used his aerodynamics expertise to create functional front and rear spoilers, plus rear window slats. The Boss needed a strong gearbox and Borg Warner's four-speed T10 'Toploader' was the chosen unit. All the Boss 302s used a Hurst shifter with T-handle, adding driver involvement. Produced into 1970, it won the Transmission-Am manufacturers' title that year.

Top speed:	128 mph (205 km/h)
0–60 mph (0–96 km/h):	6.5 sec
Engine type:	V8
Displacement:	302 ci (4,948 cc)
Transmission:	4-speed manual
Max power:	290 bhp (216 kW) @ 5,800 rpm
Max torque:	290 lb ft (393 Nm) @ 4,300 rpm
Weight:	3,227 lb (1,466 kg)
Economy:	14 mpg (4.96 km/l)

Ford Mustang Mach 1 (1969)

The Mach 1 sat between the mighty Boss 429 and the highly strung 302, and with the great 428 Cobra Jet engine, it was just what many Mustang fans were waiting for. The Cobra Jet motor had a strong bottom end, which made it ideal for performance use, and in 1969 it came in three states of tune, the Drag Pack being the top version, with the Super Cobra Jet engine. Inside, the Mach 1 had specially designed instruments heavily set into the dash, plus a split dash top and high-backed bucket seats. Externally the style was more evident with a Shaker hood that attached an intake directly to the engine-top through the hood, thus you could see the engine 'shaking' as it idled. The spring and shock rates were firmed up, and the rear shocks were staggered either side of the axle to reduce wheel hop which was prevalent on high-bhp Mustangs.

Top speed:	121 mph (194 km/h)
0–60 mph (0–96 km/h):	5.3 sec
Engine type:	V8
Displacement:	428 ci (7,013 cc)
Transmission	3-speed auto
Max power:	335 bhp (250 kW) @ 5,200 rpm
Max torque:	440 lb ft (596 Nm) @ 3,400 rpm
Weight:	3,420 lb (1,554 kg)
Economy:	20 mpg (7.08 km/l)

Ford Mustang Boss 429 (1969)

Ford needed a new engine for NASCAR, but to qualify its use, it had to go into 500 production cars. Instead of putting their new 429ci (7.2-litre) into the mid-sized Torinos they were racing, they shoehorned it into the fastback Mustang. Trouble was, being designed to rev over 6,000rpm, the engine didn't make the Mustang the incredible performer it promised on paper. The 429 motor was unlike any other Ford motor, being much wider in the cylinder head, thanks to its semi-Hemi combustion chamber design, and this meant strut towers needed widening and the battery relocating to the trunk. The Boss used the 'Top Loader' close-ratio, four-speed manual because the autos couldn't handle the torque. The suspension had uprated springs and shocks plus an anti-roll bar. While the Boss 429 was the most expensive non-Shelby Mustang produced, the 428 Cobra Jet was a better street car.

Top speed:	118 mph (188 km/h)
0–60 mph (0–96 km/h):	6.8 sec
Engine type:	V8
Displacement:	429 ci (7,030 cc)
Transmission	4-speed manual
Max power:	375 bhp (280 kW) @ 5,200 rpm
Max torque:	450 lb ft (610 Nm) @ 3,400 rpm
Weight:	3,870 lb (1,759 kg)
Economy:	13.8 mpg (4.89 km/l)

Lincoln Continental Mk III (1969)

Henry Ford II put his personal stamp on this design of Lincoln's luxury coupe. It was very long for a two-door coupe and in fact had the longest hood ever produced on a US car (over 6ft or 1.8m). Under it was 150lb (68kg) of sound-deadening to quieten the 460ci (7,538cc) V8, though it couldn't dampen the performance, thanks to the huge torque produced. The suspension was set deliberately soft, so the car floated in style over the worst of surfaces, while the interior wrapped the driver in leather-lined luxury and wood trim, with a distinctly stately like dash. The engine – unusually for a luxury vehicle but typical for the late 1960s – ran 10.5:1 compression and a four-barrel carburettor for tremendous performance, and the car was brought down in speed by the power-assisted 11.7-inch (280mm) front discs and huge rear drum brakes.

Top speed:	123 mph (196 km/h)
0–60 mph (0–96 km/h):	10.3 sec
Engine type:	V8
Displacement:	460 ci (7,538 cc)
Transmission	3-speed auto
Max power:	365 bhp (272 kW) @ 4,600 rpm
Max torque:	500 lb ft (678 Nm) @ 2,800 rpm
Weight:	4,475 lb (2,034 kg)
Economy:	13 mpg (4.60 km/l)

Shelby Mustang GT500 (1969)

If too much power was considered just enough, the Shelby GT500 went overboard when it joined the GT350 in production in 1967. It was a sales success, outselling the smaller-engined model two to one. Based on the standard Mach 1 Mustang, it differed visually with a new grille, different tail lights, Shelby stripes and square tailpipes. Like the Mach 1, the Shelby used the 428 Cobra jet big-block V8 engine, but it had massive handling improvements. Heavy-duty springs and shocks, wider tyres, thicker anti-roll bars and a roll cage to stiffen the shell gave the Shelby great balance. The exclusivity cost though, at three times the price of Ford's regular Mach 1. Although the factory rated the Cobra Jet motor at 335bhp (250kW) to appease insurance companies who were charging $1000 to insure young males, the output was actually closer to 400bhp (298kW).

Top speed:	130 mph (208 km/h)
0–60 mph (0–96 km/h):	5.5 sec
Engine type:	V8
Displacement:	428 ci (7,013 cc)
Transmission	3-speed auto
Max power:	335 bhp (250 kW) @ 5,200 rpm
Max torque:	440 lb ft (596 Nm) @ 3,400 rpm
Weight:	3,100 lb (1,409 kg)
Economy:	8 mpg (2.83 km/l)

AMC Rebel Machine (1970)

AMC were small compared to the big three muscle-car producers in 1970. They'd released the patriotic-coloured SC Rambler in conjunction with Hurst in 1969 which packed 315bhp (235kW) for 14-second quarter-miles, but only 1,512 were made. In 1970 the SC/Rambler replaced it, but again it only lasted for a year and just 2,326 were made. The Rambler was a good muscle car, and AMC stuffed their largest engine into the new mid-sized saloon. It was a strong motor with a forged steel crank and it could spring the car to mid-14-second times on the quarter, through a Borg Warner Muncie gearbox. At the rear a 3.54:1 moderate gear was fitted, but AMC offered up to 5.00:1 acceleration gears and a Twin Grip limited-slip differential for racers. The Rambler had very stiff suspension, and grossly overpowered steering, which didn't help reviews and, hence, sales.

Top speed:	115 mph (184 km/h)
0–60 mph (0–96 km/h):	6.4 sec
Engine type:	V8
Displacement:	390 ci (6,390 cc)
Transmission	4-speed manual
Max power:	340 bhp (254 kW) @ 5,100 rpm
Max torque:	430 lb ft (583 Nm) @ 3,600 rpm
Weight:	3,650 lb (1,659 kg)
Economy:	11 mpg (3.89 km/l)

Buick GSX (1970)

While most muscle-car enthusiasts were content with the mid-sized GS 455, for others it was too dual, so Buick launched the uprated 1970 GSX. This car had the power of the regular GS 455, but with better suspension and younger, dynamic looks, thanks to Magnum 500 wheels, spoilers, scoops and stripes. The suspension used independent wishbones at the front and coil springs out back (all heavy-duty), and anti-roll bars at both ends to improve cornering. The brakes comprised 11-inch (280mm) discs and finned drums for better cooling. The 455ci (7.5-litre) was the biggest engine Buick produced, and standard in the base GSX, though most buyers opted for the Stage 1 conversion with a four-barrel carb, high-lift camshaft, larger valves and a 10.5:1 compression. It had a real rating of around 400bhp (298kW) and massive torque, making it one of the most powerful muscle-car big-block motors.

Top speed:	123 mph (197 km/h)
0–60 mph (0–96 km/h):	5.5 sec
Engine type:	V8
Displacement:	455 ci (7,456 cc)
Transmission:	4-speed manual
Max power:	360 bhp (268 kW) @ 4,600 rpm
Max torque:	510 lb ft (691 Nm) @ 2,800 rpm
Weight:	3,561 lb (1,618 kg)
Economy:	7.1 mpg (2.51 km/l)

Chevrolet Chevelle SS454 (1970)

At the height of the muscle-car wars, Chevrolet played its trump card with the launch of the LS-6 454 V8. At the same time, GM lifted its displacement on mid-sized cars which meant that they could be finally fitted with engines over 400ci (6.5-litres). The result was the Chevelle SS454. The car was basic underneath with coil springs all around, but the SS package included the F41 suspension which had stiffer front springs to cope with the big-block's weight. Maganum 500 wheels were fitted to every SS Chevelle but even being wide, fitted with Polyglas tyres barely provided traction. The engine had high compression pistons, rectangular port heads and solid lifters so could rev well for a big engine. It received high-pressure air while on the move through a vacuum-operated flap on the cowl induction. Just 4,475 SS454s made it out of the factory, but all were 13-second quarter-mile cars.

Top speed:	125 mph (200 km/h)
0–60 mph (0–96 km/h):	6.1 sec
Engine type:	V8
Displacement:	454 ci (7,439 cc)
Transmission	4-speed manual
Max power:	450 bhp (336 kW) @ 5,600 rpm
Max torque:	500 lb ft (678 Nm) @ 3,600 rpm
Weight:	4,000 lb (1,818 kg)
Economy:	12.5 mpg (4.43 km/l)

Dodge Challenger T/A (1970)

Dodge jumped in headfirst to the SCCA's Trans Am racer series with its aptly named Challenger, as it was going up against the likes of Ford's Mustang and Chevrolet's Camaro. It was built for just one year and featured a spec sheet that would get any gasoline head revved up. The car stuck with a small-block engine, thus keeping weight down and handling at the optimum, thanks to better balance. The suspension was uprated torsion bar at the front and a live axle rear on leaf springs, while discs came standard on the front. The engine came from the art Swinger and, though advertised at 290bhp (216kW) output, was well over 300bhp (223kW). To reinforce the racing theme a four-speed was fitted, with an auto optional. Also, to aid traction, bigger rear tyres were fitted than at the front, and this was the first Detroit muscle car to have such a set-up.

Top speed:	125 mph (200 km/h)
0–60 mph (0–96 km/h):	5.8 sec
Engine type:	V8
Displacement:	340 ci (5,571 cc)
Transmission:	3-speed auto
Max power:	290 bhp (216 kW) @ 5,000 rpm
Max torque:	345 lb ft (467 Nm) @ 3,200 rpm
Weight:	3,650 lb (1,659 kg)
Economy:	12 mpg (4.25 km/l)

Dodge Coronet R/T (1970)

The Coronet was introduced in 1967 and had sales of over 10,000 in its first year. It was the package people wanted, thanks to the high-performance, no-frills approach. In 1970 the Coronet R/T (Road and Track) didn't enjoy continued success, but it was still a great combination for the street- or strip-racing enthusiast. In base trim it used the 440ci (7.2-litre) Wedge engine which was a more reliable and easier to maintain engine than the famed 'Hemi', though that was an option. Even in stock form, the 440ci had 375bhp (279kW) with a single carb, or 390bhp (291kW) with the 'Six Pack' carb option. A torsion bar front and live axle rear, as per most in the Chrysler group, kept its ride quality high. In 1970 the car was only just surviving, as other powerful cars – most from Chrysler, in fact – took over. Its sales dropped to 2,615 and of those, only 13 had the Hemi installed.

Top speed:	123 mph (197 km/h)
0–60 mph (0–96 km/h):	6.6 sec
Engine type:	V8
Displacement:	440 ci (7,210 cc)
Transmission	3-speed auto
Max power:	375 bhp (279 kW) @ 4,600 rpm
Max torque	480 lb ft (650 Nm) @ 3,200 rpm
Weight:	3,546 lb (1,611 kg)
Economy:	10.6 mpg (3.75 km/l)

Mercury Cougar Eliminator (1970)

Two years after the Mustang, Mercury launched its own pony car and named it the Cougar. Underneath it basically a stretched Mustang platform, which in turn was based on a Falcon, so it held nothing new suspension-wise. The top-rated Eliminator came in 1969 and use an independent front with double wishbones and coil springs, plus a live axle rear on leaf springs, with staggered shocks to limit wheel hop under hard acceleration. It was fast, no matter what engine choice you made, the Boss 302 or 428 Cobra Jet being the options. The smaller of the two made 290bhp (216kW) while the bigger was rated at 335bhp (250kW) to fool the insurance companies, though it was more like 410bhp (305kW). The 428 could also be ordered with a ram air system, and if the owner specified the 'Drag Pak', the car would receive an oil cooler and 4.3:1 axle gears.

Top speed:	106 mph (170 km/h)
0–60 mph (0–96 km/h):	5.6 sec
Engine type:	V8
Displacement:	428 ci (7,013 cc)
Transmission:	3-speed auto
Max power:	335 bhp (250 kW) @ 5,200 rpm
Max torque:	440 lb ft (596 Nm) @ 3,400 rpm
Weight:	3,780 lb (1,718 kg)
Economy:	6.2 mpg (2.19 km/l)

Olds Cutlass Rallye 350 (1970)

Insurance premiums were turning into a nightmare for many drivers in the 1960s, especially on the more powerful big-block muscle cars. So, manufacturers offered more small-block alternatives. The Oldsmobile Rallye 350 was one of the best but was available only for 1970. It was based on the Cutlass and featured a double wishbones up front end and a live axle rear on coil springs and located by upper and lower control arms. However, front and rear anti-roll bars, heavy-duty springs and shocks meant good handling and more balance with less weight up front. And the 350ci (5.7-litre) produced plenty of power and impressive torque for its displacement. All the Rallyes came in Sebring Yellow and featured the functional cold-air intake hood from the W-30 model. For 1971 the Rallye was dropped and power on the small-block Cutlass was reduced to 260bhp (194kW).

Top speed:	122 mph (196 km/h)
0–60 mph (0–96 km/h):	7.0 sec
Engine type:	V8
Displacement:	350 ci (5,735 cc)
Transmission	3-speed auto
Max power:	310 bhp (231 kW) @ 4,600 rpm
Max torque:	390 lb ft (529 Nm) @ 3,200 rpm
Weight:	3,574 lb (1,624 kg)
Economy:	14 mpg (4.96 km/l)

Plymouth Hemi 'Cuda (1970)

The Hemi 'Cuda represents one of the best of all Chrysler muscle cars, having a handsome bodystyle and the awesome Hemi V8 with its hemispherical combustion chambers. In standard form, the car used a unitary body/chassis, though this owner has modified his car to what is termed as 'back-halving' which means the back half of the car has had its stock suspension cut out to be replaced by a drag-racing four-bars suspension. Also, to house the 18.5-inch (470mm) wide Mickey Thompson street/strip racing tyres, the car has been fitted with sheet aluminium 'tubs' (the term for arches) which means the back seat and most of the trunk space has gone. The engine here has been modified by Dick Landy Industries and output is up by around 50 percent on the stock Hemi. A four-speed manual and 4.56:1 geared rear end catapult it down the quarter-mile in 11 seconds.

Top speed:	137 mph (219 km/h)
0–60 mph (0–96 km/h):	4.3 sec
Engine type:	V8
Displacement:	432 ci (7,079 cc)
Transmission	4-speed manual
Max power:	620 bhp (462 kW) @ 6,500 rpm
Max torque:	655 lb ft (888 Nm) @ 5,100 rpm
Weight:	3,945 lb (1,793 kg)
Economy:	9.4 mpg (3.33 km/l)

Plymouth Superbird (1970)

The 1970 Superbird was built to win NASCAR. Ford had dominated the series in the late 1960s with their Talladegas and even the Superbird's twin, the 1969 Dodge Daytona, couldn't take enough wins off them. The 1970 Superbird offered slightly better aerodynamics than the Dodge, to give good downforce at 200mph (322km/h). Under the hood the 426ci (6.9-litre) Hemi was fitted, and it made the Superbird so quick that it won 21 races and the whole championship in its first season. The NASCAR officials stepped in, however, to keep competition even, and thus imposed engine-size restrictions on cars with rear wings, hence the Superbird was banned. Plymouth had trouble selling the street versions because of their radical looks, so many had the nose cones and rear spoilers stripped off to be sold as standard Road Runners.

Top speed:	140 mph (224 km/h)
0-60 mph (0–96 km/h):	6.1 sec
Engine type:	V8
Displacement:	426 ci (6,980 cc)
Transmission	4-speed manual
Max power:	425 bhp (317 kW) @ 5,000 rpm
Max torque:	490 lb ft (664 Nm) @ 4,000 rpm
Weight:	3,841 lb (1,745 kg)
Economy:	13.8 mpg (4.89 km/l)

Chevrolet Monte Carlo 454 (1970)

The Monte Carlo was supposed to be luxurious more than sporty, and it was built on the Chevelle platform but used a slightly longer wheelbase. It had extra rubber mounts fitted between the body and chassis to reduce vibration from the street, plus extra sound-deadening inside. The option RPO Z20 made you the SS454 model, and that incorporated the largest big-block Chevy had on offer, the infamous 'Rat'. The long stroke of the LS-5 motor produced the torque, giving the car endless power through the rev range. The following year's version of the same engine, coded LS-6, produced even more power with 450bhp (335kW). Underneath the car ran with the Chevelle's wishbone front and coil-sprung rear suspension, with an Automatic Level Control system and on-board air compressor to control ride height. Inside it featured soft vinyl bucket seats and a simulated walnut burr dash.

Top speed:	132 mph (211 km/h)
0–60 mph (0–96 km/h):	7.1 sec
Engine type:	V8
Displacement:	454 ci (7,439 cc)
Transmission	3-speed auto
Max power:	360 bhp (268 kW) @ 4,400 rpm
Max torque:	500 lb ft (678 Nm) @ 3,200 rpm
Weight:	3,860 lb (1,754 kg)
Economy:	11.5 mpg (4.07 km/l)

Dodge Challenger R/T SE (1970)

Dodge's own pony car finally arrived in 1970 and was well named with the likes of the Cougar, Mustang and Camaro around on the street. It came with a huge list of options including 12 engines, and in Dodge tradition, the R/T (Road/Track) package was the high performance model. The base engine was the 335bhp (250kW) 383ci (6.3-litre) V8, but the car could be ordered with the mighty 426ci (7-litre) Street Hemi or 440ci (7.2-litre) V8s, which gave out 425bhp (317kW) and 375bhp (280kW). The Challenger was built on Chrysler's brand new E-body platform, sharing its firewall and front subframe with the bigger B-body cars like the Charger. The new car used Chrysler's proven torsion bar front suspension with beefed up anti-roll bar, and rear leaf springs on a live axle, the latter requiring the Sure-Grip limited-slip differential option to make use of all the torque.

Top speed:	128 mph (205 km/h)
0–60 mph (0–96 km/h):	7.2 sec
Engine type:	V8
Displacement:	440 ci (7,210 cc)
Transmission	4-speed manual
Max power:	390 bhp (291 kW) @ 4,700 rpm
Max torque:	490 lb ft (664 Nm) @ 3,200 rpm
Weight:	3,437 lb (1,562 kg)
Economy:	9 mpg (3.19 km/l)

Ford Torino Cobra (1970)

While the new-for-1970 Torino GT was a good muscle car, the Cobra was the bare-knuckle fighter version. It was based on said sporty GT, but instead of the small-block, it featured a 429ci (7-litre) big-block but it wasn't the Boss 429, even though it made a lot of power, thanks to 11.3:1 compression, upgraded heads, a high-lift cam and high-flow Holley carburettor. If the Drag Pack was ordered the engine received solid lifter cam, oil cooler, forged pistons, a four-bolt main cap block, and an even larger carb for 375bhp (280kW) and a lot more durability in racing. To cope with the power the Cobra could be ordered with either a Traction Lok limited-slip differential with 3.91:1 gears, or for more serious racers there was the harsher, more noisy Detroit Locker with 4.30:1 gearing for best acceleration. The Shaker hood scoop even had a ram air system for more power on the move.

Top speed:	118 mph (189 km/h)
0–60 mph (0–96 km/h):	5.9 sec
Engine type:	V8
Displacement:	429 ci (7,030 cc)
Transmission	4-speed manual
Max power:	370 bhp (276 kW) @ 5,400 rpm
Max torque:	450 lb ft (610 Nm) @ 3,400 rpm
Weight:	4,000 lb (1,818 kg)
Economy:	12 mpg (4.25 km/l)

Mercury Cyclone Spoiler (1970)

Allll Ford group cars were redesigned in 1970s, and this included Mercury with its Cyclone. Besides smoother lines and contours, it got a new engine, the 429ci (7-litre) big-block Ford, which packed huge torque. Mercury being a premium Ford brand meant the ride quality was very good, though the car was happier going quickly in a straight line than cornering. Underneath it used Mercury's Montego unitary platform, stretched to improve the ride on the heavy-duty coil sprung front and leaf sprung rear, with front anti-roll bar. The styling was the, by then, popular fastback muscle-car styling and a hidden light front grille with distinctive gunsight-type grille centre. Adding the Dragpack option gave a Hurst shifted four-speed plus higher rear end gearing, making the Spoiler a low-14-second quarter-mile machine. The Cyclone only lasted another year before being axed.

Top speed:	126 mph (202 km/h)
0–60 mph (0–96 km/h):	6.2 sec
Engine type:	V8
Displacement:	429 ci (7,030 cc)
Transmission	4-speed manual
Max power:	370 bhp (276 kW) @ 5,400 rpm
Max torque:	450 lb ft (610 Nm) @ 3,400 rpm
Weight:	3,773 lb (1,715 kg)
Economy:	9 mpg (3.19 km/l)

Chevrolet Camaro SS396 (1970)

The redesign of the Camaro came early in 1970 so these models are often referred to as the 70 1/2 Camaros. It was an instant hit on the streets, especially when Chevy announced the performance version, top of which was the SS396. The engine was actually 402ci (6.6 litres) through an increase in bore size, even though GM badged it still as a 396. Two states of tune were available, in the L-34 with 350bhp (261kW) or L-78 with 375bhp (280kW), and while the 350 version came with 10.25:1 compression and a Rochester four-barrel carb, the 385 went higher still on compression, adding an aluminium intake and a Holley four-barrel. Underneath, the extras included a heavy-duty F41 suspension package with front and rear anti-roll bars, a 12-bolt rear axle with choice of ratios and 7x14-inch (178x356mm) wheels. Cars ordered with the four-speed Muncie gearbox also got a Hurst shifter.

Top speed:	128 mph (205 km/h)
0–60 mph (0–96 km/h):	6.2 sec
Engine type:	V8
Displacement:	402 ci (6,587 cc)
Transmission	4-speed manual
Max power:	375 bhp (280 kW) @ 5,600 rpm
Max torque:	415 lb ft (562 Nm) @ 3,200 rpm
Weight:	3,550 lb (1,613 kg)
Economy:	14 mpg (4.96 km/l)

Chevrolet El Camino SS454 (1970)

Some muscle machines are best remembered because they show the pinnacle of the model, and the El Camino SS454 is no different. The El Camino hadn't been seen four years early in the 1960s, but by 1964 it returned with a 396ci (6.5-litre) engine option, then had a makeover and facelift in 1968 with softer, rounded lines, yet the 396ci remained. In 1970 the El Camino followed the Chevelle SS by having only the 454ci (7.4-litre) big-block 'Rat' V8 available. The engine came in two different versions, the mild one being the LS5 with 10.25:1 compression and 360bhp (268kW), while the wild one was the LS6 with forged aluminium pistons, a special cam, forged steel crank and rods, and 11.5:1 compression for 450bhp (336kW). With a Positraction live-axle and very little rear end weight, the El Camino's back wheels could easily overtake the front with a heavy right foot.

Top speed:	130 mph (208 km/h)
0–60 mph (0–96 km/h):	7.0 sec
Engine type:	V8
Displacement:	454 ci (7,439 cc)
Transmission	3-speed auto
Max power:	360 bhp (268 kW) @ 4,400 rpm
Max torque:	500 lb ft (678 Nm) @ 3,200 rpm
Weight:	4,270 lb (1,940 kg)
Economy:	14 mpg (4.96 km/l)

Plymouth Road Runner (1970)

The good thing about so many muscle cars is that although nowadays they can be beaten by some modern machines, they can be made to run quicker still thanks to the healthy aftermarket. Often the performance parts available today far exceed the benefits of parts available over 30 years ago, so making more power in these old brutes is not difficult. This Road Runner has gone through an increase in compression and has been fitted with a Mopar Performance camshaft plus high-flow exhaust and electronic ignition, for an extra 65bhp (48kW) over stock. The rear end has wider alloys to fit 12-inch (305mm) wide rubber, which helps traction dramatically. The stock suspension remains, albeit lowered by one spline on the front torsion bars, but otherwise it remains very similar, so retains excellent value too. On the strip it can regularly produce low 13-second quarter miles.

Top speed:	137 mph (219 km/h)
0–60 mph (0–96 km/h):	5.0 sec
Engine type:	V8
Displacement:	440 ci (7,210 cc)
Transmission	3-speed auto
Max power:	440 bhp (328 kW) @ 5,500 rpm
Max torque:	500 lb ft (678 Nm) @ 4,000 rpm
Weight:	3,475 lb (1,579 kg)
Economy:	10.2 mpg (3.61 km/l)

AMC Javelin AMX (1971)

While the new-for-1971 Javelin wasn't as small nor as sharp looking as its previous incarnation, with the range of V8s available, it could still be made to perform. The new car was bigger than the previous model which meant four seats instead of two, and rode on a 1-inch (25mm) longer wheelbase. The 'Go Package' gave it heavy-duty suspension, power front disc brakes, a cowl induction set-up and 7x15-inch (178x381mm) rims with Goodyear tyres. The AMX was the high-performance version of the Javelin so had the option of either a 360ci (5,899cc) or 401ci (6,571cc) V8, the top model producing 335bhp (250kW) and 360lb ft (487Nm) torque. Javelins came with a 3-speed manual transmission, but a 4-speed was optional and recommended for the bigger engines. A Shift Command automatic option was available, buyers choosing between floor or column shift.

Top speed:	114 mph (182 km/h)
0–60 mph (0–96 km/h):	6.9 sec
Engine type:	V8
Displacement:	360 ci (5,899 cc)
Transmission	4-speed manual
Max power:	285 bhp (213 kW) @ 5,000 rpm
Max torque:	315 lb ft (427 Nm) @ 3,400 rpm
Weight:	3,244 lb (1,474 kg)
Economy:	10 mpg (3.54 km/l)

Buick Riviera Gran Sport (1971)

Jerry Hirshberg styled the 1971 Riviera and forgot about the ultra-conservative Buicky styling which had happened up until 1971. The new model was larger and heavier than previous models, but the dramatic design, which brought the car to a boat-style point at the rear, led to the car being nicknamed the 'boat tail Buick'. The Riviera rode on a separate chassis, with an A-arm independent front end plus live axle rear using coil springs. The Gran Sport package added uprated springs, stiffer shocks and a fatter front anti-roll bar, With fuel very cheap at 30 cents per gallon, Buick didn't concern buyers by fitting in their 455ci (7.4-litre) big-block engine which, with its long stroke, made huge torque and the car more of a luxury cruiser than straight-line performer. The Riviera was produced for just two years before being redesigned then axed.

Top speed:	120 mph (192 km/h)
0–60 mph (0–96 km/h):	8.1 sec
Engine type:	V8
Displacement:	455 ci (7,456 cc)
Transmission	3-speed auto
Max power:	330 bhp (246 kW) @ 4,600 rpm
Max torque:	455 lb ft (616 Nm) @ 2,800 rpm
Weight:	4,325 lb (1,965 kg)
Economy:	8 mpg (2.83 km/l)

Chevrolet Camaro RS/SS (1971)

Camaros have always been modified, and when the new 1970 1/2 model was introduced, it addressed some of the former models' shortcomings so improved the breed and potential still further. Many styles have developed over time, but one that has been popular in the 1990s and into the 21st century is Pro Touring. This uses classic muscle-car bodies but with all the handling and finesse of a modern-day supercar. Upgraded road/race suspension, massive Baer Claw disc brakes, and large rims with modern wide and low-profile rubber are fitted on this Camaro. Inside there are modern bucket race seats, harnesses and also a modern sound system. Usually Pro Touring cars run at least five but sometimes six-speed gearboxes, but this owner has opted for a high-tech four-speed overdrive gearbox with ratchet-style shifter which provides minimal shifter movement for each gear change.

Top speed:	143 mph (229 km/h)
0–60 mph (0–96 km/h):	5.4 sec
Engine type:	V8
Displacement:	400 ci (6,554 cc)
Transmission	4-speed auto
Max power:	425 bhp (317 kW) @ 4,800 rpm
Max torque:	330 lb ft (447 Nm) @ 3,000 rpm
Weight:	3,320 lb (1,509 kg)
Economy:	17 mpg (6.02 km/l)

Dodge Charger R/T (1971)

In 1971 the Charger, which had set the standards for full-sized sedan muscle-car performance, got a restyle. The front end was wider and had a one-piece fender for better crash protection, and this was matched at the rear where there was also a sharper roofline slope. The car was virtually unchanged on the chassis, still with torsion bars at the front and multi-leaf rear springs on the Dana 60-equipped rear axle. The 440ci (7.2-litre) Magnum engine was a racer's dream, with an ultra-strong crankshaft and connecting rods, plus a rigid cast-iron block. It also had high flow cylinder heads and an effective intake manifold with triple two-barrel carbs (the famous 'Six Pack'), so it's easy to see how the cars were so effective in NHRA Super Stock drag-racing class. Just 3,118 R/Ts were built in 1971, and only 63 had the extra option of the legendary Hemi.

Top speed:	125 mph (200 km/h)
0–60 mph (0–96 km/h):	6.0 sec
Engine type:	V8
Displacement:	440 ci (7,210 cc)
Transmission:	4-speed manual
Max power:	385 bhp (287 kW) @ 4,800 rpm
Max torque:	490 lb ft (664 Nm) @ 3,200 rpm
Weight:	3,785 lb (1,720 kg)
Economy:	12 mpg (4.25 km/l)

Ford Mustang Boss 351 (1971)

The Boss Mustang was based on a the new-for-1971 fastback design model, or 'SportsRoof' as Ford called it. It superseded the Boss 302 and 429 versions and, though bigger, was both quicker and equally good in cornering. The suspension remained conventional with coil sprung wishbones and a thick anti-roll bar at the front, plus a leaf spring rear with staggered shocks to prevent wheel hop. The Boss got stiffer suspension, however, and continued the previous model's stiffer spindles and reinforced shock towers for improved durability under hard cornering. The brakes were better too with 11.3-inch (287mm) vented discs at the front that could stop the car from 80mph (129km/h) in 250ft (76.2m). Optional 7x15-inch (178x381mm) Magnum wheels also improve the Boss. Inside, the dash had a wraparound feel with instruments in the centre console and a large, T-handle shifter.

Top speed:	116 mph (186 km/h)
0-60 mph (0–96 km/h):	5.8 sec
Engine type:	V8
Displacement:	351 ci (5,751 cc)
Transmission	4-speed manual
Max power:	330 bhp (246 kW) @ 5,400 rpm
Max torque:	370 lb ft (502 Nm) @ 4,000 rpm
Weight:	3,550 lb (1,613 kg)
Economy:	12 mpg (4.25 km/l)

Plymouth 'Cuda 383 (1971)

The 'Cuda was a winner for Chrysler and was their most successful 'E-body' car. It used the same front end as the full-sized B-body cars and so was well suited for the biggest V8s on offer from Dodge and Plymouth. The 1971 'Cuda 383 had a 383ci (6.3-litre) V8 which shared the block, heads, exhaust and camshaft from the 440, with the crankshaft having less stroke, which meant less displacement. Although not the quickest muscle car out, the 'Cuda 383 did put out huge torque and could still produce mid-14 second quarters. The chassis was conventional Chrysler, using torsion bars up front and leaf springs on the Dana 60-equipped rear axle. Stiffer springs all around improved handling and the Sure-Grip differential helped traction. Because of less demand, the 'Cuda 383 was produced only for two years, then axed. Today, however, collectors pay high prices for them.

Top speed:	120 mph (192 km/h)
0–60 mph (0–96 km/h):	7.8 sec
Engine type:	V8
Displacement:	383 ci (6,276 cc)
Transmission	4-speed manual
Max power:	300 bhp (224 kW) @ 4,800 rpm
Max torque:	410 lb ft (556 Nm) @ 3,400 rpm
Weight:	3,475 lb (1,579 kg)
Economy:	12 mpg (4.25 km/l)

Plymouth Duster 340 (1971)

Muscle cars started getting out of reach financially to many people, so Chrysler brought in a new entry-level model. The Duster combined their 340ci (5.6-litre) small-block engine with a lightweight, two-door version of the Valiant body. The result, though regarded as a budget racer, could easily give trouble to bigger-engined cars. Chrysler's torsion bar front suspension was used, and leaf springs out back held the live axle in place, the latter coming with 3.23:1 gears and the option of a Sure Grip differential. The stock gearbox was a three-speed manual, though a four-speed was on the option list, as was the Torqueflite three-speed automatic. Externally the car looked best with the optional matt black hood with '340 Wedge' graphic. Inside, the Duster had a very simple interior with a bench seat and multi-dial dash, with optional steering-column mounted rev counter.

Top speed:	120 mph (192 km/h)
0–60 mph (0–96 km/h):	6.0 sec
Engine type:	V8
Displacement:	340 ci (5,571 cc)
Transmission	3-speed auto
Max power:	275 bhp (205 kW) @ 5,000 rpm
Max torque:	340 lb ft (461 Nm) @ 3,200 rpm
Weight:	3,500 lb (1,590 kg)
Economy:	16 mpg (5.66 km/l)

Plymouth Road Runner (1971)

The original road Runner in 1968 was a runaway success for Chrysler, and when the new car was designed in 1971, it continued with much the same proven options as before. Underneath, it wasn't changed at all, save for a slightly shorter wheelbase and wider track which improved handling response. Also changed was the interior with a much-improved layout of the dash, pistol grip shifter and high back seats which offered better support. The base engine was the 383ci (6.2-litre), but this particular car was fitted with the famous Street Hemi from the factory. Just 55 Road runners made it out of the factory with this engine and for this year the valves got hydraulic lifters in place of slid ones, which made maintenance easier and the engine quieter. This motor, through the standard-issue four speed Muncie gearbox, could push the Road Runner deep into 13-second quarter-mile times.

Top speed:	125 mph (200 km/h)
0–60 mph (0–96 km/h):	5.7 sec
Engine type:	V8
Displacement:	426 ci (6,980 cc)
Transmission	4-speed manual
Max power:	425 bhp (317 kW) @ 4,700 rpm
Max torque:	490 lb ft (664 Nm) @ 3,200 rpm
Weight:	3,640 lb (1,654 kg)
Economy:	11 mpg (3.89 km/l)

Pontiac GTO Judge (1971)

Pontiac were one of the other manufacturers holding onto the muscle era as long as they possibly could before the fuel-conscious early 1970s took over. The GTO name had started when John DeLorean installed a 389ci (6.3-litre) big-block into Pontiac's intermediate Tempest sedan, and the car reached its peak in 1969, but wasn't about to got out without a bang come 1971. The car got a slight restyle around the nose section with a more protruding grilled surround, and used large vents at the front of the hood for the Ram Air intake. The car changed little in the suspension department except for revalved shocks, but wider alloy wheels at 7x14 inches (178x356mm) helped the handling. The interior had individual bucket seats and optional was a hood-mounted rev counter. The new engine was the 455ci (7.4-litre), which lost power through low compression to comply with emissions.

Top speed:	108 mph (173 km/h)
0-60 mph (0–96 km/h):	7.0 sec
Engine type:	V8
Displacement:	455 ci (7,456 cc)
Transmission	3-speed auto
Max power:	335 bhp (250 kW) @ 4,800 rpm
Max torque:	412 lb ft (558 Nm) @ 3,200 rpm
Weight:	3,894 lb (1,770 kg)
Economy:	10.2 mpg (3.61 km/l)

Ford Grand Torino Sport (1972)

The redesigned Torino became a single model series in 1972 split into just two options: the base and Grand Torino. While not as sharp-looking as their previous incarnations, they had the trademark muscle-car swept-back roofline and the classic formula of a V8 engine mounted up front and driving the rear wheels. This modified version has received a 351ci (5.75-litre) Cleveland V8, now displacing 357ci (5.8 litres) thanks to a rebore. Fitted are high compression pistons, modified heads, a high-lift cam, roller rockers (for increased rpm use) and electronic ignition. The car has received changes in the suspension, too, with lowered springs and uprated shocks. Along with modern radial tyres on wide Magnum 500 optional rims, they make the Torino far better than the standard car at taking corners. Inside it sports a multi-gauge dash and a modern sound system.

Top speed:	130 mph (208 km/h)
0–60 mph (0–96 km/h):	7.2 sec
Engine type:	V8
Displacement:	357 ci (5,850 cc)
Transmission	3-speed auto
Max power:	340 bhp (254 kW) @ 6,200 rpm
Max torque:	360 lb ft (488 Nm) @ 4,200 rpm
Weight:	3,496 lb (1,589 kg)
Economy:	14 mpg (4.96 km/l)

Oldsmobile Hurst/Olds (1972)

George Hurst became famous in the 1960s through his speed shop and in 1968 one of his employees, Jack 'Doc' Watson, built him a special Oldsmobile 4-4-2. George was convinced the car could be a sales winner so approached Oldsmobile with the notion of tuning muscle cars for them. The result was the Hurst/Olds, and in 1972 a convertible was picked to pace the 56th Indianapolis 500. This was based on the W-30 model which was fitted with the 455ci (7.4-litre) engine. This had seen 500lb ft (677Nm) torque previously, though emissions reduced power for 1972, even with the hood's functional cold-air induction scoops. A special Hurst shifter allowed manual shifts through the three-speed automatic, while the suspension used uprated springs and shocks, with front and rear anti-roll bars, for balanced handling. In typical Oldsmobile luxury, the hood dropped at the touch of a button.

Top speed:	132 mph (211 km/h)
0–60 mph (0–96 km/h):	6.8 sec
Engine type:	V8
Displacement:	455 ci (7,456 cc)
Transmission	3-speed auto
Max power:	300 bhp (224 kW) @ 4,700 rpm
Max torque:	410 lb ft (556 Nm) @ 3,200 rpm
Weight:	3,844 lb (1,747 kg)
Economy:	8 mpg (2.83 km/l)

Oldsmobile 4-4-2 W-30 (1972)

The 1968 and 1969 4-4-2 cars had been awesome but were limited by the GM ban on any engine over 400ci (6.5 litres) in its mid-sized cars. By 1970 they'd lifted that ban and Buick were free to slot in their 455ci (7.4-litre) big-block, which made the new 4-4-2 very quick on the street. As standard, the 4-4-2 had heavy-duty springs and shocks, plus thick front and rear anti-roll bars, but the W-30 also added a glass-fibre hood with cold-air induction, a rear trunk spoiler, an increase in power, in part thanks to an aluminium intake, and 7x14 (178x356mm) Rallye wheels which gave great handling. Typical for Buick, they retained luxury inside the car, with high-backed bucket seats, tuck 'n' roll vinyl, wood veneer and power windows. Performance extras included a Muncie manual gearbox which, though a little tricky to use off the line, didn't sap so much engine power.

Top speed:	129 mph (206 km/h)
0–60 mph (0–96 km/h):	7.1 sec
Engine type:	V8
Displacement:	455 ci (7,456 cc)
Transmission	4-speed manual
Max power:	300 bhp (224 kW) @ 4,700 rpm
Max torque:	410 lb ft (556 Nm) @ 3,200 rpm
Weight:	3,828 lb (1,740 kg)
Economy:	8 mpg (2.83 km/l)

Oldsmobile Vista Cruiser (1972)

Muscle cars were predominantly two-door hardtop coupes or convertibles, but such was the list of options available with many models, that a shrewd and wealthy buyer could come up with something completely different. That's what's happened with this full-specification Oldsmobile wagon, kitted out with a full 4-4-2 W-30 package. Only three of these cars were ever built and the package options have equipped it with heavy-duty suspension, front and rear anti-roll bars, a glass-fibre hood with cold-air intake for the huge 455ci (7,456cc) engine, a Positraction limited-slip differential, and 3.73:1 gears, plus it has the practicality of a family hauler with rear massive luggage space and a roof rack. In this particular car the engine has been fully balanced and blueprinted, meaning it puts out at least the factory-rated figures, but more likely it's actually slightly higher.

Top speed:	120 mph (192 km/h)
0–60 mph (0–96 km/h):	6.5 sec
Engine type:	V8
Displacement:	455 ci (7,456 cc)
Transmission	3-speed auto
Max power:	300 bhp (224 kW) @ 4,700 rpm
Max torque:	410 lb ft (556 Nm) @ 3,200 rpm
Weight:	4,150 lb (1,886 kg)
Economy:	7 mpg (2.48 km/l)

Pontiac GP Hurst SSJ (1972)

The looks might have been a long way from the muscle Pontiacs of the 1960s, but the 1972 Grand Prix at least had some of those classics' traits, thanks to the front V8 and rear-wheel-drive format. This was the third year for Hurst's involvement with the Grand Prix, and their additions included heavy-duty suspension and power front disc brakes, plus on the majority of cars, a Hurst shifted auto gearbox. The standard engine was the 400ci (6,554cc) D-port unit, underrated at 250bhp (186kW) with a dual plane intake and four-barrel carb. Buyers could opt for the mighty 455ci (7.4-litre) which was modified by Hurst Performance Research. It received blueprinting, a more aggressive camshaft and reworked cylinder heads, hence though rated at 250bhp (186kW), it was more like 350bhp (261kW). The interior had a curved dash facing the driver and centre console splitting high-back bucket seats.

Top speed:	125 mph (200 km/h)
0–60 mph (0–96 km/h):	8.0 sec
Engine type:	V8
Displacement:	455 ci (7,456 cc)
Transmission	3-speed auto
Max power:	250 bhp (186 kW) @ 3,600 rpm
Max torque:	375 lb ft (508 Nm) @ 2,400 rpm
Weight:	3,898 lb (1,771 kg)
Economy:	8 mpg (2.83 km/l)

Chevrolet Nova SS (1973)

The restyle in 1968 pumped up the Nova to make a bigger car, more intermediate sized but still a performance machine. It used the popular design style of a fastback roofline too, thus dispensing with the dull, regular sedan looks. Though the car was available with a big-block V8, by 1973 only the small-block V8 was on the option list. The Novas make great drag cars as they have much room under the hood for big engines and the owner of this street machine has installed a 454ci (7.4-litre) 'Rat' motor, bored out to 468ci and fully balanced internally. It has an Iskendarian performance camshaft, rare L88 big-block aluminium manifold and a Holley carburettor. Regular 454s are only rated at 450bhp (336kW), so with this one's upgrades, it'll do the quarter mile in 12.5 seconds. It uses the stock suspension, but lowered and stiffened, and a pair of traction bars at the rear launch the car straight.

Top speed:	144 mph (230 km/h)
0–60 mph (0–96 km/h):	4.8 sec
Engine type:	V8
Displacement:	468 ci (7,669 cc)
Transmission	3-speed auto
Max power:	525 bhp (391 kW) @ 6,200 rpm
Max torque:	520 lb ft (705 Nm) @ 4,200 rpm
Weight:	3,250 lb (1,477 kg)
Economy:	6 mpg (2.12 km/l)

Ford Mustang Mach 1 (1973)

Biggest of all Mustangs, the Mach 1 was a long way from the sporty pony car of the mid–1960s. But not only was it larger (rear passengers had space), it was heavier and more luxurious, but still handled, thanks to uprated suspension which included heavy-duty springs, front and rear anti-roll bars and revalved shocks. The car was strangled because of emissions compliance and as such the 302ci (5-litre) engine offered a fraction of the performance available in 1969 with the first Mach 1. Buyers could opt for the 351ci (5.8-litre) engine with a four-barrel carburettor if they wanted better performance. The 1973 Mach 1's stylish fastback lines and comfortable ride made it a hit, and over 35,000 cars were produced, which was good, considering the fuel crisis was hurting gas-guzzler sales. This model stayed for just one year more before the compact Mustang II made its debut.

Top speed:	110 mph (176 km/h)
0–60 mph (0–96 km/h):	10.4 sec
Engine type:	V8
Displacement:	302 ci (4,948 cc)
Transmission	3-speed auto
Max power:	136 bhp (101 kW) @ 4,200 rpm
Max torque:	232 lb ft (315 Nm) @ 2,200 rpm
Weight:	3,090 lb (1,404 kg)
Economy:	14 mpg (4.96 km/l)

Plymouth Road Runner (1973)

Less powerful and less handsome than its predecessors, the later Road Runners nonetheless did have all the right ingredients to turn them into performance machines. The Hemi had been dropped the previous year, but the 440ci (7.2-litre) top engine option came as part of the GTX package and could at least deliver an ultra reliable 280bhp (209kW). This car has been treated to a hefty engine reworking, with an overbore to 446ci (7,308cc), a full balanced rotating assembly, Offenhauser intake and dual Edelbrock four-barrel carburettors. Nitrous adds around 150bhp (112kW) to the set-up to make the car capable of 10-second quarter-miles. To lower power, the rear chassis rails are narrowed so 18.5-inch (470mm) Mickey Thompson tyres can fit under the stock arches. The chassis uses a six-point roll cage, and despite torsion bars up front, a drag-racing set-up is used out back.

Top speed:	135 mph (216 km/h)
0–60 mph (0–96 km/h):	4.9 sec
Engine type:	V8
Displacement:	446 ci (7,308 cc)
Transmission	3-speed auto
Max power:	430 bhp (321 kW) @ 6,200 rpm
Max torque:	515 lb ft (698 Nm) @ 3,800 rpm
Weight:	3,525 lb (1,602 kg)
Economy:	7 mpg (2.48 km/l)

Pontiac Formula 400 (1973)

Many manufacturers had given up with their muscle cars with the advent of stringent emissions laws, but Pontiac persevered with their Firebird and Trans Am models, de-tuning the engines where necessary. The thing was, while bhp was easy to limit with intake and fueling restrictions, torque often survived the changes unaffected, so the cars were still quick off the mark and gave drivers a good 'seat of the pants' feel. This made the Firebirds popular for those who either didn't mind paying extra for fuel or for people who simply wanted them as a second car. They still handled well with unitary construction and uprated double wishbone front suspension (with anti-roll bar) plus a leaf sprung live rear axle, and 11-inch (280mm) front discs helped too, as did 7x14-inch (178x356mm) five-spoke steel wheels. The car kept its energy-absorbing front fender, and even had a cold-air intake hood.

Top speed:	118 mph (188 km/h)
0–60 mph (0–96 km/h):	9.4 sec
Engine type:	V8
Displacement:	400 ci (6,554 cc)
Transmission	3-speed auto
Max power:	230 bhp (172 kW) @ 4,400 rpm
Max torque:	277 lb ft (375 Nm) @ 3,200 rpm
Weight:	3,766 lb (1,711 kg)
Economy:	12.4 mpg (4.39 km/l)

Chevrolet C10 (1974)

For 1973 Chevrolet's trucks were redesigned for a smoother and more modern appearance. Off came the dated drip rails, and on went doors which opened into the roof, using curved side glass. The truck's waistline was a sculpted curve which promoted a wide, brutal feel, and with their large engine bays, the new C10s soon became favourites for modification. This vehicle has been lowered with new springs at the front and blocks between the leaf springs and axle at the rear. More modern lightweight alloys plus radial tyres sit at each corner to further improve the handling. Under the hood there's now a 1970 454ci (7.4-litre) Corvette big-block which uses high-flow heads, a high-lift camshaft and a free- flowing dual exhaust. It all helps to push out enough to get this pick-up down the quarter-mile in 15 seconds at over 90mph (145km/h).

Top speed:	122 mph (195 km/h)
0–60 mph (0–96 km/h):	7.8 sec
Engine type:	V8
Displacement:	454 ci (7,439 cc)
Transmission	3-speed auto
Max power:	425 bhp (317 kW) @ 6,200 rpm
Max torque:	500 lb ft (678 Nm) @ 3,400 rpm
Weight:	4,045 lb (1,838 kg)
Economy:	7 mpg (2.48 km/l)

Pontiac Grand Ville (1974)

Pontiac, like many manufacturers, had reduced the number of performance models drastically by the mid-1970s. It had also reduced the number of convertibles it produced down to just one car (from six in the mid-1960s): the Grand Ville. Car peaked in size in the mid-1970s and the Grand Ville was no exception, being just short of 19ft (5.8m) in length and 6.5ft (2m) wide. For the first time ever the cars were fitted with radial tyres, a major development in road holding and safety, and as such the Grand Ville got RTS (Radial Tuned Suspension). Another first was the 5mph (8km/h) fenders which could absorb impacts up to the that speed, while a final bow was the use of leaded fuel which at least gave a modest horsepower increase to the 455ci (7.4-litre) engine. Luxury equipment included the power hood, double bench for six passengers, wood veneer and sound system.

Top speed:	124 mph (198 km/h)
0–60 mph (0–96 km/h):	7.8 sec
Engine type:	V8
Displacement:	455 ci (7,456 cc)
Transmission	3-speed auto
Max power:	250 bhp (186 kW) @ 4,000 rpm
Max torque:	370 lb ft (502 Nm) @ 2,800 rpm
Weight:	4,476 lb (2,034 kg)
Economy:	11 mpg (3.89 km/l)

Pontiac Trans Am SD455 (1974)

If you wanted a muscle car of the old school in 1974, there was only one manufacturer who you could go to, and that was Pontiac. They offered the SD455 (Super Duty) in limited numbers (just 953 were made) but the car was built almost as if the fuel crisis had never happened. Underneath it used a raised transmission tunnel, so the body could be mounted lower on the suspension, thus improving the centre of gravity for better handling, and the drive train was pure muscle, thanks to a 455ci (7.4-litre) with four-bolt main caps, forged pistons and a massive 800cfm Quadrajet carburettor. Inside it still looked 1970s, but it still showed the way dash layout was going, with a flat aluminium plate housing several dials for maximum driver information, plus a sporty three-spoke wheel. The car's performance meant the limited-slip differential and front disc brakes were much needed.

Top speed:	132 mph (211 km/h)
0–60 mph (0–96 km/h):	5.4 sec
Engine type:	V8
Displacement:	455 ci (7,456 cc)
Transmission	3-speed auto
Max power:	310 bhp (231 kW) @ 4,000 rpm
Max torque:	390 lb ft (529 Nm) @ 3,600 rpm
Weight:	3,655 lb (1,661 kg)
Economy:	13 mpg (4.60 km/l)

Lincoln Continental Coupe (1975)

Featuring every idea that improved luxury, the Lincoln Continental of 1975 was truly a masterpiece in high-class motoring. The chassis was separate in order to best insulate the cabin from road noise, and the springs and shocks were suitably soft to cushion the ride. The 9-inch (229mm) live axle was located by trailing arms, a torque arm and a transverse link to ensure good stability despite the wallowing ride, and 11.8-inch (300mm) vented discs were fitted at the front with optional anti-lock drums at the rear to stop the heavyweight. Externally, the styling remained conservative with classy lines, hidden headlights behind vacuum-operated panels, plus covered rear arches to emphasize the long and low appearance. Inside there was power everything and deep button velour bench seats, plus walnut veneer trim. An auxiliary fuel tank allowed an extra 100 miles (160km) of motoring.

Top speed:	118 mph (189 km/h)
0-60 mph (0–96 km/h):	10.4 sec
Engine type:	V8
Displacement:	460 ci (7,538 cc)
Transmission	3-speed auto
Max power:	215 bhp (160 kW) @ 4,000 rpm
Max torque:	338 lb ft (458 Nm) @ 2,800 rpm
Weight:	5,219 lb (2,372 kg)
Economy:	9 mpg (3.19 km/l)

Jeep CJ-7 (1977)

Jeep were owned by the American Motor Company (AMC) in the mid-1970s, and they responded to the growth of the leisure industry by building a modern version of the military Jeep: the CJ-7. The new vehicle had a longer wheelbase and got six-cylinder power, and was also the first jeep to become available with a Turbo-Hydramatic gearbox. Hard top and soft top versions were available, but they all used the same rugged separate ladder-style frame which was almost identical to that used on the World War II Jeeps. Semi-elliptical springs were used all around on the twin-live axle set-up, with part-time four-wheel drive coming on the manual version and the Quadratrac permanent four-wheel drive being optional on both the manual and automatic. As many were used off-road, the Jeep came with a four-point roll cage, but otherwise was little changed styling-wise from the original Jeep shape.

Top speed:	73 mph (117 km/h)
0–60 mph (0–96 km/h):	11.4 sec
Engine type:	In-line six
Displacement:	232 ci (3,801 cc)
Transmission	4-speed manual
Max power:	100 bhp (74 kW) @ 3,600 rpm
Max torque:	185 lb ft (251 Nm) @ 1,800 rpm
Weight:	3,100 lb (1,409 kg)
Economy:	17.2 mpg (6.09 km/l)

Pontiac Can Am (1977)

Refusing to let go of the notion that people liked their muscle cars, Pontiac developed the Cam Am in 1977 by dropping their 400ci (6,554cc) V8 engine into the Le Mans. The limited-edition car had just 3,177 models made, but they were great performers in their day. While the suspension was conventional, coming from the Le Mans, the Can Am received the RTS (Radial Tuned Suspension) package, and this included stiffer springs and shocks, front and rear anti-roll bars, and steel belted radial tyres. If sold in California the engine was the 185bhp (138kW) 403ci (6.6-litre) Oldsmobile V8, though everywhere else got the W-72 code high-output 400ci (6.5-litre) Pontiac V8 with dual-plane intake manifold and four-barrel carburettor. Inside, the dash housed multiple circular gauges and enclosed the driver. The three-spoke wheel and bucket seats boasted sporting intentions.

Top speed:	120 mph (192 km/h)
0–60 mph (0–96 km/h):	8.6 sec
Engine type:	V8
Displacement:	400 ci (6,554 cc)
Transmission	3-speed auto
Max power:	200 bhp (149 kW) @ 3,600 rpm
Max torque:	325 lb ft (440 Nm) @ 2,400 rpm
Weight:	4,140 lb (1,881 kg)
Economy:	11 mpg (3.89 km/l)

Lincoln Continental Mk V (1978)

The Lincoln range had always concentrated on luxury before light weight, but in 1978 that changed with the launch of the Mk V Continental. While looking almost identical to its predecessor the Lincoln Coupe, it was almost 500lb (227kg) lighter, which made it perform and handle better. This didn't stop designers having a field day with the options list, however, as the Mk V featured every possible extra to pamper the occupants. The Diamond Jubilee edition as shown celebrated the start of the Lincoln company 60 years earlier in 1918, after Henry Martyn Leland walked out of Cadillac having disagreed with GM boss William C. Durant about wartime production. Leland named the company after the president whom he had first voted for in 1864, and over a century later the Cadillac bearing the anniversary edition displayed glitz on wheels and sold over 72,000 in total for 1978.

Top speed:	118 mph (189 km/h)
0–60 mph (0–96 km/h):	9.8 sec
Engine type:	V8
Displacement:	460 ci (7,538 cc)
Transmission	3-speed auto
Max power:	210 bhp (157 kW) @ 4,200 rpm
Max torque:	357 lb ft (484 Nm) @ 2,200 rpm
Weight:	4,567 lb (2,075 kg)
Economy:	9 mpg (3.19 km/l)

Chevrolet Camaro modified (1978)

Camaros have seen modifications to make them faster, handle better, more luxurious, into glitzy show winners, and they've even been turned into automotive art pieces in museums. But the majority of them are still used to go down the drag strip very fast and this 1978 example does exactly that. It's been modified in a Pro Street style, meaning the larger race wheels are all sitting under the stock bodywork, but there's drag-racing suspension front and rear to keep weight down and help the car react to get the best possible traction off the startline. It can cover the quarter in just 9.8 seconds at a speed of over 140mph (225km/h), but is something of a crowd pleaser too, because it has exhaust headers facing upwards that have special fuel injectors and spark plugs in each pipe to shoot flames skywards. The front sits low, courtesy of adjustable airbag springs.

Top speed:	165 mph (264 km/h)
0–60 mph (0–96 km/h):	3.8 sec
Engine type:	V8
Displacement:	468 ci (7,669 cc)
Transmission:	3-speed auto
Max power:	540 bhp (403 kW) @ 6,800 rpm
Max torque:	510 lb ft (692 Nm) @ 4,200 rpm
Weight:	N/A
Economy:	7 mpg (2.48 km/l)

Chevrolet Corvette Pace Car (1978)

The Corvette was 25 years old in 1978, and to celebrate a limited edition Silver Anniversary model was produced. This car was also chosen to pace the 62nd Indianapolis and more than 6,000 replica cars were built and sold through select dealers. While the styling was all new, the chassis was carried over but the new car got the FE7 Gymkhana package which included heavy-duty front and rear shocks, fatter front and rear anti-roll bars, and higher rated springs. Front and rear discs were power assisted and all the chassis upgrades gave the Corvette tremendous grip and handling. Standard fitment was the L82 high-performance 350ci (5,735cc), with greater power than in other 'Vettes thanks to high-lift camshaft, special heads with bigger valves, and forged pistons. Induction comprised a four-barrel carb and dual snorkel air cleaner, while the dual exhaust was larger, for more flow.

Top speed:	125 mph (200 km/h)
0–60 mph (0–96 km/h):	8.2 sec
Engine type:	V8
Displacement:	350 ci (5,735 cc)
Transmission	3-speed auto
Max power:	220 bhp (164 kW) @ 5,200 rpm
Max torque:	260 lb ft (352 Nm) @ 3,600 rpm
Weight:	3,401 lb (1,545 kg)
Economy:	16 mpg (5.66 km/l)

Pontiac Trans Am (1978)

Displaying a large Firebird hood decal meant the 1978 Trans Am had to live up to expectations. The car had already satisfied owners with its handling, which it was praised for back in 1970, but the owner of this car has gone further still to enhance the cornering potential with uprated gas shocks, larger anti-roll bars front and rear, plus lowering springs. The brakes have a rear-disc upgrade and all are now vented. The engine is Pontiac's awesome big-block 455ci (7,456cc), tuned here with an Edelbrock intake, Crane high-lift camshaft, high-flow carburettor and dual exhaust with performance mufflers. The wheels are 8x16-inch (203x406mm) cross-spoke alloys with 255/50ZR rated tyres, a nice compromise between ride quality and handling. A front spoiler with air dam helps airflow over the car instead of underneath, while the rear spoiler provides downforce and stability at speed.

Top speed:	125 mph (200 km/h)
0–60 mph (0–96 km/h):	5.1 sec
Engine type:	V8
Displacement:	455 ci (7,456 cc)
Transmission	3-speed auto
Max power:	350 bhp (261 kW) @ 4,800 rpm
Max torque:	360 lb ft (488 Nm) @ 3,300 rpm
Weight:	3,511 lb (1,596 kg)
Economy:	9 mpg (3.19 km/l)

Chevrolet Monte Carlo (1979)

For the lowrider scene, the Monte Carlo is one of the most chosen cars to modify. Its suspension is ideal, being double wishbone front and a live axle rear supported on coil springs, to use hydraulic rams in place of the coils and shocks, therefore giving a fully moving set-up capable of doing any number of lowrider tricks. Yet even within the lowrider movement, fragmentation of styles has occurred and the cars which move now have their own competitions, while the show finish machines dual it out in huge halls where they can be displayed to maximum effect. Cars such as this show machine rarely get driven; inside it features an immaculate crushed-velour interior with no dash but a 6-inch (152mm) TV screen in the centre console. The interior extends into the trunk and externally there's a meticulously detailed flake paint with pinstriping and murals.

Top speed:	118 mph (189 km/h)
0–60 mph (0–96 km/h):	9.4 sec
Engine type:	V8
Displacement:	305 ci (4,998 cc)
Transmission	3-speed auto
Max power:	120 bhp (89 kW) @ 3,800 rpm
Max torque:	240 lb ft (596 Nm) @ 2,400 rpm
Weight:	3,169 lb (1,440 kg)
Economy:	15 mpg (5.31 km/l)

Pontiac Trans Am Anniversary (1979)

After almost axing the Trans Am in 1972, Pontiac decided to continue with it through the fuel conscious mid-1970s, and eventually they had a best seller late in that decade. The car shown was the 10th Anniversary model, all in silver and featuring the W72 400ci (6.6-litre) V8 plus four-speed Borg Warner Super T10 manual transmission. Though the Trans Am had been redesigned a year before, it featured much the same suspension layout but on the Anniversary model a special upgrade of the springs and shocks took care of cornering, along with 7x15-inch (178x381mm) Turbine alloys and wide radial tyres. Braking was also exceptional, with the four-wheel discs being power assisted. The interior looked ultra-modern for the time, having a machined aluminium dash with seven sport gauges, drilled three-spoke steering wheel, and silver vinyl high-back bucket seats.

Top speed:	125 mph (200 km/h)
0–60 mph (0–96 km/h):	7.0 sec
Engine type:	V8
Displacement:	400 ci (6,554 cc)
Transmission:	4-speed manual
Max power:	220 bhp (164 kW) @ 4,000 rpm
Max torque:	320 lb ft (434 Nm) @ 2,800 rpm
Weight:	3,551 lb (1,614 kg)
Economy:	12 mpg (4.25 km/l)

Dodge Li'l Red Express (1979)

Based on the Adventurer 150 pick-up, the Li'l Red Express Truck was Dodge's attempt at a factory custom pick-up, and it was a very successful one. It uses the truck's standard and very strong separate chassis with a 360ci (5,899cc) V8 mounted up front for extraordinary pulling power, in fact the engine made this one of the fastest production vehicles in Detroit in 1979. It used a police-spec build, with high-lift camshaft, large four-barrel 850cfm, windage tray to help the crankshaft rev free of oil, plus a high-flow air filter and chrome dress-up items. The suspension was uprated with stiffer shocks for improved handling, while the brakes got power assistance to help bring down the speed. While in 1978 the truck had seen just 2,188 buyers, but the following year this more than doubled to 5,118, with the only change that year being the quad headlights.

Top speed:	118 mph (189 km/h)
0–60 mph (0–96 km/h):	6.6 sec
Engine type:	V8
Displacement:	360 ci (5,899 cc)
Transmission	3-speed auto
Max power:	225 bhp (168 kW) @ 3,800 rpm
Max torque:	295 lb ft (400 Nm) @ 3,200 rpm
Weight:	3,855 lb (1,752 kg)
Economy:	14 mpg (4.96 km/l)

Checker A11 (1980)

For 30 years the Checker cab patrolled the streets of Manhattan, and for more than four decades it's been shown in nearly every bit of TV and movie footage about New York. Checker started producing cabs back in 1956 and they were liked because of their rugged build quality, large interior and basic functionality. The A11 made its debut in 1963 and came in either a 120-inch (3.05m) or 129-inch (3.28m) wheelbase with a ultra-strong steel chassis with X-brace. Wishbones and stiff coils up front plus uprated leaf springs out back kept the suspension simple, and while most cars had drum brakes only, later versions did get front discs. In the 1950s the standard engine was a 226ci (3,703cc) straight six, but later the Chevy small-block was chosen, often set up to run on propane. Huge fenders with overriders kept cars and pedestrians at bay, while the rear had room for eight passengers.

Top speed:	98 mph (157 km/h)
0–60 mph (0–96 km/h):	15.5 sec
Engine type:	V8
Displacement:	305 ci (4,998 cc)
Transmission	3-speed auto
Max power:	155 bhp (116 kW) @ 3,800 rpm
Max torque:	250 lb ft (339 Nm) @ 2,400 rpm
Weight:	3,830 lb (1,740 kg)
Economy:	15 mpg (5.31 km/l)

Pontiac Firebird Turbo T/A (1980)

While it looked like the Anniversary model, the Turbo T/A was very different indeed as it used a turbocharged V8 under the hood. The car was deemed good enough to pace that year's Indianapolis 500, and around 7,500 replicas made it on to the road. A WS6 suspension package was optional, and this gave recalibrated shocks and stiffer springs, as was a four-wheel disc brake set-up, which many buyers went for. Pontiac's 400ci (6.5-litre) and Oldsmobiles 403ci (6.6-litre) engines were proving too tough to get through emission, so engineers started out with a 401ci (6.5-litre) from the station wagons, then bolted a turbo to it, lowering the compression in the process to aid reliability. While it took some getting over the lag, the car was great once up to speed. An all-time high in sales was reached this year with 117,109 Trans Am being sold.

Top speed:	116 mph (186 km/h)
0–60 mph (0–96 km/h):	8.2 sec
Engine type:	V8
Displacement:	301 ci (4,932 cc)
Transmission	3-speed auto
Max power:	210 bhp (157 kW) @ 4,000 rpm
Max torque:	345 lb ft (468 Nm) @ 2,000 rpm
Weight:	3,673 lb (1,669 kg)
Economy:	16 mpg (5.66 km/l)

Chevrolet Corvette (1982)

By 1982 the Corvette was at the end of its third-generation guise which had started back in the late 1960s. Despite tweaks over time and a mild facelift with moulded fenders in 1980, a redesign was well overdue, but Chevrolet engineers wanted this 'Vette to go out with a bang so they produced the 'Collector Edition'. It came with silver paint and clot, silver leather door trim, a lift-up rear window, bronze T-tops, plus tasteful finned aluminium wheels measuring 8x15 inches (203x381mm) and fitted with 255/60 Goodyear Eagle tyres. The only engine available was at least very good, featuring Cross Fire fuel injection and computer-controlled engine management for great power, plus over 20mpg (7.08km/l) at steady highway speeds. The Corvette handled like a true sportscar thanks to full independent suspension, but inside was the most civilized ride yet in the model.

Top speed:	125 mph (200 km/h)
0-60 mph (0–96 km/h):	8.0 sec
Engine type:	V8
Displacement:	350 ci (5,735 cc)
Transmission	3-speed auto
Max power:	200 bhp (149 kW) @ 4,200 rpm
Max torque:	285 lb ft (386 Nm) @ 2,800 rpm
Weight:	3,425 lb (1,556 kg)
Economy:	20 mpg (7.08 km/l)

Oldsmobile Hurst Olds (1983)

Some 15 years after the first Hurst Olds, an anniversary collaboration model was debuted. A total of 3,000 were produced and each used a tuned 307ci (5.03-litre) small-block V8, though performance was a long way from the muscle cars available first time around. The cars were based on the mid-sized Cutlass, and though somewhat smaller than the first cars, retained the front-engined rear-drive format. Upgrades to the suspension included thicker anti-roll bars, stiffer springs and shocks, quicker ratio steering, shorter gearing and 7x15-inch (178x381mm) wheels. The emphasis was more on handling than power; the small-block was tuned with Delco electronic ignition, a Rochester carb and low restriction exhaust. Power went from 140bhp (104kW) to 180bhp (134kW). Typically Hurst was the shifter; the triple Lightning Rods meant first, second, and third gears could be selected manually.

Top speed:	120 mph (192 km/h)
0–60 mph (0–96 km/h):	8.4 sec
Engine type:	V8
Displacement:	307 ci (5,030 cc)
Transmission	Hurst 4–speed auto
Max power:	180 bhp (134k kW) @ 4,000 rpm
Max torque:	245 lb ft (332 Nm) @ 3,200 rpm
Weight:	3,535 lb (1,606 kg)
Economy:	17 mpg (6.02 km/l)

Chevrolet S10 pick-up (1984)

During the 1980s many imported trucks started to arrive in the US and were being snapped up as reliable, cheap work vehicles. Chevrolet responded by releasing the S10 and it soon became a best seller and a favourite with customizers. They started a trend known as minitrucks, where the pick-ups lost their utilitarian roots in favour of smooth street style and more radical modifications for performance and handling. This truck gets its lowered ride through drop spindles at the front and lowering blocks out back, but retains the stock springs as they're stiff as standard. The exterior mods feature a cowl induction hood, front and rear valance extensions, bullet tail lights and graphics. Billet aluminium wheels with low-profile radials help it corner with the best factory hot rod pick-ups, while the Vortech V6 engine is strong at low rpm and ideal for cruising.

Top speed:	108 mph (172 km/h)
0–60 mph (0–96 km/h):	11.2 sec
Engine type:	V6
Displacement:	262 ci (4,300 cc)
Transmission	4–speed auto
Max power:	160 bhp (119 kW) @ 4,000 rpm
Max torque:	230 lb ft (312 Nm) @ 2,800 rpm
Weight:	3,140 lb (1,427 kg)
Economy:	21 mpg (7.43 km/l)

Ford Mustang SVO (1984)

After years of being V8 or at least V6 powered, Ford's Special Vehicle Operations installed a four-cylinder engine, trying to convince people it was a high-performance model. Ford was reacting to high fuel prices and the demand for economy, so using the 'Fox' Mustang platform, fitted a turbo version of its 140ci (2.3-litre) engine. A drop in compression plus the forced induction gave it 143bhp (107kW). It wasn't enough, so power was upped further for 1985 1/2 cars to 175bhp (130kW) with 15psi boost. In 1986 power was increased to 205bhp (153kW) and 240lb ft (325Nm) torque. Handling was exceptional, thanks to light weight and a stiffer front anti-roll bar, rear anti-roll bar, uprated springs, and adjustable Koni shocks. Four-wheel disc brakes brought the stopping power up to scratch. Cheaper fuel brought the V8 back into fashion and the SVO was discontinued after 1986.

Top speed:	140 mph (224 km/h)
0–60 mph (0–96 km/h):	6.7 sec
Engine type:	In-line four
Displacement:	140 ci (2,294 cc)
Transmission	5-speed manual
Max power:	205 bhp (153 kW) @ 5,000 rpm
Max torque:	240 lb ft (325 Nm) @ 3,000 rpm
Weight:	3,036 lb (1,380 kg)
Economy:	25 mpg (8.85 km/l)

Mercury Capri 5.0L (1986)

Based on the Fox platform, the new-for-1979 Mercury Capri ran alongside its more successful Mustang stablemate during the 1980s. It was offered only as a hatchback with a bulbous back window, and came with slightly widened arches, and these less attractive points saw its sales gently decline throughout the 1980s. However, it still represented something of a performance bargain, thanks to a strong and revvy V8 with sequential fuel injection and excellent economy, plus it was at least practical, thanks to the hatchback rear. The RS package gave the car gas shocks and a pair of Quad shocks which were arranged horizontally to the rear axle to control wheel hop, plus meaty Goodyear Eagle 2125/60 tyres on 7x15-inch (244x381mm) alloy rims. With a very positive T5 Borg Warner manual gearbox, it made quite a driver's car, one which would accept all the same mods as a Mustang.

Top speed:	134 mph (214 km/h)
0–60 mph (0–96 km/h):	6.5 sec
Engine type:	V8
Displacement:	302 ci (4,948 cc)
Transmission	5-speed manual
Max power:	200 bhp (149 kW) @ 4,000 rpm
Max torque:	285 lb ft (386 Nm) @ 3,000 rpm
Weight:	3,150 lb (1,431 kg)
Economy:	23 mpg (8.14 km/l)

Shelby Omni GLH-S (1986)

Compacts made a big impact as soon as the VW Rabbit (Golf in Europe) debuted in 1975. Chrysler fought back in 1977 with its European-acquired Talbot, altering it for the US market and calling it the Omni. It was significant as it was the first front-wheel drive compact from a US manufacturer. Things hotted up when VW launched the GTi, but Dodge fought back with their 1984 134ci (2.2-litre) Omni GLH, tuned by Carroll Shelby. A year on they turbocharged the engine for 146bhp (109kW), then in 1986 released just 500 of their hottest version: the GLH-S. It ran an intercooler and different intake for the extra power and could do the quarter-mile in 14.9 seconds. Strut suspension with uprated springs and shocks made it handle like a dream, but torque steer was a problem under boost, barely controllable with the 205/50 Goodyear Eagle tyres.

Top speed:	130 mph (208 km/h)
0–60 mph (0–96 km/h):	6.4 sec
Engine type:	In-line four
Displacement:	135 ci (2,212 cc)
Transmission:	5-speed manual
Max power:	175 bhp (130 kW) @ 5,200 rpm
Max torque:	168 lb ft (227 Nm) @ 3,600 rpm
Weight:	2,300 lb (1,045 kg)
Economy:	20 mpg (7.08 km/l)

Chevy MC SS Aerocoupe (1987)

Performance started to make a welcome return to many American vehicles in the mid-1980s, and this saw the rebirth of the SS range on Chevrolet's Monte Carlos. The Aerocoupe had been designed and released in 1986 to compete with Ford's Thunderbird on the NASCAR tracks. Just 200 were built that year but it was well known the fastback style rear window and sloping nose could give the Monte Carlo a few extra mph on the top speed, much needed in NASCAR. More than 6,000 were built in 1987 and featured a separate chassis with stiffer springs, a larger front anti-roll bar, gas shocks and 7x15-inch (224x381mm) forged alloy rims with 225/60 tyres rated to 150mph (241km/h). The small-block engine got a hotter camshaft, new cylinder heads and intake, and an electronically controlled Rochester four-barrel carburettor. Monte Carlos outnumbered the Aerocoupe; 125,000 were produced.

Top speed:	130 mph (208 km/h)
0–60 mph (0–96 km/h):	8.2 sec
Engine type:	V8
Displacement:	305 ci (4,998 cc)
Transmission	4-speed auto
Max power:	190 bhp (142 kW) @ 4,800 rpm
Max torque:	240 lb ft (325 Nm) @ 3,200 rpm
Weight:	3,526 lb (1,602 kg)
Economy:	18 mpg (6.37 km/l)

Buick GNX (1987)

Something of a 'Q' car, the Buick GNX to many looked like just another US coupe car with a low-power V8. Those in the know gave it respect, because it had help from ASC/McLaren in developing its turbocharged V6 engine, which put huge horsepower and an even bigger hit of torque. The car started life in 1978 as a Buick Regal with turbo V6 producing just 150bhp (112kW). Four years later just 215 Grand Nationals (hence the 'GN') made it on the street, and by 1984 the power had been upped to 200bhp (149kW). Revised computer management and an air-to-air intercooler pushed power to 235bhp (175kW) for 1986, then a year on came McLaren's involvement for 276bhp (206kW). Although just 547 made it out in this guise, the GNX was worth searching out; it had modified and uprated suspension for better handling, with Panhard rod added to increase its cornering capability.

Top speed:	125 mph (198 km/h)
0–60 mph (0–96 km/h):	5.5 sec
Engine type:	V6
Displacement:	231 ci (3,785 cc)
Transmission	4-speed auto
Max power:	276 bhp (206 kW) @ 4,400 rpm
Max torque:	360 lb ft (488 Nm) @ 3,000 rpm
Weight:	3,545 lb (1,611 kg)
Economy:	23 mpg (8.14 km/l)

Buick T-Type (1987)

Buick built its T-Type through the mid-1980s and it was forerunner to the GNX. It was a tuner-friendly car and got a reputation for being able to blow away the eight-cylinder cars as soon as its turbo started to whistle and the boost came on strong. The T-Type shown has taken the forced induction to a whole new level, featuring a Ken Duttweiler race engine with variable boost for anything between 10-24psi. The gearbox is a specially prepared GM Turbo-Hydramatic, while the rear axle is an aftermarket Lenco unit located on three spherical-joint arms as per NASCAR racers. The chassis is made from tubular chrome-moly steel, so is light but extremely rigid, just what this car needs, as it can accelerate to 200mph (322km/h) in just 44 seconds. The windscreen has support bars for extra strength at high speeds, while the brakes are 13-inch (330mm) vented units all around.

Top speed:	226 mph (361 km/h)
0–60 mph (0–96 km/h):	2.8 sec
Engine type:	V6
Displacement:	260 ci (4,260 cc)
Transmission	3-speed auto
Max power:	967 bhp (721 kW) @ 6,500 rpm
Max torque:	877 lb ft (1,189 Nm) @ 5,200 rpm
Weight:	3,200 lb (1,454 kg)
Economy:	6 mpg (2.12 km/l)

Ford Mustang GT (1987)

Whearn the 'Fox' Mustang debuted in 1979, the public quickly warmed to it, and Ford knew they'd got themselves a winner. In fact they sold over a million up to 1993. The sheer amount on the road meant an aftermarket for performance parts quickly grew, and modifications go from the likes of a high-flow air filter to blown 700bhp (522kW) road cars which can cover the quarter-mile in under 10 seconds. This particular car is a heavily altered road machine, having been fitted with IMSA-style fender bulges to fit the 10-inch (250mm) and 13-inch (330mm) wide wheels, a new nose section, huge rear wing to aid downforce and some good engine mods to boost the already powerful V8. A larger throttle body to allow more air in plus a performance camshaft and free-flow exhaust help this car to run in 13.4 seconds on the quarter. Racecraft uprated suspension lowers the car and improves handling.

Top speed:	150 mph (240 km/h)
0–60 mph (0–96 km/h):	5.2 sec
Engine type:	V8
Displacement:	306 ci (5,014 cc)
Transmission	5-speed manual
Max power:	370 bhp (276 kW) @ 4,800 rpm
Max torque:	300 lb ft (406 Nm) @ 3,000 rpm
Weight:	3,560 lb (1,618 kg)
Economy:	17 mpg (6.02 km/l)

Ford T-bird Turbo Coupe (1987)

Ford's Thunderbird looked very dated and a way too conservative to be successful in the early 1980s. However, Ford was quick to realize it needed a change, so a restyle was in order for 1983. The new look was dramatic and it stirred up much interest again. The car looked dynamic and modern, but even so, in the rapidly changing 1980s, by 1987 it need a facelift. While the car's profile didn't change, it did get significant upgrades with flush-fitting lights and side glass, plus all new sheet metal. Ford also introduced two sporty versions: the 5.0L V8 and the Turbo Coupe. The latter used the former Mustang SVO unit, a turbo four-cylinder engine with intercooler, forged pistons and an oil cooler. Riding on the well-established Fox platform, it used upgraded suspension and 16-inch (406mm) rims. Through its Borg Warner T5 the car could attain 15-second quarter-miles.

Top speed:	137 mph (219 km/h)
0–60 mph (0–96 km/h):	7.1 sec
Engine type:	In-line four
Displacement:	140 ci (2,300 cc)
Transmission	5-speed manual
Max power:	190 bhp (142 kW) @ 4,600 rpm
Max torque:	180 lb ft (244 Nm) @ 3,600 rpm
Weight:	3,380 lb (1,536 kg)
Economy:	23 mpg (8.14 km/l)

Pontiac Fiero Formula (1988)

Conceived as competition to the forthcoming MR2 from Toyota, Pontiac's Fiero was launched in 1983 and was well designed, and proved a good seller for the company. It even paced the Indianapolis 500 in 1985, which inspired the launch of the GT model with low drag nose from the pace car. The Fiero used mainly parts-bin components, with a Chevrolet Chevette front strut set-up and the front subframe, including transaxle and engine mountings, from GM's X-body cars but adapted for the rear. This planted the engine mid-ships and gave the Fiero great handling. Just two motors were available, the first being the 'Iron Duke' four pot, so called because it was all-iron and ruggedly reliable, and the GM corporate 60-degree V6. The GT got this engine and a whole lot more, but the Formulas were the same in the drive train and suspension, yet slightly faster and cheaper.

Top speed:	120 mph (192 km/h)
0-60 mph (0–96 km/h):	7.4 sec
Engine type:	V6
Displacement:	173 ci (2,834 cc)
Transmission	5-speed manual
Max power:	135 bhp (101 kW) @ 5,200 rpm
Max torque:	170 lb ft (230 Nm) @ 3,600 rpm
Weight:	2,778 lb (1,262 kg)
Economy:	26 mpg (9.20 km/l)

Zimmer Quicksilver (1988)

Zimmer was a well-known van conversion company who in 1980 decided to produce a nostalgia coupe called the Golden Spirit. It used Ford running gear and that decade produced sales of 1,500. In 1986 GM designer Don Johnson penned the striking Quicksilver for the company, and while it was first shown that summer, it didn't start production until 1987. The car was based on the Pontiac Fiero so, unusually for a large coupe, it had its engine mid-mounted and handling was very good. The long nose was purely there for styling and was deceptive as there was no huge engine under it, though it did give incredible luggage space. The retro-styling also featured with the massive chrome fenders, as a nod to the glitzy cars like Lincolns and Cadillacs of the 1970s. The front suspension used wishbones, while the rear had struts, and discs front and rear uprated the braking.

Top speed:	121 mph (193 km/h)
0–60 mph (0–96 km/h):	9.7 sec
Engine type:	V6
Displacement:	173 ci (2,834 cc)
Transmission	3-speed auto
Max power:	140 bhp (104 kW) @ 5,200 rpm
Max torque:	170 lb ft (230 Nm) @ 3,600 rpm
Weight:	2,920 lb (1,327 kg)
Economy:	24 mpg (8.50 km/l)

Pontiac Turbo Trans Am (1989)

Built to commemorate the first production Trans Am of 1969, the Turbo Trans Am had echo that original car by being powerful, ground-breaking, and a driver's machine. Pontiac came up with the Turbo Trans Am, loaded with extras not just for performance but comfort too. All of the 20th anniversary models came with the WS6 handling package which comprised uprated springs and shocks, thicker anti-roll bars front and rear, a torque arm for better rear traction, and Panhard rod to locate the axle. These modifications benefited the car because it could pull 0.89g on a skid pad. The powerplant was straight from the previous year's Buick Grand National and used a Garrett turbo, intercooler and engine management for massive power comparable to a V8, though the V6 made the Trans Am lighter. All bar 50 of the 1,555 cars came with T-tops.

Top speed:	157 mph (251 km/h)
0–60 mph (0–96 km/h):	5.1 sec
Engine type:	V6
Displacement:	231 ci (3,785 cc)
Transmission	4-speed auto
Max power:	255 bhp (190 kW) @ 4,000 rpm
Max torque:	340 lb ft (461 Nm) @ 2,800 rpm
Weight:	3,406 lb (1,548 kg)
Economy:	27 mpg (9.56 km/l)

Saleen Mustang SSC (1989)

Steve Saleen modified his own racing Mustang in 1984 and soon became respected. That same year he produced three modified road Mustangs for buyers, then in 1985 modified and sold 139 hatchbacks and two convertibles. The following year sales grew, and on the strength of this, Saleen formed a racing team. By 1989 the race and road experience had led to the production of the SSC (Saleen Super Car). This was based on the 5.0L LX, and Saleen modified the suspension by adding stiffer springs and adjustable shocks, and upgraded the chassis by fitting a strut brace and four-point roll cage. A special Saleen leather interior and bodykit were also added. In the drive train the standard 5.0L had reworked heads, a larger throttle body, upgraded cam and bigger exhaust. The stock T5 transmission stayed, but the axle gears were swapped for 3.55:1 ratio, plus rear discs were fitted.

Top speed:	156 mph (250 km/h)
0–60 mph (0–96 km/h):	5.6 sec
Engine type:	V8
Displacement:	302 ci (4,948 cc)
Transmission	5-speed manual
Max power:	290 bhp (216 kW) @ 5,200 rpm
Max torque:	325 lb ft (440 Nm) @ 3,500 rpm
Weight:	3,425 lb (1,556 kg)
Economy:	22 mpg (7.79 km/l)

Shelby Dakota (1989)

The 1980s compact Dodge Ram Mini pick-up was actually a Mitsubishi truck, simply rebadged for sale in the USA. But this changed in 1987 when Dodge release their replacement, the home-grown Dakota. It was larger than most of its rivals and ran a 238ci (3.9-litre) V6, so was powerful. Two years on, Dodge offered a Sport version of the same truck, with blacked-out trim and alloys. Carroll Shelby took this one stage further with his Shelby Dakota later that same year, which had the V6 swapped for Chrysler's 318ci (5.4-litre) V8, giving it far more power. But it wasn't all about straight line acceleration, because Shelby also added stiffer springs and dampers, Goodyear Eagle tyres and a limited-slip differential, which meant that it handled very well. A sport steering wheel plus Shelby trim inside made this a new breed of sport truck.

Top speed:	119 mph (190 km/h)
0–60 mph (0–96 km/h):	8.5 sec
Engine type:	V8
Displacement:	318 ci (5,211 cc)
Transmission	4-speed auto
Max power:	175 bhp (130 kW) @ 4,000 rpm
Max torque:	270 lb ft (366 Nm) @ 2,000 rpm
Weight:	3,610 lb (1,640 kg)
Economy:	15 mpg (5.31 km/l)

Ford Thunderbird SC (1990)

The Thunderbird SC (Super Coupe) was introduced in 1989 and won Motor Trend magazine's 'Car of the Year'. The new super sleek styling was just part of the deal, as the car sat on an all-new platform with A-arms up front and a full independent rear with pivoting axle halfshafts. The SC was a celebration of 35 years of the Thunderbird, and came with black wheel and paint. It also had beefier springs and gas shocks, plus four-wheel disc brakes which were vented at the front to aid cooling. While T-birds of the past had used four cylinders, V6s or V8s, the new car was exclusively V6 powered, and the SC used an Eaton supercharger in conjunction with sequential fuel injection to boost output. Dual tailpipes was one way of telling the SC from regular Thunderbirds, along with the 7x16-inch (178x406mm) alloys on 225/60 Goodyear Eagle tyres.

Top speed:	141 mph (226 km/h)
0–60 mph (0–96 km/h):	7.4 sec
Engine type:	V6
Displacement:	231 ci (3,600 cc)
Transmission	5-speed manual
Max power:	210 bhp (157 kW) @ 4,000 rpm
Max torque:	315 lb ft (427 Nm) @ 2,600 rpm
Weight:	3,701 lb (1,682 kg)
Economy:	17 mpg (6.02 km/l)

Lincoln Mk VII LSC (1990)

Marketed as a grown-up Mustang, the Lincoln LSC ran on an identical Fox platform and came with the same specification engine as the street-brawling 5.0 GT Mustang. Although somewhat heavier than the smaller car, the LSC (luxury super coupe) had tremendous pick up and the standard auto gearbox harnessed the power well. Where it was vastly superior to other cars on the same platform (such as the earlier Thunderbird and Mercury Cougar) was with its ride quality, which was super smooth, thanks to air suspension. It was still an okay handler because of fattened anti-roll bars, ABS-assisted disc brakes all around and 7x16-inch (178x406mm) alloys with Goodyear Eagle 225/60 tyres. Inside it had luxury features such as climate control, 12-way power seats, cruise control, tilt column, plus power windows, mirrors, door locks and steering. The only optional was leather seats.

Top speed:	137 mph (219 km/h)
0–60 mph (0–96 km/h):	8.0 sec
Engine type:	V8
Displacement:	302 ci (4,948 cc)
Transmission	4-speed auto
Max power:	225 bhp (168 kW) @ 4,200 rpm
Max torque:	300 lb ft (407 Nm) @ 3,000 rpm
Weight:	3,779 lb (1,717 kg)
Economy:	16 mpg (5.66 km/l)

Callaway Speedster (1991)

Unusually, it was a 1987 twin turbo Alfa Romeo GTV6 which had impressed Chevrolet bosses enough to call on the services of Reeves Callaway. With his Alfa boasting 230bhp (172kW), well up on the stock model, he was asked to do the same with a Corvette, and three years later the Callaway 'Sledgehammer' was debuted. It was an 880bhp (656kW) supercar with the body redesigned by French-Canadian stylist Paul Deutschman. The Speedster's appearance at the Los Angeles Auto Show in 1991 led to 50 orders. Underneath the dramatic low body, with 7 inches (178mm) chopped out of the stock Corvette's screen, were adjustable coil-over shocks, plus Brembo brakes using vented discs and four-pot callipers. The engine was stripped and fitted with a forged crankshaft and new pistons to allow the fitting of RotoMaster turbos. Although pricey at $107,000 new, the cars have only ever gone up in value.

Top speed:	185 mph (296 km/h)
0–60 mph (0–96 km/h):	4.5 sec
Engine type:	V8
Displacement:	350 ci (5,735 cc)
Transmission	6-speed manual
Max power:	420 bhp (313 kW) @ 4,250 rpm
Max torque:	562 lb ft (762 Nm) @ 2,500 rpm
Weight:	3,200 lb (1,454 kg)
Economy:	10.4 mpg (3.68 km/l)

Chevrolet 454SS (1991)

When the general public started to become less concerned about fuel costs in the 1980s, manufacturers once again began a power chase and with America's pick-up obsession, a new market was soon born: the muscle truck. Chevrolet was one of the first to indulge the market with its 1989 454 C1500 truck, which had been restyled just a year before, so looked very modern. Underneath the SS454 was still very trucklike, with a strong ladder frame chassis and carlike wishbone suspension, but a leaf spring rear. All spring rates were stiffened and Bilstein shocks were fitted to improve handling. Also modified was the steering, with quicker gearing to aid response through the new 225/60 tyres. The 454ci (7.4-litre) came from the standard C/K 3/4 and 1-ton pick-ups, and with its long stroke was designed for low rpm torque. The rear end was fitted with 4.10:1 gears for acceleration.

Top speed:	120 mph (192 km/h)
0–60 mph (0–96 km/h):	7.2 sec
Engine type:	V8
Displacement:	454 ci (7,439 cc)
Transmission	3-speed auto
Max power:	255 bhp (190 kW) @ 4,000 rpm
Max torque:	405 lb ft (549 Nm) @ 2,400 rpm
Weight:	4,535 lb (2,061 kg)
Economy:	10 mpg (3.54 km/l)

Chevrolet Corvette ZR1 (1991)

The most advanced engine ever in a Corvette was the LT5 V8, developed by Lotus for the limited edition ZR1. The model began production a year prior to this model after much hype, and looked different to regular 'Vettes because of the widened rear bodywork which allowed the fitting of 11x17-inch (279x432mm) alloys with 315/35 tyres. Lotus based the engine on Chevy's small-block V8, but started with an aluminium-alloy block. Scratch-built heads used two-cams-per-bank operating on four valves per cylinder. The induction also had two ports and injectors per cylinder and only one of each operated below 3,500rpm. Above this on the throttle the other port and injector would open up and allow the full 405bhp (302kW) on later models to be unleashed. Other high-tech gadgetry included the suspension; the driver could select Touring, Sport and Performance settings.

Top speed:	180 mph (288 km/h)
0–60 mph (0–96 km/h):	5.0 sec
Engine type:	V8
Displacement:	350 ci (5,735 cc)
Transmission	6-speed manual
Max power:	405 bhp (302 kW) @ 5,800 rpm
Max torque:	371 lb ft (503 Nm) @ 4,800 rpm
Weight:	3,519 lb (1,599 kg)
Economy:	14.7 mpg (5.20 km/l)

Dodge Spirit R/T (1991)

The first Sprit came about in 1988 as a replacement for the ageing Aries compact, but unlike the Aries, came only as a four-door sedan. It looked like any other sedan around at the time, but Dodge turned up the wick when they debuted the limited edition R/T late in 1990. It used the engine which had been developed throughout the 1980s and which had already seen duty in the Omni GLH-S and Shelby Charger GLH, this being a 134ci (2.2-litre) turbocharged engine with twin balancer shafts to keep vibration to a minimum. Through an intercooler and with twin overhead camshaft, its output was enough to beat many of the original muscle cars on the quarter-mile, but the Spirit still had the practicality of a four-door sedan. Inside the driver's car they continued with sporty bucket seats and a Getrag five-speed manual shift. Just 1,300 models were made in the one year.

Top speed:	130 mph (208 km/h)
0-60 mph (0–96 km/h):	6.9 sec
Engine type:	In-line four
Displacement:	135 ci (2,212 cc)
Transmission	5-speed manual
Max power:	224 bhp (167 kW) @ 6,000 rpm
Max torque:	217 lb ft (294 Nm) @ 2,800 rpm
Weight:	3,060 lb (1,390 kg)
Economy:	25 mpg (8.85 km/l)

GMC Syclone (1991)

Based on GMC's Sonoma truck, the Syclone might not have had a great deal of load space, but buyers weren't after that, nor was GMC trying to sell them a load lugger. The truck was Ferrari quick though, in fact faster than a Ferrari 348 and even the mighty Corvette ZR-1. But it wasn't all about straight-line performance, because with four-wheel drive, the Syclone was also incredibly able in corners too. GMC kept the bias towards rear-wheel drive with a 35:65 front/rear split of torque, and added a limited-slip differential in the live rear axle to ensure the best possible traction. They also fitted the truck with lowered/uprated springs and shocks to further enhance its sporting feel. The Syclone quickly built up a strong following in the USA, and while as standard it could run the quarter-mile in 14 seconds, the current quarter-mile record for a road-going Syclone stands in the 10s.

Top speed:	125 mph (200 km/h)
0–60 mph (0–96 km/h):	5.2 sec
Engine type:	V6
Displacement:	262 ci (4,293 cc)
Transmission:	4-speed auto
Max power:	280 bhp (209 kW) @ 4,400 rpm
Max torque:	350 lb ft (474 Nm) @ 3,600 rpm
Weight:	3,422 lb (1,555 kg)
Economy:	25 mpg (8.85 km/l)

Pontiac Firebird GTA (1991)

The GTA stood for Gran Turismo Americano and was a development of the original Pontiac GTO name which meant so much to muscle-car enthusiasts. Hence, the GTA for 1987–1992 had to be good. With the 350ci (5.7-litre) high-output engine, it finally got the power that early-1980s versions had lacked, and once again represented a great muscle machine which was quick in a straight line, and also was economical and could handle with the best supercar exotica. Although still a live axle chassis, the rear end was held in check well, thanks to a torque arm, Panhard rod and lower trailing arms. Being on the same platform as the Camaro meant MacPherson struts up front, and disc brakes were fitted all around, completing the very axle package. The engine got Tuned Port Injection which increased power while retaining impressive mpg, considering the car's potential.

Top speed:	150 mph (240 km/h)
0–60 mph (0–96 km/h):	6.7 sec
Engine type:	V8
Displacement:	350 ci (5,735 cc)
Transmission	4-speed auto
Max power:	240 bhp (179 kW) @ 4,400 rpm
Max torque:	340 lb ft (461 Nm) @ 3,200 rpm
Weight:	3,519 lb (1,599 kg)
Economy:	18 mpg (6.37 km/l)

Chevrolet Camaro Z28 (1992)

In 1982 Chevrolet had released the third-generation Camaro and it had sold well, lasting for 10 years and growing in power during that time. As always, the Z28 was the performance option, and in 1992 it was the 25th anniversary of the model, but also the last year for that generation, so the car went out with a bang. It received a Heritage appearance package in either red, white or black and this consisted of bolt-on spoilers plus side skirts to modernize its appearance. The live rear axle came with a limited-slip differential and 3.42:1 gears, and was located on lower trailing arms plus a Panhard rod for better cornering feel. The 305ci (5-litre) V8 had electronic Tuned Port Injection with an individual runner for each cylinder, and Chevrolet made the car into more of a driver's machine by fitting a five-speed manual gearbox.

Top speed:	137 mph (219 km/h)
0–60 mph (0–96 km/h):	6.5 sec
Engine type:	V8
Displacement:	305 ci (4,998 cc)
Transmission	5-speed manual
Max power:	235 bhp (175 kW) @ 4,400 rpm
Max torque:	300 lb ft (406 Nm) @ 3,200 rpm
Weight:	3,105 lb (1,411 kg)
Economy:	13.8 mpg (4.89 km/l)

Chevrolet Caprice modified (1992)

The Caprice, which was first launched 1990, had ultra-smooth styling and lent itself well to customizing. Being a practical car, too, and coming with a V8 as standard meant it soon got the attention of hot rodders. Station-wagon versions often got used as aftermarket manufacturers' show vehicles come parts haulers, and this is one has been built along those lines but has gone a step forward and backward at the same time. This Caprice features styling touches from a 1957 Chevy Nomad, including the rear three-quarter panels and tail lights, side trim, hood spears and a classic set of polished American Racing Torque-Thrust rims on 275/50 Pirelli tyres. The interior continues on a 1950s theme with red and white tuck 'n' roll, but has rearward-facing back seats to best utilize the huge rear space. Power comes from Throttle Body fuel-injected small-block Chevy V8.

Top speed:	120 mph (192 km/h)
0–60 mph (0–96 km/h):	9.8 sec
Engine type:	V8
Displacement:	350 ci (5,735 cc)
Transmission	4-speed auto
Max power:	180 bhp (134 kW) @ 4,000 rpm
Max torque:	300 lb ft (406 Nm) @ 2,400 rpm
Weight:	4,120 lb (1,872 kg)
Economy:	18 mpg (6.37 km/l)

Dodge Stealth R/T Turbo (1992)

The Stealth began production in 1990, and although called a Dodge, was actually a rebodied Mitsubishi 3000GT and, as such, a brilliant driver's machine. It was even put together on Mitsubishi's assembly line in Japan. An identical chassis, engine, gearbox and suspension was shared between the two. MacPherson struts all around with trailing arms at the rear and anti-roll bars at each end kept handling sharp. The iron engine had extra ribs for rigidity, while the top end featured alloy dual cam 24v heads. In R/T guise it managed 222bhp (166kW) but the most powerful was the R/T Turbo, which had twin Mitsubishi TD04 turbos with intercoolers for 10psi boost and 300bhp (224kW). The hi-tech gadgetry included four-wheel drive and four-wheel steer, front spoiler lowering at 50mph (80km/h) to re-direct airflow around the car, and a rear spoiler changing its angle to increase downforce at speed.

Top speed:	151 mph (241 km/h)
0–60 mph (0–96 km/h):	5.3 sec
Engine type:	V6
Displacement:	181 ci (2,966 cc)
Transmission	5-speed manual
Max power:	300 bhp (224 kW) @ 6,000 rpm
Max torque:	307 lb ft (416 Nm) @ 2,500 rpm
Weight:	3,803 lb (1,728 kg)
Economy:	18 mpg (6.37 km/l)

Dodge Viper (1992)

Initially a concept at the 1989 Detroit international Auto Show, the Viper had a massive public response, and Dodge knew it would have to go into production. Theory was that it would be a modern-day 427 Cobra, and in fact it had a similar layout and, like the original 427 model, huge torque thanks to the biggest production engine in the world at the time. The monster motor was caged in a tubular steel chassis which also had independent wishbone suspension front and rear. Drive was through the rear wheels and torque went through a specially designed Borg Warner gearbox with a lockout shift mechanism to go from first gear straight to fourth under light throttle. The motor was so tractable it could pull from as little as 500rpm in sixth gear. The body was constructed in reinforced glass-fibre to help keep it light, while the brakes were 13-inch (330mm) Brembo discs and callipers.

Top speed:	162 mph (260 km/h)
0-60 mph (0–96 km/h):	5.4 sec
Engine type:	V10
Displacement:	488 ci (7,998 cc)
Transmission	6-speed manual
Max power:	400 bhp (298 kW) @ 4,600 rpm
Max torque:	488 lb ft (661 Nm) @ 3,600 rpm
Weight:	3,477 lb (1,580 kg)
Economy:	12 mpg (4.25 km/l)

Ford Mustang 5.0 LX (1992)

There are few cars which can claim as big an impact on the 1980s muscle-car scene as the 5.0L Mustang. For a bargain price it gave enthusiasts a torquey V8 engine, enough luxury and good handling, exactly what buyers wanted, hence it was a massive hit. Although the 1987–93 GT was touted as the performance version, the base LX model came without the range-topping GT's bodykit, hence it weighed less and was quicker. Motoring magazines which had the car on test had the T5 manual five-speed versions running low-14-second quarter-miles, surpassing many higher powered muscle cars of the 1960s and 1970s. It was definitely much better in handling too because of progressive rate springs and 'Quadra-shock' horizontal shocks at either side of the axle to prevent wheel hop and therefore improve traction. The LX was so good that the US police chose it for high-speed patrol work.

Top speed:	138 mph (220 km/h)
0–60 mph (0–96 km/h):	6.2 sec
Engine type:	V8
Displacement:	302 ci (4,948 cc)
Transmission	5-speed manual
Max power:	225 bhp (168 kW) @ 4,400 rpm
Max torque:	300 lb ft (406 Nm) @ 3,000 rpm
Weight:	3,145 lb (1,429 kg)
Economy:	22 mpg (7.79 km/l)

GMC Typhoon (1992)

GMC had plans to improve its image among performance enthusiasts, so in 1991 started by creating the ultimate hi-power pick-up, the GMC Syclone. A year later, with the continuing popularity of Sport Utility Vehicles, it debuted the Typhoon, which had far more room; enough for five adults plus their luggage, in fact. The Typhoon sat on the same separate chassis, with live rear axle and 11-inch (279mm) ABS-assisted vented discs. The engine was from the GMC Jimmy, all cast-iron but uprated from the stock 165bhp (123kW) thanks to an intercooled turbo and altered engine management. The torque was split 35:65 front/rear with a mechanical centre differential and viscous coupling, though the live rear axle also had a limited-slip differential for better traction. The four-speed auto could only just handle the power, evident from the interior sticker that read: 'Do not tow with this vehicle.'

Top speed:	124 mph (198 km/h)
0–60 mph (0–96 km/h):	5.4 sec
Engine type:	V6
Displacement:	262 ci (4,293 cc)
Transmission	4-speed auto
Max power:	280 bhp (209 kW) @ 4,400 rpm
Max torque:	350 lb ft (474 Nm) @ 3,600 rpm
Weight:	3,822 lb (1,737 kg)
Economy:	25 mpg (8.85 km/l)

Cadillac Allanté (1993)

The 1987–1993 Allanté was certainly no ordinary Cadillac. For a start, it was styled by Italian design house Pininfarina, and while it used a modified Eldorado platform, the all-start suspension was much tweaked in order to make the car feel more European. Sales were slow for the first few years, and so GM made changes to try and improve the situation, including more power and active suspension, but the most significant model came in 1993 with the fitting of the incredible 32v Northstar V8 in the front-wheel drive configuration. This engine was so advanced it could run for 100,000 miles (160,000km) without servicing. It worked well in conjunction with a four-speed automatic which was also computer-managed and could retard the engine's timing slightly before each gear change to smooth out the shifts. Vented discs all around and 16-inch (406mm) wheels ensured great handling too.

Top speed:	145 mph (232 km/h)
0–60 mph (0–96 km/h):	7.0 sec
Engine type:	V8
Displacement:	279 ci (4,571 cc)
Transmission	4-speed auto
Max power:	290 bhp (216 kW) @ 5,600 rpm
Max torque:	290 lb ft (393 Nm) @ 4,400 rpm
Weight:	3,720 lb (1,690 kg)
Economy:	17 mpg (6.02 km/l)

Chevrolet Suburban (1993)

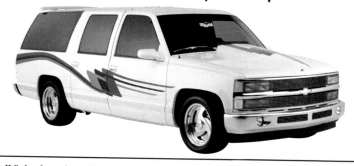

All Suburbans from Chevrolet have been massive, and over time (they've been in production for nearly 40 years) they have gradually taken on more luxury and style and now represent one of the best SUVs (Sport Utility Vehicle) in a packed and ever-growing market. While they offer a great deal as standard, as always for some people it's not enough, and this example show just how well the vehicles receives modifications. The car has gone through massive lowering, being some 3.5 inches (89mm) down at the front, but a huge 5 inches (127mm) lower at the rear. This helps handling, as do the 8x17-inch (203x432mm) billets with 255/50 tyres. But it's inside where most changes have occurred: power leather seats, a 56-piece Bahia Rosewood overlay set, and huge in-car entertainment system with TV, VCR and video game player. Power is via full-dressed computer-managed small-block Chevy.

Top speed:	98 mph (157 km/h)
0–60 mph (0–96 km/h):	11.2 sec
Engine type:	V8
Displacement:	350 ci (5,735 cc)
Transmission	4–speed auto
Max power:	210 bhp (157 kW) @ 4,000 rpm
Max torque:	300 lb ft (406 Nm) @ 2,800 rpm
Weight:	4,675 lb (2,125 kg)
Economy:	14.4 mpg (5.10 km/l)

Ford Mustang Cobra (1993)

Having debuted in 1979, the Series 3 Mustang was well overdue for replacement come 1993. To show what a performer it could be, Ford made the best version possible with their aftermarket performance equipment. Its engineers used the 215bhp (160kW) GT as a base then added a new grille, sill panel mouldings, rear valance and spoiler, and gave the model special 17-inch (432mm) wheels and low-profile tyres. Lowered suspension, with softer linear rate springs, improved the car's handling and gave a more civilized ride. Power was up to 235bhp (175kW) thanks to the addition of GT40 heads, a special intake, bigger throttle body, larger injectors, a higher-lift roller camshaft and roller rockers. Disc brakes all around improved braking significantly, but the car was like the GT. The Cobra R was a race-only version with air-con, radio and rear seats removed, thus saving weight.

Top speed:	151 mph (242 km/h)
0–60 mph (0–96 km/h):	5.8 sec
Engine type:	V8
Displacement:	302 ci (4,948 cc)
Transmission:	5-speed manual
Max power:	235 bhp (175 kW) @ 5,000 rpm
Max torque:	285 lb ft (386 Nm) @ 4,000 rpm
Weight:	3,225 lb (1,465 kg)
Economy:	21 mpg (7.43 km/l)

Callaway Camaro C8 (1994)

Callaway's Corvettes had already established his name as top in the high performance league during the early 1990s, but in 1994 turned his attention to the new Camaro and produced the C8. This was based on the stock Camaro but featured many aftermarket upgrades already available, plus many designed by Callaway themselves. The chassis used a strut brace across the engine to stiffen the front end and a subframe connectors to make the unitary structure more rigid. Eibach springs and Koni shocks at each corner stiffened the ride and enabled 0.94g on the skid pad, while the vented disc brakes came from Brembo and were 13 -inch (330mm) at the front and 11-inch (279mm) at the rear. The bodykit was designed by Paul Deutschman, and providing the performance to back the looks was a stroked small-block Chevy with special Callaway induction and electronics.

Top speed:	172 mph (275 km/h)
0-60 mph (0–96 km/h):	4.7 sec
Engine type:	V8
Displacement:	383 ci (6,276 cc)
Transmission	6-speed manual
Max power:	404 bhp (301 kW) @ 5,750 rpm
Max torque:	412 lb ft (558 Nm) @ 4,750 rpm
Weight:	3,373 lb (1,533 kg)
Economy:	17 mpg (6.02 km/l)

Chevrolet Corvette modified (1994)

The Corvettes through all its generations has always been a tuner's dream. A lightweight bodyshell, powerful V8 and (from the late 1960s) fully independent suspension, means all the right ingredients are there in stock form. As the car went into the 1990s, it increasingly became high-tech, but so did the aftermarket with it, hence instead of a carburettor or ignition upgrade, the engines of the generation-four cars got chipped instead, meaning their engine management was improved for more performance. This example has received not just an engine chip, but Chevy's own Performance Handling Package and a set of 1996 Corvette 17-inch (432mm) alloys. An upgraded exhaust releases more power and makes this Corvette into a more finely tuned driver's car which can do the quarter-mile in low-13-second times and pull 0.9 lateral g. The bodywork has a subtle, but effective, trunk spoiler.

Top speed:	158 mph (252 km/h)
0–60 mph (0–96 km/h):	5.0 sec
Engine type:	V8
Displacement:	350 ci (5,735 cc)
Transmission:	4-speed auto
Max power:	330 bhp (246 kW) @ 5,500 rpm
Max torque:	340 lb ft (461 Nm) @ 4,000 rpm
Weight:	3,504 lb (1,592 kg)
Economy:	14 mpg (4.96 km/l)

Boyd Smoothster (1995)

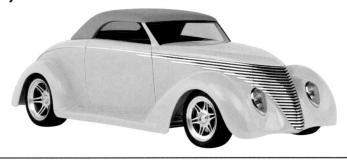

Boyd Coddington's name became synonymous with high-tech, high-buck hot rodding during the 1980s and this continued into the 1990s while his projects grew increasingly wild. His aim was to build hot rods which used classic looks but with a modern twist, and the majority of the machines his company made went out to win trophies and garner the Coddington name more recognition. The Smoothster was designed to win the prestigious 'America's Most Beautiful Roadster' award and did so in 1995. It featured hand-made sheet aluminium bodywork over a custom steel frame with one-off billet aluminium A-arms at either end for fully independent suspension. The Corvette engine is untouched except for a rework of its looks but is powerful in stock trim. The 17-inch (432mm) and 18-inch (457mm) wheels' six-spoke pattern is replicated in the twin tailpipes. The roof is a removable Carson-style top.

Top speed:	122 mph (195 km/h)
0–60 mph (0–96 km/h):	6.0 sec
Engine type:	V8
Displacement:	350 ci (5,735 cc)
Transmission	4-speed auto
Max power:	300 bhp (224 kW) @ 5,000 rpm
Max torque:	330 lb ft (447 Nm) @ 2,400 rpm
Weight:	N/A
Economy:	17 mpg (6.02 km/l)

Chevrolet Camaro Z28 (1995)

From 1993 to 1997 the fourth-generation Camaro appeared and carried on with the Z28 high performance option. Chevrolet gave purchasers a lot of bang-for-the-buck for the sticker price of less than $20K. The car was still of unitary construction with chassis subframes at each end, but in Z28 form gas-pressurized shocks were fitted all around and a torque arm plus Panhard rod at the rear located the live axle well for improved handling. Up front once again the venerable small-block Chevy was fitted, but in the latest LT1 guise which meant multi-point fuel injection, aluminium heads, a roller camshaft, 10.4:1 compression and an Optispark ignition system. The Z28 made excellent use of this motor through a six-speed manual. To reduce weight as much as possible all panels except the rear fenders, hood and roof were manufactured from plastic.

Top speed:	155 mph (248 km/h)
0–60 mph (0–96 km/h):	6.1 sec
Engine type:	V8
Displacement:	350 ci (5,735 cc)
Transmission	6-speed manual
Max power:	275 bhp (205 kW) @ 5,000 rpm
Max torque:	325 lb ft (440 Nm) @ 2,400 rpm
Weight:	3,475 lb (1,579 kg)
Economy:	19 mpg (6.73 km/l)

Dodge Ram (1995)

The first of the brand new Rams from Dodge came along in 1994 and made the outgoing model seem well past it sell-by date. The new Ram's styling was very bold but made it easily distinguishable on the street. The raised hood and low-down headlights was a popular style, and became the look for Dodge's later Dakota SUV. The top Ram model used a cast-iron version of the Dodge Viper's V10 engine, and this made it the biggest motor ever in a production pick-up, something which Dodge proudly advertised. The powerplant was designed to be a torquey low rpm unit, running sequential fuel injection and 8.6:1 compression. Underneath, a strong ladder-type chassis was separate to the body and the suspension comprised front double wishbones, a rear live axle rear on leaf springs, all basic but functional and rugged, with optional 4WD.

Top speed:	113 mph (180 km/h)
0–60 mph (0–96 km/h):	7.5 sec
Engine type:	V10
Displacement:	488 ci (7,998 cc)
Transmission	4-speed auto
Max power:	300 bhp (224 kW) @ 4,000 rpm
Max torque:	440 lb ft (596 Nm) @ 2,800 rpm
Weight:	5,383 lb (2,446 kg)
Economy:	13.6 mpg (4.81 km/l)

Ford Mustang Cobra R (1995)

The 'R' stood for race and Ford's Special Vehicle Team (SVT) made sure they had the fastest Mustang ever built on their hands. Based on a regular Cobra, the R was stripped of its sound-deadening, radio, rear seats, rear-window defrost, electric windows and air-conditioning to save as much weight as possible. The car even came with basic trim seats, as Ford knew these would be changed for race versions by owners. The suspension used uprated Eibach progressive rate springs along with Koni adjustable shocks, while up front sat a thicker anti-roll bar. The engine came from Ford's Lightning truck, this being a 351ci (5.8-litre) V8, upgraded with GT40 heads, a special Cobra intake, SVO camshaft and larger mass air meter. The motor put out so much torque that Ford had to fit the stronger Tremec 3550 gearbox. With racing slicks the R could easily do 12-second quarter-mile passes.

Top speed:	150 mph (240 km/h)
0-60 mph (0–96 km/h):	5.5 sec
Engine type:	V8
Displacement:	351 ci (5,751 cc)
Transmission:	5-speed manual
Max power:	300 bhp (224 kW) @ 4,800 rpm
Max torque:	365 lb ft (494 Nm) @ 3,750 rpm
Weight:	3,325 lb (1,511 kg)
Economy:	17 mpg (6.02 km/l)

Lincoln Mk VIII (1995)

Lincoln has long been Ford's premium brand, with a strong luxury bias. When the Mk VIII came along in 1992 (it remained in production until 1999) it was luxury to a new level. Using developments from the Mk VII, the new model was superior and also had swoopy modern looks which meant it could go head-to-head with the import luxury cars such as Lexus and BMW. It sat on Thunderbird platform and received much praise for it, but testers also praised the all-alloy 32-valve Modular engine which, coupled to the new 4R70W automatic overdrive transmission, made the Mk VIII very swift yet refined. Handling was accomplished, the car feeling sporty whilst retaining good ride quality on air springs. The car required a code before the door handle would operate, then once inside there was a very modern and ergonomic dash layout, full of gadgets and power extras.

Top speed:	123 mph (197 km/h)
0-60 mph (0–96 km/h):	7.0 sec
Engine type:	V8
Displacement:	281 ci (4,601 cc)
Transmission	4-speed auto
Max power:	290 bhp (216 kW) @ 5,750 rpm
Max torque:	285 lb ft (386 Nm) @ 4,500 rpm
Weight:	3,765 lb (1,711 kg)
Economy:	22 mpg (7.79 km/l)

Saleen Mustang S351 (1995)

While Ford has its top-line Cobra for high-performance junkies, Saleen used their knowledge to go a huge step up with its S351. Started in 1995 with this set-up, the S351 used a truck block but with modifications like aluminium heads, roller rockers, a bigger throttle body, upgraded fuel system, bigger fuel injectors and, best of all, the 'S' in the name stood for supercharged which meant a Vortech 6psi centrifugal blower. To contain the power a Tremec gearbox was fitted, with new rear end gears and an uprated limited-slip differential. The brakes featured huge discs with Alcon four-pot callipers, with 18-inch (457mm) Speedline rims plus 255/35 and 295/35 BF Goodrich tyres. The special Saleen bodykit and graphics weren't matched inside, as it was mostly Mustang, but with the important addition of Recaro seats. Mid-12-second quarter-miles were possible in full street trim.

Top speed:	177 mph (283 km/h)
0–60 mph (0–96 km/h):	4.5 sec
Engine type:	V8
Displacement:	351 ci (5,751 cc)
Transmission	6-speed manual
Max power:	495 bhp (369 kW) @ 5,700 rpm
Max torque:	490 lb ft (664 Nm) @ 3,500 rpm
Weight:	3,450 lb (1,568 kg)
Economy:	11.7 mpg (4.14 km/l)

Chevrolet Camaro Z28 (1996)

As soon as the fourth-generation Corvette came along in 1992, it started getting modified. It mattered not that the model was high-tech, because the aftermarket just grew increasingly high-tech to cope with the changes. This Camaro uses modern touches combined with a period-type paint scheme featuring flames, just like hot rods of the 1960s. The owner has fitted 18-inch (457mm) rims with 35-series tyres for handling, while the suspension has SLA lowering springs and uprated anti-roll bar. Under the hood much work has gone on too, with a Vortech 7psi supercharger now feeding in more air and fuel through Edelbrock aluminium heads and a larger throttle body. Being a 1996 model, this also has Chevy's own tweaked exhaust for an extra 10bhp (7kW). The interior features additional boost and fuel-pressure gauges, plus white gauges and re-trimmed flame seats.

Top speed:	168 mph (269 km/h)
0–60 mph (0–96 km/h):	4.5 sec
Engine type:	V8
Displacement:	350 ci (5,735 cc)
Transmission	4-speed auto
Max power:	430 bhp (321 kW) @ 5,200 rpm
Max torque:	490 lb ft (664 Nm) @ 3,400 rpm
Weight:	3,650 lb (1,659 kg)
Economy:	14 mpg (4.96 km/l)

Chevrolet Corvette GS (1996)

Afifth-generation Corvette was due to be debuted in 1997, so Chevrolet wanted to say farewell to the fourth-generation car in style. Designers and engineers collaborated and came up with the 1996 Grand Sport, which was a nod to the 1960s' Grand Sport race cars which had been successful in SCCA racing. The striped paint was just part of the deal, as the car had many upgrades. On the suspension there were thicker anti-roll bars, plus stiffer springs and shocks to improve handling. Special arch extensions were put on the rear to house larger 315/35 tyres, which were much needed with the new power on tap. The 405bhp (302kW) LT5 engine was to be used, but Chevrolet had axed it the previous year, so engineers fitted the 350ci (5.7-litre) LT4 and hotted it up via modified pistons, larger valves, modified cylinder heads, a high-lift camshaft and roller rockers.

Top speed:	168 mph (269 km/h)
0–60 mph (0–96 km/h):	4.7 sec
Engine type:	V8
Displacement:	350 ci (5,735 cc)
Transmission	6-speed manual
Max power:	330 bhp (246 kW) @ 5,800 rpm
Max torque:	340 lb ft (461 Nm) @ 4,500 rpm
Weight:	3,298 lb (1,499 kg)
Economy:	21 mpg (7.43 km/l)

Chevrolet Impala SS (1996)

At first the Impala SS was debuted purely as a concept, but as with many such ideas, GM knew it would have a winner if the public responded well. They did. The car made the showroom floors by 1996 and showed how much modern technology could improve a muscle car. The SS was fitted with the LT1 small-block 350ci (5.7-litre) V8, with multi-point fuel injection and revised engine management. It could push the Impala to sub-7-second 0–60mph (0–96km/h) times and impressive top speed, while giving 21mpg (7.43km/l) on a run. A heavyweight at just under 2 tons (2.03 tonnes), it could handle very well, thanks to thicker anti-roll bars, stiffer springs and de Carbon shocks. Heavy-duty police front spindles and huge 12-inch (305mm) disc brakes all around helped the inspiring feel, and owners didn't go without extras on the interior, with power everything and leather seats.

Top speed:	140 mph (224 km/h)
0–60 mph (0–96 km/h):	6.6 sec
Engine type:	V8
Displacement:	350 ci (5,735 cc)
Transmission	4-speed auto
Max power:	260 bhp (194 kW) @ 5,000 rpm
Max torque:	330 lb ft (447 Nm) @ 3,200 rpm
Weight:	4,230 lb (1,922 kg)
Economy:	21 mpg (7.43 km/l)

AM General Hummer (1997)

Nicknamed the 'Humvee' after its initials HMMWV which stood for High Mobility Multi-purpose Wheeled Vehicle, this vehicle debuted in 1980. It had been designed in just 11 months and had its thorough testing in the Nevada desert. The US Army thought it very impressive and ordered 55,000 within a couple of years. But it wasn't until the much-televised Gulf War of 1991 that the public demanded a road version. Starting with a small-block Chevy engine, the Humvee soon got GM's new-for-1994 378ci (6.4-litre) turbo-diesel V8. The car was designed for military use, so weight was not an issue, hence there's a massive ladder-style chassis. Raised independent suspension was utilized to give plenty of travel and ground clearance, while four-wheel drive was standard with a four-speed auto transmitting drive to a two-speed transfer case and centre differential.

Top speed:	87 mph (139 km/h)
0–60 mph (0–96 km/h):	17.3 sec
Engine type:	V8
Displacement:	395 ci (6,472 cc)
Transmission	4-speed auto
Max power:	195 bhp (145 kW) @ 3,400 rpm
Max torque:	430 lb ft (583 Nm) @ 1,700 rpm
Weight:	6,620 lb (3,009 kg)
Economy:	10.7 mpg (3.79 km/l)

Panoz Roadster (1997)

It's appropriate to call the Panoz roadster a modern Shelby Cobra, because it had a similar build specification and borrowed many components from Ford's Mustang. Danny Panoz had taken over the Irish motorsport company in 1994 and wanted to produce a car which offered raw driving thrills, and the Roadster debuted that same year. Two years on it had developed further into the AIV (aluminium-intensive vehicle) Roadster, so called because it featured aluminium in the body, engine and chassis. The frame was conceived by racing-car engineer Frank Costin (the 'cos' in Marcos) and comprised large-bore aluminium tubes with tubular backbone, off of which hung race A-arm suspension either end with either a standard or sport setting. The 13-inch (330mm) ABS disc brakes gave the Panoz astonishing stopping power, while the 32v engine gave it amazing go, both from the Mustang Cobra.

Top speed:	131 mph (210 km/h)
0–60 mph (0–96 km/h):	4.5 sec
Engine type:	V8
Displacement:	281 ci (4,604 cc)
Transmission	5-speed manual
Max power:	305 bhp (227 kW) @ 5,800 rpm
Max torque:	300 lb ft (406 Nm) @ 4,800 rpm
Weight:	2,459 lb (1,117 kg)
Economy:	19.9 mpg (7.04 km/l)

Plymouth Prowler (1997)

The public's response to the concept Prowler blew Chrysler away. They knew they had to make it, but it also took some time to get into production as the concept was so radical. When it appeared, demand was overwhelming, to the point where the $40,000 price doubled within months on the second-hand market. The design was led by Chrysler head Tom Gale, a hot rodder at heart, who wanted to give the public a modern slant rod. The design sheet said it had to be light, so an aluminium chassis was built with slender A-arms at either end for independent suspension. At the front, coilover shocks were mounted inboard like a race car, while the rear used a multi-link arrangement which made for brilliant handling. To distribute weight the gearbox was part of the rear transaxle and the engine set well back in the frame. The only let down was the lack of power.

Top speed:	140 mph (224 km/h)
0–60 mph (0–96 km/h):	7.0 sec
Engine type:	V6
Displacement:	215 ci (3,523 cc)
Transmission:	4-speed auto
Max power:	214 bhp (160 kW) @ 5,850 rpm
Max torque:	221 lb ft (300 Nm) @ 3,100 rpm
Weight:	2,862 lb (1,300 kg)
Economy:	20 mpg (7.08 km/l)

Dodge Viper GTS-R (1997)

Chrysler's road-going GTS was every bit a race car developed for the street, so it was a natural move to produce the GTS-R, where the 'R' stood for 'racing'. In 1997 two cars were entered in the GT2 class in World Sportscar Racing, and they came first and second at the Le Mans 24 Hours. The GTS-R went on to take the World GT2 Championship, which was the first time an American production car had done so. The R was quite different from the road GTS, having the engine positioned further back to aid weight distribution and fully balanced for reliability. Internally it was given 12:1 compression, plus stronger forged-steel connecting rods use. A dry sump oiling system was essential to maintain oil pressure under cornering loads. The suspension used spherical joints for maximum response, and carbon-fibre panels were fitted and the bodywork deepened to improve aerodynamics.

Top speed:	203 mph (325 km/h)
0–60 mph (0–96 km/h):	3.1 sec
Engine type:	V10
Displacement:	488 ci (7,998 cc)
Transmission	6-speed manual
Max power:	650 bhp (485 kW) @ 6,000 rpm
Max torque:	650 lb ft (881 Nm) @ 5,000 rpm
Weight:	2,750 lb (1,250 kg)
Economy:	N/A

Cadillac Catera (1998)

Import cars are big competition for American manufacturers and Cadillac decided in 1996 that the best way to fight them was to have one of its own. So it started using an Opel model sold in Europe as the Omega, and named it the Catera. The only differences visually were the front and rear light clusters, which went full width on the rear and at the front were separated by a grille more akin to previous Cadillacs. The suspension was fully independent and had struts up front plus a strut and multi-link rear for exceptional ride quality and handling – enough to rival BMW, Mercedes, and Lexus. The engine was a compact 183ci (3-litre) V6 with 24 valves, twin overhead camshafts and three-stage intake runner lengths to boost torque production throughout the rev range. Powerful braking is available, thanks to vented and ABS-assisted discs all around. The Catera remains in production.

Top speed:	125 mph (200 km/h)
0–60 mph (0–96 km/h):	8.5 sec
Engine type:	V6
Displacement:	180 ci (2,962 cc)
Transmission	4-speed auto
Max power:	200 bhp (149 kW) @ 6,000 rpm
Max torque:	192 lb ft (260 Nm) @ 3,600 rpm
Weight:	3,800 lb (1,727 kg)
Economy:	22 mpg (7.79 km/l)

Chevrolet Camaro SS (1998)

As always, the Camaro's SS badge stood for Super Sport, and way back in 1967 the original Camaro SS had the 295bhp (220kW) Turbo-Fire 350ci (5.7-litre) V8 engine, plus special SS hood, badges and stripes. The newer version's output might not seem much higher, but with the high-tech all-aluminium powerplant the SS could launch hard and get to 60mph (96km/h) in just five seconds, then down the quarter-mile in 13 seconds. The brand new LS1 engine featured Ram Air induction to increase power from the usual 305bhp (227kW), and a six-speed gearbox was standard. While a live axle remained at the rear, up front the SS was fitted with unequal-length wishbones and uprated suspension. Huge 9x17-inch (229x432mm) alloys and 275/40 tyres meant the SS could pull 0.9gs on a skid pad. Being the fastest ever SS too makes the 1998 SS by far Chevrolet's most complete Camaro ever.

Top speed:	161 mph (257 km/h)
0–60 mph (0–96 km/h):	5.2 sec
Engine type:	V8
Displacement:	347 ci (5,686 cc)
Transmission	6-speed manual
Max power:	320 bhp (239 kW) @ 5,200 rpm
Max torque:	325 lb ft (440 Nm) @ 4,400 rpm
Weight:	3,593 lb (1,633 kg)
Economy:	27 mpg (9.56 km/l)

Chevrolet Corvette C5 (1998)

The fifth- generation, or C5, Corvette had a lot to live up to. When debuted in 1998 it had over 40 years behind it as America's only mass-produced supercar, the longest run of any supercar. The all-new small-block V8 engine, coded LS1, was designed especially for the C5, and marked a return to pushrod-operated valves. However, with new cylinders heads, a composite induction system, electronic fuel injection and electronic throttle control, the motor revved like a race-tuned V8 and was powerful right through the rev range. The tradition of a glass-fibre body continued, this time aided by magnesium wheels for more weight loss. The floor was constructed in wood sandwiched between steel sheets to stiffen the structure, while the steel chassis had alloy suspension arms and composite monoleaf rear spring. The gearbox was in the rear transaxle to help distribute weight.

Top speed:	175 mph (280 km/h)
0–60 mph (0–96 km/h):	4.7 sec
Engine type:	V8
Displacement:	347 ci (5,686 cc)
Transmission	6-speed manual
Max power:	345 bhp (257 kW) @ 5,400 rpm
Max torque:	350 lb ft (474 Nm) @ 4,400 rpm
Weight:	3,220 lb (1,463 kg)
Economy:	20.2 mpg (7.15 km/l)

Chrysler Sebring (1998)

The Sebring's roots go back to 1995 when Chrysler released the Cirrus and Stratus sedans to replace their ageing A-body cars. A year on they went one further by replacing their Le Baron top-selling drop-top with the new Sebring. While the sheet metal was all-new, the Sebring convertible's chassis and suspension came from the Cirrus and Stratus, which meant unitary construction and double wishbones up front plus a complex rear wishbone arrangement with trailing arms. The convertible got uprated springs and shocks plus 6.5x16-inch (165x406mm) alloys and 215/55 tyres, so the handling was top notch and made the car dynamic to drive as well as in looks. The V6 from Mitsubishi, while smooth and refined, had much weight to pull around. The car was more a cruiser than sports machine. Luxury and refinement made the Sebring America's best-selling convertible.

Top speed:	122 mph (195 km/h)
0–60 mph (0–96 km/h):	10.2 sec
Engine type:	V6
Displacement:	152 ci (2,490 cc)
Transmission	4-speed auto
Max power:	168 bhp (125 kW) @ 5,800 rpm
Max torque:	170 lb ft (230 Nm) @ 4,350 rpm
Weight:	3,382 lb (1,537 kg)
Economy:	23 mpg (8.14 km/l)

Dodge Viper GTS (1998)

The first Viper was shown as a concept in 1989 at the Detroit Motor Show and the public's hunger for it meant one was pacing the Indy 500 in 1991. The following year the RT/10 version was on sale, with buyers queuing up. Then Chrysler repeated the process with a Viper GTS coupe concept, and again it was well received. The first production GTS coupe appeared in 1996 and addressed many of the roadster's shortcomings. Every body panel was new, as was the engine up to a point, and it had been re-cast in aluminium and featured many new components. Power was up, but overall weight was down by over 40lb (18kg), thanks to composite bodywork and all-aluminium suspension. The GTS was practical too because of the rear window hatch and generous trunk space. The 11x17-inch (279x432mm) rims out back could just about cope with the incredible torque.

Top speed:	179 mph (286 km/h)
0–60 mph (0–96 km/h):	4.7 sec
Engine type:	V10
Displacement:	488 ci (7,998 cc)
Transmission	6-speed manual
Max power:	450 bhp (336 kW) @ 5,200 rpm
Max torque:	490 lb ft (664 Nm) @ 3,700 rpm
Weight:	3,384 lb (1,538 kg)
Economy:	24 mpg (8.50 km/l)

Ford Mustang GT (1998)

Aprogression of the body style which had debuted in 1994, the 1998 Mustang GT looked every bit a sports coupe. While heavier due to extra stiffening in the shell structure, the new model felt more solid and better planted on the road, and tweaks to the suspension vastly improved its handling. The biggest change was the 281ci (4.6-litre) 'Modular' V8 which first arrived in 1996. Massively improved refinement made up for the lack of torque, even though by 1998 the GT was putting out 225bhp (168kW) and 285lb ft (386Nm) torque and the engine was very keen at high rpm. The GT stuck with a live axle and front strut arrangement, using four locating bars and separate coil springs and shocks at the rear for an excellent ride and sporty handling. Retro-feel Ford added scoops on the side bodywork and vertically segmented rear lights, while the grille carried the running horse badge.

Top speed:	141 mph (225 km/h)
0–60 mph (0–96 km/h):	6.3 sec
Engine type:	V8
Displacement:	281 ci (4,604 cc)
Transmission	5-speed manual
Max power:	225 bhp (168 kW) @ 4,400 rpm
Max torque:	285 lb ft (386 Nm) @ 3,500 rpm
Weight:	3,462 lb (1,573 kg)
Economy:	20 mpg (7.08 km/l)

Ford Taurus SHO (1998)

The name SHO stood for Super High Output; Ford wanted this model to compete against the imports from both Europe and Japan. The drive train consisted of a V8, transversely mounted and with heads developed and built in Japan by Yamaha, as with previous SHO models. With four valves per cylinder and a balancer shaft to smooth out the dynamics, the engine was a keen revver all the way through the 7,000rpm redline. The only downside was the engine produced most of its best power above 4,500rpm, so low-speed response wasn't as good, though Ford made sure at least 80 percent of the torque was available at 2,000rpm. The suspension had a strut front and multi-link rear, with computer-controlled shock absorbers. Inside, the SHO came fully equipped with air-conditioning, cruise control, plus power windows, steering seats, mirrors and sunroof, making it a luxurious fast tourer.

Top speed:	139 mph (222 km/h)
0–60 mph (0–96 km/h):	7.8 sec
Engine type:	V8
Displacement:	208 ci (3,408 cc)
Transmission	3-speed auto
Max power:	235 bhp (175 kW) @ 6,100 rpm
Max torque:	230 lb ft (311 Nm) @ 4,800 rpm
Weight:	3,395 lb (1,543 kg)
Economy:	19 mpg (6.73 km/l)

Jeep Grand Cherokee (1998)

Chrysler cleverly used the heritage of the Jeep name when it launched the 1993 Jeep Grand Cherokee in 1993. It went through little change until 1997, when it was facelifted and equipped with the 360ci (5.8-litre) V8. However, it wasn't changed underneath with a Uni-frame structure which was a steel monocoque, and Quadra Coil suspension on live front and rear axles, equipped with anti-roll bars and gas shocks. The new Quadra-Trac 4WD was brilliant, being an on-demand system with a viscous coupling centre differential with torque split varyingly between front and rear axles, depending on conditions. A more rounded body meant the Cherokees had one of the most aerodynamic shapes of any Sport Utility Vehicle. Also, with its short overhangs it could approach slopes of 37 degrees or leave them at 30 degrees. The V8 made the Grand Cherokee a sportscar on the road.

Top speed:	125 mph (198 km/h)
0–60 mph (0–96 km/h):	8.2 sec
Engine type:	V8
Displacement:	360 ci (5,899 cc)
Transmission	4-speed auto
Max power:	237 bhp (177 kW) @ 4,050 rpm
Max torque:	345 lb ft (467 Nm) @ 3,050 rpm
Weight:	4,218 lb (1,917 kg)
Economy:	13 mpg (4.60 km/l)

Jeep Wrangler (1998)

The Jeep is well known as a wartime vehicle which kept American servicemen on the move; in fact it's often referred to as the original off-roader. The car and name developed through the decades, and Chrysler bought the right to produce it in 1988, when they took bought the American Motor Company. That spurred the release of the Jeep Wrangler Renegade, with wider arch extensions and a 244ci (4-litre) straight-six. The Sahara was simply a limited edition of the same Jeep Wrangler, even though it looked slightly different, thanks to new sheet metal (all bar the doors, in fact) and round headlamps, fitted from 1996-on models. Like the original Jeep, the Sahara used a strong ladder frame underneath with front and rear live axles. The gearboxes available were a 5-speed manual or 3-speed auto, with standard low and high four-wheel drive ratios.

Top speed:	112 mph (179 km/h)
0–60 mph (0–96 km/h):	8.8 sec
Engine type:	In-line six
Displacement:	244 ci (4,000 cc)
Transmission:	5-speed manual
Max power:	184 bhp (137 kW) @ 4,600 rpm
Max torque:	220 lb ft (298 Nm) @ 3,600 rpm
Weight:	3,349 lb (1,522 kg)
Economy:	12 mpg (4.25 km/l)

Cadillac STS (1998)

The Cadillacs of the 1980s had suffered dreadfully from old age and hence the company lost many sales to the likes of BMW and Mercedes. This continued through to 1992 until Cadillac completely revamped their line-up and included a new STS. This won Automobile magazine's 'Car of the Year' in 1992, but it didn't end there as Cadillac worried the competition more with the introduction of its high-tech Northstar V8 in 1993. From 1997 a new STS (Seville Touring Sedan) arrived, and it was by far the best yet, with the company so confident they even built them in right-hand-drive form to sell in Europe. The suspension used MacPherson struts and a multi-link rear, with variable shocks. The interior was fully loaded even in basic trim, while the engine could run 100,000 miles (160,000km) between tune-ups and could limp home 60 miles (96km) without coolant.

Top speed:	155 mph (248 km/h)
0–60 mph (0–96 km/h):	6.8 sec
Engine type:	V8
Displacement:	279 ci (4,571 cc)
Transmission	4-speed auto
Max power:	300 bhp (224 kW) @ 6,000 rpm
Max torque:	295 lb ft (400 Nm) @ 4,400 rpm
Weight:	4,010 lb (1,822 kg)
Economy:	26 mpg (9.20 km/l)

Dodge Durango (1998)

The Sport Utility Vehicle became very competitive in the late 1990s and Dodge regularly sat among the top three manufacturers sales-wise. Its 1997 to present Dakota might have used a truck chassis but it handled more like a road car, thanks to a stiffened frame and a great 4WD system. Suspension was based around the Dakota's set-up, with double wishbones acting on a torsion bar springs up front and a live axle rear sitting on leaf springs. The 4x4 capabilities were obvious looking at the ride height, and while a driver had low or high ratio full-time 4WD available, for the road they could select rear drive only to save fuel. Three engine options were available, the 238ci (3.9-litre) V6, the better 318ci (5.2-litre) V8, or the range-topping 360ci (5.9-litre), which gave excellent performance. Inside there was seating for up to eight people.

Top speed:	115 mph (184 km/h)
0–60 mph (0–96 km/h):	8.7 sec
Engine type:	V8
Displacement:	360 ci (5,898 cc)
Transmission	4-speed auto
Max power:	250 bhp (186 kW) @ 4,000 rpm
Max torque:	335 lb ft (454 Nm) @ 3,200 rpm
Weight:	5,050 lb (2,295 kg)
Economy:	15 mpg (5.31 km/l)

Lincoln Navigator (1998)

Sitting at the top of the SUV market as soon as it arrived in 1998 was the Lincoln Navigator. Using the floorpan and running gear of the Ford Expedition, which itself could be traced back to the F-150 pick-up, the Lincoln developed the chassis further with the addition of adjustable air springs which were controlled by an automatic load-levelling facility. When off-road this set-up lifted the car by an inch for extra clearance. The live axle was the only dated part, but it was strong and improved by extra locating links featuring upper and lower trailing arms plus a Panhard rod. The engine was a larger version of the Ford's modular unit. Called the 'Triton', it had a single cam per bank and sequential fuel injection and was highly reliable, going for 100,000 miles (160,000km) between service stops. It was competitively priced in top trim at $43,000.

Top speed:	109 mph (174 km/h)
0–60 mph (0–96 km/h):	11.4 sec
Engine type:	V8
Displacement:	330 ci (5,400 cc)
Transmission	4-speed auto
Max power:	230 bhp (171 kW) @ 4,250 rpm
Max torque:	325 lb ft (440 Nm) @ 3,000 rpm
Weight:	5,557 lb (2,525 kg)
Economy:	14.7 mpg (5.20 km/l)

Saleen-Allen RRR Mustang (1998)

With Saleen's name well respected on the circuit racing scene, and on the street, the company decided in 1997 to take an SR Mustang to Le Mans for endurance racing. The company became a force to be reckoned with and so in 1998 in the US Speedvision World Challenge Series, Saleen, in conjunction with Tim Allen from 'Home Improvement' (who also drove this car), entered and dominated with their 1998 Mustang RRR. Using a stripped SN 95, the car got a tubular spaceframe chassis with double A-arm suspension, Howe springs and Bilstein shocks. The engine was replaced with a Windsor 351ci (5.7-litre), and on to this went GT40 aluminium heads to give 10:1 compression, and a Holley 600cfm carburettor. Carbon-fibre was used for the doors, trunk lid, hood, fenders and nose. A tough Jerico gearbox handled the power and helped Saleen win the manufacturer's trophy in 1998.

Top speed:	210 mph (336 km/h)
0–60 mph (0–96 km/h):	3.2 sec
Engine type:	V8
Displacement:	357 ci (5,850 cc)
Transmission	Jerico 4-speed manual
Max power:	525 bhp (391 kW) @ 6,800 rpm
Max torque:	N/A
Weight:	N/A
Economy:	N/A

Saleen Explorer (1998)

Being well-known for their Mustang tuning meant it was only natural for Saleen to offer a performance version of Ford's Explorer, especially so because SUVs were becoming so popular in the late 1990s. It was 1996 that the first one appeared and in this they used the former Mustang pushrod 5.0L engine. Saleen launched their new version in 1998 and concentrated on giving it enhanced driver appeal and making it more dynamic visually. The separate steel chassis and live axle were retained, but stiffer bushes were fitted throughout the suspension, plus the springs were both lowered and uprated and the shocks revalved. Thicker anti-roll bars replaced the stock units, and thanks to lightweight magnesium 18-inch (457mm) rims and low-profile tyres, the car could pull an astonishing 0.80g on a skidpad. The body was fitted with a Saleen styling kit, and optional was a supercharger, which this one has.

Top speed:	125 mph (200 km/h)
0–60 mph (0–96 km/h):	7.9 sec
Engine type:	V8
Displacement:	302 ci (4,948 cc)
Transmission	4-speed auto
Max power:	286 bhp (213 kW) @ 4,500 rpm
Max torque:	333 lb ft (451 Nm) @ 3,200 rpm
Weight:	4,500 lb (2,045 kg)
Economy:	15 mpg (5.31 km/l)

Chevrolet Corvette hardtop (1998)

Corvettes had long been available both in the T-top and convertible form, but when the C5 arrived in the late 1990s, the company decided to produce a new version which would attract the real driving enthusiasts. It offered a hardtop-only version which came without such interior accessories as air-conditioning, power seats, electric door mirrors or a sound system. It also lost weight with the fixed top, some 70lb (52kg) in fact, because adding the roof meant the car didn't need so much strengthening in other areas. The car got the Z51 package which consisted of stiffer springs, anti-roll bars and shocks, and special 17-inch (432mm) magnesium alloy rims with ultra low-profile tyres. The engine went unchanged in output, but the only option gearbox was the manual six-speed. Standard brakes were four-wheel vented discs that could stop the car from 60mph (96km/h) in just 126ft (38m).

Top speed:	168 mph (268 km/h)
0–60 mph (0–96 km/h):	5.3 sec
Engine type:	V8
Displacement:	347 ci (5,686 cc)
Transmission	6-speed manual
Max power:	345 bhp (257 kW) @ 5,600 rpm
Max torque:	350 lb ft (474 Nm) @ 4,400 rpm
Weight:	3,245 lb (1,475 kg)
Economy:	21 mpg (7.43 km/l)

Chrysler 300M (1999)

The 300M pays homage to the great 'letter cars' from Chrysler of the 1950s and 1960s. Cars like the 300C and 300G were amazing luxury sedans which also had huge power, and the 300M replicates those, while providing unsurpassed ride quality. More of a sports sedan than cruiser, the M had handling package option designed for it, which meant its cornering ability was higher than any of its competitors'; up to 0.83 lateral g in fact. As it was destined to be sold internationally, the design used typical 'cab-forward' styling which meant interior space was excellent; the other effect was to push the wheel out to each corner, which aided handling. The suspension was struts all around, which further enhanced the driver appeal. The original letter cars had a Hemi engine and the new one at least used the same design of engine internally, but with two cylinders less.

Top speed:	118 mph (188 km/h)
0–60 mph (0–96 km/h):	7.7 sec
Engine type:	V6
Displacement:	215 ci (3,523 cc)
Transmission	4-speed auto
Max power:	253 bhp (189 kW) @ 6,400 rpm
Max torque:	255 lb ft (345 Nm) @ 3,950 rpm
Weight:	3,567 lb (1,621 kg)
Economy:	23 mpg (8.14 km/l)

Ford F-350 Super Duty (1999)

America's obsession with trucks means they have excellent sales figures. And with so many of the vehicles on the road, it's understandable that people want to personalize their vehicles. This Super Duty might be just a few years old but the owner has gone through the vehicle and added many modifications. To start with, the truck has received an 8-inch (203mm) lift kit allowing the body and chassis more travel, and a bolt-in cage has been added to the rear should the inevitable happen while off-road. At each corner sit huge 12x16.5-inch (305x419mm) American Egle rims with Dick Cepek 38-inch (965mm) tall tyres, giving the F-350 a baby monster truck look. The engine is Ford's immense Triton V10 which can return great economy given the size and provides incredible pulling power. Chassis hardware consist of Ford's twin Traction beams, live axles and a central viscous coupling.

Top speed:	96 mph (153 km/h)
0–60 mph (0–96 km/h):	10.2 sec
Engine type:	V10
Displacement:	415 ci (6,800 cc)
Transmission	4-speed auto
Max power:	275 bhp (205 kW) @ 4,250 rpm
Max torque:	410 lb ft (556 Nm) @ 2,650 rpm
Weight:	6,710 lb (3,050 kg)
Economy:	14 mpg (4.96 km/l)

Lincoln Town Car Cartier (1999)

This is a full-sized car of the old school, with an emphasis on maximum luxury and minimum driver fatigue. But it's built with modern standards and technology, hence is barely over 2 tons (2.03 tonnes) – excellent, given the specification. The Two Car had first received its more rounded lines in 1997 but underneath it continued with a double wishbone front and live axle rear. What the car did have to help ride was a Watts linkage on the back axle and air springs to smooth out the bumpiest of surfaces. The Town Car used the same engine as it had done since the early 1990s, that being the Ford Modular unit with single cam per bank, sequential multi-point fuel injection, and Ford's high-tech EEC-V engine management. It's whisper-quiet, even at speed. The Cartier edition shown means leather, and every other optional extra is fitted as standard.

Top speed:	130 mph (208 km/h)
0–60 mph (0–96 km/h):	7.9 sec
Engine type:	V8
Displacement:	281 ci (4,604 cc)
Transmission:	4-speed auto
Max power:	220 bhp (164 kW) @ 4,500 rpm
Max torque:	290 lb ft (393 Nm) @ 3,500 rpm
Weight:	4,015 lb (1,825 kg)
Economy:	23 mpg (8.14 km/l)

Mercury Cougar (1999)

First shown as the MC2 concept at the 1997 Detroit Motor Show, the Mercury Cougar got a very positive public reaction so was put into production immediately. It used the Contour sedan platform but with significantly altered springs, bushing and shocks rates to make the Cougar more sporting. The car was also lowered by 1.5 inches (38mm) to get the centre of gravity down and hence improve handling. Power came from the Ford Duratec V6, with a 60-degree V and short stroke. The block and heads are alloy and four overhead camshaft hollow to help make the powerplant very lightweight. What brought buyers back to the car was its radical styling, or, as Ford called it: 'New Edge'. Unusually, the car was known under the same name in Europe where it successfully took over from the ageing Probe and had not just a V6 but a Zetec 16v 130bhp (97kW) engine.

Top speed:	135 mph (216 km/h)
0–60 mph (0–96 km/h):	8.0 sec
Engine type:	V6
Displacement:	155 ci (2,540 cc)
Transmission	5-speed manual
Max power:	170 bhp (127 kW) @ 6,250 rpm
Max torque:	165 lb ft (224 Nm) @ 4,250 rpm
Weight:	3,065 lb (1,393 kg)
Economy:	29 mpg (10.27 km/l)

Pontiac Firebird Firehawk (1999)

Street Legal Performance (SLP) was started by ex-drag racer Ed Hamburger in 1987 and he did a deal with GM to design and fit a performance package for the Pontiac Firebird. It was known as the SLP 'Firehawk' and it debuted in 1992. Come 1995 it was using the 315bhp (235kW) LT1 engine in both coupe and convertible bodies, then in 1998 a new Firehawk was released and featured the Corvette's all-aluminium LS1 engine, being available only with the six-speed manual. On the SLP options owners got the choice of Bilstein Ultra Performance Suspension which could make the Firehawk achieve 0.91 lateral g on a skidpad. SLP's design cleverly incorporated heat-extracting vents in the top of the hood plus functional Ram Air intakes on the nose. The 9x17-inch (229x432mm) alloys hid 11.8-inch (300mm) vented discs, ABS-assisted and making the car an awesome all-round sportscar.

Top speed:	157 mph (251 km/h)
0–60 mph (0–96 km/h):	5.1 sec
Engine type:	V8
Displacement:	347 ci (5,686 cc)
Transmission	6-speed manual
Max power:	327 bhp (244 kW)@ 5,200 rpm
Max torque:	345 lb ft (467 Nm) @ 4,400 rpm
Weight:	3,520 lb (1,600 kg)
Economy:	22 mpg (7.79 km/l)

Pontiac Grand Prix GTP (1999)

While the Grand Prix name had been around for many years, it didn't use much in the way of modern technology nor looks until it switched to front-wheel drive in 1988. It got sporty styling that year, marking it out significantly, and the looks were backed up by performance, thanks to the same basic turbocharged engine as in the fire-breathing Grand Nationals from just a couple of years before. Into the 1990s the car was renamed the GTP instead of Turbo, then in 1994 got new styling, then again in 1996, which has since become the car's most successful guise. In GPX form it used a supercharger but remained front-wheel drive. The suspension had revised geometry with more negative camber on the front wheels to improve cornering. A GM first was the heads-up display, which projected the speed and other functions onto the windshield.

Top speed:	142 mph (227 km/h)
0–60 mph (0–96 km/h):	6.6 sec
Engine type:	V6
Displacement:	231 ci (3,785 cc)
Transmission	4-speed auto
Max power:	240 bhp (179 kW) @ 5,200 rpm
Max torque:	280 lb ft (380 Nm) @ 3,200 rpm
Weight:	3,396 lb (1,543 kg)
Economy:	23 mpg (8.14 km/l)

Roush Mustang (1999)

The team of Jack Roush and Ford go back to 1988 when Roush built a 351ci (5.8-litre) twin-turbo 400bhp (298kW) Mustang as a 25th Anniversary edition. Unfortunately, Ford rejected the idea of selling it due to the expense, but Roush Racing continued and in 1995 Roush Performance was formed. They again chose the Mustang to make a high-performance street car. Years later the same happened on the new 1999 Mustang, as Roush developed a number of models in various stages of tune. Shown is a Stage II, given minor but very effective tweaks for more driver involvement. The shocks and springs were uprated and lowered and stiffer anti–roll bars fitted. Roush control arms replaced the stock items locating the live rear axle. Brembo 13-inch (330mm) vented discs were added at the front to go with the stock ABS system. Finishing the body was a full skirt kit with side exhausts.

Top speed:	150 mph (240 km/h)
0–60 mph (0–96 km/h):	5.8 sec
Engine type:	V8
Displacement:	281 ci (4,604 cc)
Transmission	5-speed manual
Max power:	260 bhp (194 kW) @ 5,250 rpm
Max torque:	302 lb ft (410 Nm) @ 4,000 rpm
Weight:	3,471 lb (1,577 kg)
Economy:	16 mpg (5.66 km/l)

Glossary

9-inch (228mm) axle: Size of ring gear within axle housing; also a popular Ford high-performance axle.

Alloys: Aluminium wheel rims, used as lightweight alternatives to pressed steel rims.

Bhp (bhp): Brake horsepower, measurement used for engine power output. Power output can also be measured in kW (kilowatts).

Big-block: Generic term given to large-displacement American V8 engines, usually 383 ci (6,276 cc) or under. Also refers to larger physical size of engine compared to small-block.

Cam: Abbreviation of camshaft, the component which controls the opening and closing of valves, thus controlling air/fuel flow into an engine.

Coilovers: Type of spring and shock-absorber suspension arrangement, whereby the shock is located within the coil spring.

Crank: Abbreviation of crankshaft, the main component in an engine's rotating assembly which, via connecting rods, is attached to pistons.

Ci (ci): Cubic inches – measurement of engine displacement most commonly used in the USA.

Cc (cc): Cubic centimetres – measurement of engine displacement as used throughout Europe and Japan.

Diff: Abbreviation of differential, this being the unit which turns drive (via gears in the axle) into rotation of the wheels.

Fourbar: Four parallel arms used, two per side, to locate the front or rear axle on a car.

Hot rod: Car which is stripped and tuned for speed (usually associated with pre-1949 American cars). A Hot rodder is person who does such work.

Inline four: Engine configuration whereby the engine's four cylinders sit in a straight line. Such engines can be mounted longitudinally in a car or transversely, the latter in the case of most frontwheel-drive vehicles.

Intercooler: Radiator which cools intake charge of air to an engine, therefore creating denser air for more power.

Lb ft (lb ft): Measurement of engine torque output, representing pounds per feet force. Torque outputs can also be measured in Nm (Newton Metres).

Leaf spring: Strip (or strips) of spring steel used to support a car's weight. Development of 19th-century horseless carriage cart spring. Often referred to as semi-elliptical spring because of shape.

Live axle: Solid rear axle through which rearwheel-drive is provided.

Lowrider: Car which sits very low to the ground and uses hydraulic suspension rams for radical changes in body height/angles.

Muscle car: Car built in the era between 1964 and 1972, when large-displacement V8 engines were put into medium-sized sedans for high power-to-weight ratios and fast acceleration.

Pro Street: Style of street car whereby drag-racing suspension and wide rear tyres are used under stock bodywork.

Quarter-mile: Measured distance over which drag cars are raced in a straight line to determine speed.

Rear end: Generic term for rear axle or suspension arrangement on a car.

Small-block: Generic term given to small displacement American V8 engines, usually 380 ci (6,227 cc) or under.

Supercharger/turbocharger: Device which forces more air and fuel into an engine, the supercharger being crankshaft driven, while the turbo is spun via exhaust gas.

Traction bars: Modification bars which attach to the rear axle to prevent wheel hop on leaf sprung, rearwheel-drive cars.

Transaxle: A transmission combined in the same housing as the rear axle.

V8: Engine configuration whereby eight cylinders sit in a V fashion, usually at 60 degrees in the case of the V8 engines from the US.

Wheel hop: Bouncing of wheel under hard acceleration, usually suffered on leaf spring-equipped, rearwheel-drive cars.

Wishbone: Suspension locating arm, name deriving from chicken wishbone shape. Also referred to as A-arm.

Index

Note: Page numbers in **bold** refer to main entries